LOUISIANA COLLEGE LIBRARY DUP

3 9448 1001 7318 2

D1125516

Language Awareness

SECOND EDITION

SECOND EDITION

Language Awareness

EDITORS

Paul Eschholz

Alfred Rosa

Virginia Clark

RICHARD W. NORTON
MEMORIAL LIBRARY
Louisiana College
Pineville, Louisiana

ST. MARTIN'S PRESS   New York

Cover design by Melissa Tardiff

Library of Congress Catalog Card Number: 77-86011
Copyright © 1978 by St. Martin's Press, Inc.
All Rights Reserved.
Manufactured in the United States of America.
09
fedc
For information, write: St. Martin's Press, Inc.,
175 Fifth Avenue, New York, N. Y. 10010
ISBN: 0-312-46691-9

ACKNOWLEDGMENTS

I DISCOVERING LANGUAGE

"Coming to an Awareness of Language" by Malcolm X, from *The Autobiography of Malcolm X* by Malcolm X with the assistance of Alex Haley. Reprinted by permission of Grove Press, Inc. Copyright © 1964 by Alex Haley and Malcolm X. Copyright © 1965 by Alex Haley.

"Does a Finger Fing?" by Nedra Newkirk Lamar, from The *Christian Science Monitor* (February 29, 1970). Reprinted by permission of *The Christian Science Monitor.* Copyright © 1970 The Christian Science Publishing Society. All rights reserved.

"The Power of Words" by Bergen Evans. From *The Word-A-Day Vocabulary Builder*, by Bergen Evans. Copyright © 1963 by Bergen Evans. Reprinted by permission of Random House, Inc.

Acknowledgments and copyrights continue on pages 295–297, which constitute an extension of the copyright page.

98.042
74l

PREFACE

Most of us accept language as we accept the air we breathe: we cannot get along without it, and we take it for granted almost all of the time. Few of us are aware of the extent to which language is used dishonestly to mislead and manipulate. Few of us are fully conscious of the ways, subtle or not so subtle, in which our use of language may affect others. Still fewer of us recognize that our very perceptions of the world are influenced, and our thoughts at least partially shaped, by language.

These would be reasons enough, we believe, for a book such as *Language Awareness;* for if it is true that we are all in some sense prisoners of language, it is equally true that liberation begins with an awareness of that fact. To foster such an awareness is one of the goals of this book.

But we are, of course, the beneficiaries of language far more than we are its victims. Language is in fact one of mankind's greatest achievements and most important resources, and it is a subject endlessly fascinating in itself. We very much hope that the readers of *Language Awareness* will gain a heightened appreciation of the richness, flexibility, and vitality of their language and will wish to explore it further.

Above all, our purpose in this second edition of *Language Awareness* is to continue to encourage its readers to use language more responsibly and effectively. Although the book might appropriately be used in any of several courses, we have developed it with writing courses particularly in mind. It seems to us that the study of language is the best possible basis for courses in writing, for the common denominator of all good writing is the writer's conscious concern for language. This concern is emphasized, in different ways, by all of the selections in *Language Awareness.*

In this new edition of *Language Awareness,* we have increased the number of topical sections, thus both increasing the range of interests and sharpening the focus of each section. We have retained a number of articles that we feel have a certain timelessness about them, as well as those that students and teachers have found most entertaining and helpful. In selecting new articles, we have again

v

130441

emphasized high-interest topics and readability. We feel that the selections in this collection are well written and provide students of composition with practical illustrations of rhetorical principles and techniques.

In addition to questions on content for each selection, the second edition provides a set of questions that focus on rhetorical considerations. Writing-related classroom activities designed to take ten to fifteen minutes of class time accompany each selection. From our own experience in the classroom, we have found these activities helpful in promoting discussion of language and writing issues. At the end of each section we have included writing suggestions for 500-word essays. Finally, we have provided, at the end of the collection, a list of possible topics for longer research papers.

All of our aims in *Language Awareness* are serious ones, but a serious book need not be humorless. Readers may rightly be appalled by examples here of the ways in which language is used to classify, dehumanize, deceive, and control human beings; but Marianne Moore's correspondence with the Ford Motor Company not only teaches us a number of things about language and something about our culture but is funny besides. So, we think, are Nedra Newkirk Lamar's "Does a Finger Fing?" Thomas Fensch's catalog of CB jargon, and Bil Gilbert's "Fast as an Elephant, Strong as an Ant"—among others. Indeed, we like to think that readers of *Language Awareness* will have as much fun using this new edition as we have had in preparing it.

It is impossible to acknowledge here all our indebtedness, but for helpful advice and suggestions we wish to express our appreciation to Elizabeth Wooten Cowan, Marcia Tillotson, Leonard Vogt, and Fred Warner, as well as the many teachers who used the first edition and generously gave us the benefit of their experience with the book in their own classrooms. We also wish to give a special thanks to Judy Cota for typing our manuscript.

PAUL ESCHHOLZ
ALFRED ROSA
VIRGINIA CLARK

CONTENTS

"I suggest we abandon the word obscenity . . . and turn our attention to the social interests actually involved. Then, perhaps, some sensible law-making and law enforcement will follow."

("The words we use are changing faster today—and not merely on the slang level, but on every level. The rapidity with which words come and go is vastly accelerated.")

"Is it not possible that there is a direct correlation between a growing sense of powerlessness and futility in our lives and the jazzed-up language we use?"

"Words now seem to cut off and isolate, to cause more misunderstanding than they prevent."

On the Relation of Language to Public Policy

Resolved, That the National Council of Teachers of English find means to study the relation of language to public policy, to keep track of, publicize, and combat semantic distortion by public officials, candidates for office, political commentators, and all those who transmit through the mass media.

On Dishonest and Inhumane Uses of Language

Resolved, That the National Council of Teachers of English find means to study dishonest and inhumane uses of language and literature by advertisers, to bring offenses to public attention, and to propose classroom techniques for preparing children to cope with commercial propaganda.

Resolutions Passed by the National Council of Teachers of English

I
Discovering Language

1

Coming to an Awareness of Language

MALCOLM X

On February 21, 1965, Malcolm X, the Black Muslim leader, was shot to death as he addressed an afternoon rally in Harlem. He was thirty-nine years old. In the course of his brief life he had risen from the world of thieving, pimping, and drug pushing to become one of the most articulate and powerful blacks in America during the early 1960s.

With the assistance of Alex Haley, later the author of Roots, *Malcolm X told his story in* The Autobiography of Malcolm X, *a moving account of his search for fulfillment. In the following selection taken from the* Autobiography, *Malcolm X narrates his discovery while in prison of the power of language.*

I've never been one for inaction. Everything I've ever felt strongly   1
about, I've done something about. I guess that's why, unable to do
anything else, I soon began writing to people I had known in the
hustling world, such as Sammy the Pimp, John Hughes, the gambling house owner, the thief Jumpsteady, and several dope peddlers.
I wrote them all about Allah and Islam and Mr. Elijah Muhammad. I
had no idea where most of them lived. I addressed their letters in
care of the Harlem or Roxbury bars and clubs where I'd known
them.

I never got a single reply. The average hustler and criminal was   2
too uneducated to write a letter. I have known many slick, sharp-
looking hustlers, who would have you think they had an interest in
Wall Street; privately, they would get someone else to read a letter if
they received one. Besides, neither would I have replied to anyone
writing me something as wild as "the white man is the devil."

What certainly went on the Harlem and Roxbury wires was that   3
Detroit Red was going crazy in stir, or else he was trying some hype
to shake up the warden's office.

During the years that I stayed in the Norfolk Prison Colony,   4
never did any official directly say anything to me about those letters,
although, of course, they all passed through the prison censorship.
I'm sure, however, they monitored what I wrote to add to the files
which every state and federal prison keeps on the conversion of
Negro inmates by the teachings of Mr. Elijah Muhammad.

But at that time, I felt that the real reason was that the white man   5
knew that he was the devil.

Later on, I even wrote to the Mayor of Boston, to the Governor   6
of Massachusetts, and to Harry S. Truman. They never answered;
they probably never even saw my letters. I handscratched to them
how the white man's society was responsible for the black man's
condition in this wilderness of North America.

It was because of my letters that I happened to stumble upon   7
starting to acquire some kind of a homemade education.

I became increasingly frustrated at not being able to express   8
what I wanted to convey in letters that I wrote, especially those to
Mr. Elijah Muhammad. In the street, I had been the most articulate
hustler out there—I had commanded attention when I said something. But now, trying to write simple English, I not only wasn't
articulate, I wasn't even functional. How would I sound writing in
slang, the way I would *say* it, something such as, "Look, daddy, let
me pull your coat about a cat. Elijah Muhammad—"

Many who today hear me somewhere in person, or on television,   9
or those who read something I've said, will think I went to school far
beyond the eighth grade. This impression is due entirely to my
prison studies.

It had really begun back in the Charlestown Prison, when Bimbi   10
first made me feel envy of his stock of knowledge. Bimbi had always
taken charge of any conversation he was in, and I had tried to
emulate him. But every book I picked up had few sentences which
didn't contain anywhere from one to nearly all of the words that
might as well have been in Chinese. When I just skipped those
words, of course, I really ended up with little idea of what the book
said. So I had come to the Norfolk Prison Colony still going through
only book-reading motions. Pretty soon, I would have quit even
these motions, unless I had received the motivation that I did.

I saw that the best thing I could do was get hold of a dictionary—   11
to study, to learn some words. I was lucky enough to reason also
that I should try to improve my penmanship. It was sad. I couldn't
even write in a straight line. It was both ideas together that moved
me to request a dictionary along with some tablets and pencils from
the Norfolk Prison Colony school.

I spent two days just riffling uncertainly through the dictionary's   12
pages. I'd never realized so many words existed! I didn't know
which words I needed to learn. Finally, just to start some kind of
action, I began copying.

In my slow, painstaking, ragged handwriting, I copied into my   13 tablet everything printed on that first page, down to the punctuation marks.

I believe it took me a day. Then, aloud, I read back, to myself,   14
everything I'd written on the tablet. Over and over, aloud, to myself, I read my own handwriting.

I woke up the next morning, thinking about those words—im-   15
mensely proud to realize that not only had I written so much at one time, but I'd written words that I never knew were in the world. Moreover, with a little effort, I also could remember what many of these words meant. I reviewed the words whose meanings I didn't remember. Funny thing, from the dictionary first page right now, that "aardvark" springs to my mind. The dictionary had a picture of it, á long-tailed, long-eared, burrowing African mammal, which lives off termites caught by sticking out its tongue as an anteater does for ants.

I was so fascinated that I went on—I copied the dictionary's next   16
page. And the same experience came when I studied that. With every succeeding page, I also learned of people and places and events from history. Actually the dictionary is like a miniature encyclopedia. Finally the dictionary's A section had filled a whole tablet —and I went on into the B's. That was the way I started copying what eventually became the entire dictionary. It went a lot faster after so much practice helped me to pick up handwriting speed. Between what I wrote in my tablet, and writing letters, during the rest of my time in prison I would guess I wrote a million words.

I suppose it was inevitable that as my word-base broadened, I   17
could for the first time pick up a book and read and now begin to understand what the book was saying. Anyone who has read a great deal can imagine the new world that opened. Let me tell you something: from then until I left that prison, in every free moment I had, if I was not reading in the library, I was reading on my bunk. You couldn't have gotten me out of books with a wedge. Between Mr. Muhammad's teachings, my correspondence, my visitors . . . and my reading of books, months passed without my even thinking about being imprisoned. In fact, up to then, I never had been so truly free in my life.

QUESTIONS ON CONTENT

1. What motivated Malcolm X "to acquire some kind of a home-made education"?

2. What does Malcolm X mean when he says that he was "going through only book-reading motions"? How did he decide to solve this problem?

3. Why did the word *aardvark* spring to mind when Malcolm X recalled his study of the first page of the dictionary?

4. In what way is the dictionary like a "miniature encyclopedia"?

5. What is the nature of the freedom that Malcolm X refers to in the final sentence?

QUESTIONS ON RHETORIC

1. Malcolm X narrates his experiences as a prisoner in the first person. What are the advantages of this approach?

2. The first sentences of paragraphs 1 and 2 are both short declarative sentences. Why are they especially effective as introductory sentences?

3. Could paragraphs 12, 13, and 14 be combined into a single paragraph? What would be gained or lost if they were to be combined?

4. Why is Malcolm X's relatively simple vocabulary in this narrative appropriate?

VOCABULARY

frustrated	functional	inevitable
articulate	emulate	

CLASSROOM ACTIVITIES

1. All of us have been in situations in which our ability to use language seemed inadequate—for example, when taking an exam; being interviewed for a job; giving directions; or expressing sympathy, anger, or grief. Write several paragraphs in which you recount one such frustrating incident in your life. Compare your experiences with those of your classmates.

2. The following six sentences form a paragraph. However, the order has been changed, destroying the logical sequence. Place the sentences in what seems to you the most logical order.
    a. These circumstances and forces are largely beyond our control.
    b. A vocabulary is a tool which one uses in formulating the important

questions of life, the questions which must be asked before they can be answered.

c. At least it helps us call things by their right names.

d. To a large extent, vocabulary shapes all the decisions we make.

e. But our speech is a sort of searchlight that helps us to see these things more clearly and to see ourselves in relation to them.

f. Most decisions, of course, are shaped by our emotions, by circumstances, and by the forces which may hold us back or urge us on.

Be prepared to discuss the language signals you used to decide where each sentence should go.

NOTE: Writing assignments for "Discovering Lanaguage" appear on p. 18.

2
Does a Finger Fing?

NEDRA NEWKIRK LAMAR

Children unconsciously learn how to form new words in many different ways. They add -ment to some verbs, for example, to form nouns like excitement and development. These rules for word formation are not, of course, altogether consistent. In this article free-lance writer Nedra Newkirk Lamar reveals the incongruities that result when the "rules" are applied mechanically.

Everybody knows that a tongue-twister is something that twists   1
the tongue, and a skyscraper is something that scrapes the sky, but is an eavesdropper someone who drops eaves? A thinker is someone who thinks but is a tinker someone who tinks? Is a clabber something that goes around clabbing?

Somewhere along the way we all must have had an English   2
teacher who gave us the fascinating information that words that end in ER mean something or somebody who *does* something, like trapper, designer, or stopper.

A stinger is something that stings, but is a finger something that   3
fings? Fing fang fung. Today I fing. Yesterday I fang. Day before yesterday I had already fung.

You'd expect eyes, then, to be called seers and ears to be hear-   4
ers. We'd wear our shoes on our walkers and our sleeves on our reachers. But we don't. The only parts of the body that sound as if they might indicate what they're supposed to do are our fingers, which we've already counted out, our livers, and our shoulders. And they don't do what they sound as if they might. At least, I've never seen anyone use his shoulders for shoulding. You shoulder your way through a crowd, but you don't should your way. It's only in slang that we follow the pattern, when we smell with our smellers and kiss with our kissers.

The animal pattern seems to have more of a feeling for this   5
formation than people do, because insects actually do feel with their feelers. But do cats use their whiskers for whisking?

I've seen people mend socks and knit socks, but I've never seen   6
anyone dolage a sock. Yet there must be people who do, else how
could we have sock-dolagers?

Is a humdinger one who dings hums? And what is a hum anyway,   7
and how would one go about dinging it? Maybe Winnie the Pooh
could have told us. He was always humming hums, but A. A. Milne
never tells us whether he also was fond of dinging them. He sang
them but do you suppose he ever dang them?

Sometimes occupational names do reveal what the worker does,   8
though. Manufacturers manufacture, miners mine, adjusters adjust
—or at least try to. But does a grocer groce? Does a fruiterer fruiter?
Does a butler buttle?

No, you just can't trust the English language. You can love it   9
because it's your mother tongue. You can take pride in it because
it's the language Shakespeare was dramatic in. You can thrill to it
because it's the language Browning and Tennyson were poetic in.
You can have fun with it because it's the language Dickens and
Mark Twain and Lewis Carroll were funny in. You can revere it
because it's the language Milton was majestic in. You can be grateful to it because it's the language the Magna Carta and the Declaration of Independence were expressed in.

But you just can't trust it!   10

QUESTIONS ON CONTENT

1. Briefly identify each of the following: a *tinker*, an *eavesdropper*, *clabber*, a *sock-dolager*, and a *humdinger*.

2. People learning English as a second language often have difficulty with the irregularities in our processes of word formation. Give some examples of the kinds of errors such a person might make.

QUESTIONS ON RHETORIC

1. Why do you suppose that Lamar chose "Does a Finger Fing?" as the title for her essay?

2. What point is Lamar trying to make? What technique does she use to support that point?

3. What is Lamar's attitude toward her subject? What evidence of this attitude can you cite?

4. Does Lamar's tone in the essay help or hinder her argument? Explain.

5. Explain Lamar's use of the question as a structural device in the essay.

6. What is the effect of the repetitive parallel constructions in the next-to-last paragraph? How are they related to the final statement? Why do you feel Lamar made a separate paragraph out of the final statement?

VOCABULARY

slang   butler
fond   revere

CLASSROOM ACTIVITIES

1. Lamar tells us that "somewhere along the way we all must have had an English teacher who gave us the fascinating information that words that end in ER mean something or somebody who *does* something." Make a list of words ending in ER in which the suffix means something other than "one who does." What conclusions about the English language can you draw from your examples?

NOTE: Writing assignments for "Discovering Language" appear on p. 18.

3
The Power of Words

BERGEN EVANS

"Words are the tools for the job of saying what you want to say," writes Bergen Evans, lexicographer and professor of English at Northwestern University. With this sentence he introduces both the central point of his article and a theme that will recur in each section of this book: the importance of the word. In this selection, Evans develops his analogy of words as tools and discusses the many qualities, in addition to size, of an effective vocabulary.

Words are the tools for the job of saying what you want to say. And what you want to say are your thoughts and feelings, your desires and your dislikes, your hopes and your fears, your business and your pleasure—almost everything, indeed, that makes up *you*. Except for our vegetablelike growth and our animallike impulses, almost all that we are is related to our use of words. Man has been defined as a tool-using animal, but his most important tool, the one that distinguishes him from all other animals, is his speech.

As with other tools, the number and variety of the words we know should meet all our needs. Not that any man has ever had a vocabulary exactly fitted to his every need at all times. The greatest writers—those who have shown the rest of us how *in*adequate our own command of words is—have agonized over their verbal shortcomings. But we can approach our needs. The more words we know, the closer we can come to expressing precisely what we want to.

We can, for instance, give clear instructions, and reduce misunderstandings. If we say, "See that he does it," we should make sure that the person spoken to knows what he is to do when he *sees*, that it is clear to him who *he* is and what *it* is and what must be accomplished to *do* it.

Some of history's great disasters have been caused by misunderstood directions. The heroic but futile charge of the Light Brigade at

9

Balaclava in the Crimean War is a striking example. "Someone had blundered," Tennyson wrote. That was true, and the blunder consisted of the confusion over one word, which meant one thing to the person speaking but another to the persons spoken to.

The brigade was ordered to charge "the guns." The man who gave the order was a on a hilltop and had in mind a small battery which was very plain to him but was concealed from the soldiers in the valley by a slight rise. The only guns *they* could see were the main Russian batteries at the far end of the valley. Therefore they assumed that "the guns" referred to the batteries *they* saw. The command seemed utter madness, but it was a command and the leader of the brigade, after filing a protest, carried it out.

Fortunately, most misunderstandings don't have such disastrous consequences. But the continual confusion about such general terms as *thing, deal, it, fix,* and the like, certainly can be frustrating. Taken as a whole, the exasperation, humiliation, disappointment and quarreling caused by misunderstandings probably produce a thousand times the misery and suffering that the Light Brigade endured.

So the wise man, who wants peace of mind, and the efficient man, who wants to get on with the job, will take the trouble to use specific terms instead of doubtful ones.

Besides clarity, a large vocabulary provides variety. And that is useful; it is the basis for discrimination, since it provides a larger number of tools to choose from. A hammer won't do when a file is called for. Furthermore a large and varied vocabulary makes the speaker or writer more interesting. It allows him to avoid the dullness of repetition and to provoke attention. The interesting man is much more likely to be persuasive than the dull one. Dull people bore us. We don't listen to them. We hear them, but with a secret distaste. Instead of listening to them, we think only about getting away from them. Therefore a varied vocabulary is very useful for winning others to our point of view.

Thomas Wolfe reveled in words with more glory and gusto than perhaps any man since Shakespeare or Rabelais. On seeing a shabby little man lying dead on a subway bench, Wolfe was struck with the thought of the dull and miserable existence such a man must have had because of the sterility of his speech. "Poor, dismal, ugly, sterile, shabby little man," Wolfe wrote in his essay, "Death the Proud Brother," "with your little scrabble of harsh oaths, and cries, and stale constricted words, your pitiful little designs and feeble purposes. . . . Joy, glory, and magnificence were here for you upon this earth, but you scrabbled along the pavements rattling a few stale words like gravel in your throat, and would have none of them.''

When Caliban, the half-human monster in Shakespeare's last [10] play, *The Tempest,* furiously denies that he owes any gratitude to his master, the magician Prospero, he demands to know what Prospero has ever done for him. The magician passes over all the many benefits he has conferred on the wretched creature, to stress only one: he has taught him to speak.

> *I . . . took pains to make thee speak.*
> *When thou didst not, savage,*
> *Know thine own meaning, but wouldst gabble like*
> *A thing most brutish, I endow'd thy purposes*
> *With words that made them known.*

The simple fact is that we all begin as Calibans—and do not [11] know even our own purposes until we endow them with words. Do not, indeed, know ourselves. The pleasure you will feel as you develop your vocabulary is not solely the pleasure that comes with increased power; it is also the greater pleasure that comes with increased knowledge, especially of yourself. You will begin to appreciate expression as an art and to feel not only the advantage of commanding words but the satisfaction. You will notice that this or that phrase which someone utters in your hearing or which you see in the newspapers is very good.

And you will be pleased that it *is* good, just as you are pleased to [12] see a forward pass completed, or a long putt holed, or a dance step gracefully executed. For words are to the mind what such actions are to the body.

You will see that the rightness of a well-chosen word is not [13] merely a source of pleasure; it may provoke the most serious consequences or avoid the gravest danger. When, for example, America and Russia confronted each other during the Cuban crisis in 1962, and the world hovered for a few days on the brink of disaster, the use of the word *quarantine* instead of *blockade* was extremely important. A *blockade* is an act of war. No one knew quite what a *quarantine* meant, under the circumstances. But the very use of the word indicated that, while we were determined to protect ourselves, we wanted to avoid war. It was all a part of giving Russia some possibility of saving face. We wanted her missiles and planes out of Cuba and were prepared to fight even a nuclear war to get them out. But we certainly preferred to have them removed peacefully. We did not want to back Russia into a corner from which there could have been no escape except by violence.

Thus the use of *quarantine,* a purposefully vague word, was part of our strategy. Furthermore, it had other advantages over *blockade.* It is commonly associated with a restriction imposed by all civilized nations on people with certain communicable diseases to prevent them from spreading their disease throughout the community. It is a public health measure which, for all the inconvenience that it may impose on the afflicted individual, serves the public welfare. Thus, whereas a blockade would have been an announcement that we were proceeding aggressively to further our own interests, regardless of the rights of others, quarantine suggested a concern for the general welfare. In addition, it suggested that what was going on in Cuba was a dangerous disease which might spread.   14

So, as you develop a larger vocabulary you will be increasingly aware of what is going on. You will enjoy what you read more. New pleasures will be opened to you.   15

You will understand more. Difficult books whose meaning has been uncertain will become readable. The great poets who have enlarged our experience, the philosophers who have shaped our thoughts, the historians who have sought for patterns in the human story, the essayists whose observations have delighted men for centuries—all these and more will be available to you. And in sharing their thoughts your own world will expand. This particular benefit of an increased vocabulary is dramatically apparent in the strides that children make in comprehension as they progress in their use of language. Increased learning increases the child's word stock and the increased word stock makes learning easier. The National Conference on Research in English says "a child's ability to read, to speak, to write, and to think is inevitably conditioned by his vocabulary."   16

This goes for an adult too. Words cannot be separated from ideas. They interact. The words we use are so associated with our experiences and what the experiences mean to us that they cannot be separated. The idea comes up from our subconscious clothed in words. It can't come any other way.   17

We don't know how words are stored in our minds, but there does seem to be a sort of filing system. The filing system appears to be controlled by a perverse if not downright wacky filing clerk. Everyone has tried to remember a word and been unable to. Sometimes it is a common word, one that we *know* we know. Yet it won't come when we want it. It can be almost a form of torture trying to recall it, but no amount of fuming or fretting helps. Then suddenly,   18 usually some time later when it is no longer useful to us, it will come to mind readily. When we are searching for one of these words— often for a person's name—we will come up with others words or names that we know are close to but not exactly the one we want. This is curious in itself. For if we can't remember the word we want, how do we know the other word is very much like it? It's as though the filing clerk had seen the word we actually wanted or was even holding it in his hand but wouldn't give it to us.

Often we know that the unacceptable word has the same sound [19] or begins with the same letter as the word we can't remember. And when we finally recall the word we wanted, we find this is so. It seems as though our mental filing systems were arranged alphabetically and cross-indexed for similarity of internal sound. If we are well-read, we can call up a host of synonyms (words that mean the same thing) for many words, which suggests more crossfiling. Furthermore, words have subtle and complex associations. The speech and writing of some people who have sustained brain injuries or suffered strokes indicate a curious kind of damage. Some injured people seem to lose all proper names, some all adjectives, and many mix up capitals and small letters. This indicates that the interlocking connections of words in our minds are more complex than we can imagine. The chances are that the most spectacular computer is a simple gadget compared to the human mind.

For our purposes, our ignorance of how this intricate filing sys- [20] tem works does not matter. What matters to a person trying to enlarge his vocabulary is the many connections among the words he knows. Once we master a word, it is connected in our mind with scores of other words in what appears to be an infinite number of relationships and shades of meaning. A new word does not drop as a single addition into our word stock. Each new word learned enlarges a whole complex of thinking and is itself enlarged in meaning and significance.

A vocabularly is a tool which one uses in formulating the impor- [21] tant questions of life, the questions which must be asked before they can be answered. To a large extent, vocabulary shapes all the decisions we make. Most decisions, of course, are shaped by our emotions, by circumstances, and by the forces which may hold us back or urge us on. These circumstances and forces are largely beyond our control. But our speech is a sort of searchlight that helps us to see these things more clearly and to see ourselves in relation to them. At least it helps us call things by their right names.

To a great extent our speech affects our judgments. We don't [22] always—sometimes we can't—distinguish between words and things. A slogan, for example, especially if it rhymes, or is alliterative (that is, has a number of words that begin with the same sound), or has a strong rhythm, will move us to action. It convinces us that the action is necessary. "Motorists wise Simonize" is far more effective in promoting sales than "Simonize, wise motorists" or "Wise motorists, Simonize" would have been. It's the witchery of rhythm, one of the most subtle and dangerous of unseen forces that move and muddle our minds. Seduced by "Fifty-four forty or fight," our great-grandfathers almost went to war in 1844. And there are historians who trace much of the misery of the modern world to the fascination that Grant's "Unconditional surrender" held for four generations of Americans.

Certainly anyone who develops the valuable habit of examining   23
his own prejudices will find that many of them are, at bottom, verbal. A situation automatically calls forth a single word. The word is bathed in emotion. So whenever the situation is repeated, it produces the same emotional response. There is no effort to be rational, to see what is actually going on. The word triggers the response. But the more words one has at his command, the greater the possibility that he may be his own master. It takes words to free us from words. Removing an emotionally charged word from a phrase and substituting a neutral synonym often gives us an insight that nothing else can.

Speech is the means of relating our separate experiences and   24
emotions, of combining them, reliving them and, as far as we can, understanding them. If we did not have the words *justice, equal, radiation*—and a thousand others like them—our minds and our whole lives would be much narrower. Each new word of this kind increases the scope of thought and adds its bit to humanity. Once we have the word, of course, it seems natural and it is an effort to imagine being without it.

Consider that remarkable British phrase which Lord Broughton   25
invented during the reign of George IV (1820–1830): "His Majesty's opposition." Political parties rose in seventeenth-century England during a period of limited civil war and they behaved as if parliamentary victories were military ones. When one party gained power it immediately proceeded to impeach the leaders of the other party, demanding their very heads. But after a hundred and fifty years of peace and prosperity, men's tempers began to cool. A sense of fairness compelled them to grant their neighbor the right to a different opinion and even to grant that men who opposed them might still be loyal and honorable. But the atmosphere Lord Broughton described had to precede his phrase, just as the invention of the wheel had to precede the medieval concept of Fortune's wheel.

Once uttered, the phrase helped to further the idea it described.   26
Men saw that criticism of an administration can be as much a part of
good government as the government itself and that a man was not
necessarily a traitor because he disagreed with the party in power.

Many studies have established the fact that there is a high corre-   27
lation between vocabulary and intelligence and that the ability to
increase one's vocabulary throughout life is a sure reflection of
intellectual progress.

It is hard to stretch a small vocabulary to make it do all the things   28
that intelligent people require of words. It's like trying to plan a
series of menus from the limited resources of a poverty-stricken,
war-torn country compared to planning such a series in a prosper-
ous, stable country. Words are one of our chief means of adjusting
to all the situations of life. The better control we have over words,
the more successful our adjustment is likely to be.

QUESTIONS ON CONTENT

1. According to Evans, how can a large vocabulary help you?
Explain.

2. Does Evans feel that there is any relationship between vocabulary and intelligence? If so, what is that relationship?

3. Many newspapers carry regular "vocabulary building" columns, and the *Reader's Digest* has had for years a section called "It
Pays to Increase Your Word Power." What does the continuing
popularity of these features suggest about the attitude of many
Americans toward language?

4. Evans says, "The words we use are so associated with our experiences and what the experiences mean to us that they cannot be
separated." What associations do the following words have for you
as a result of your own experiences?

    dinner
    money
    Christmas
    fear
    success

Compare your associations with those of your classmates.

QUESTIONS ON RHETORIC

1. What is Evans's thesis and where is it stated?

2. Consider the central metaphor of Evans's essay: words as a tool.

How effective is the metaphor? What other extended metaphor does Evans use?

3. What is the purpose of Evans's reference to Caliban, a character in Shakespeare's *The Tempest?*

4. What technique does Evans use to support his generalization that "the rightness of a well-chosen word is not merely a source of pleasure; it may provoke the most serious consequences or avoid the gravest danger"?

5. How would you describe the author's tone; that is, his relationship to the reader? Would you say that the author's tone is formal, conversational, preachy, chatty, informal?

VOCABULARY

futile	inevitably	intricate
exasperation	subconscious	muddle
communicable	perverse	correlation

CLASSROOM ACTIVITIES

1. There is an important distinction between symbols and the things they stand for, that is, their referents. For example, a person should not confuse an actual chair (physical object) with the word "chair" (symbol). Evans points out, however, that "we don't always— sometimes we can't—distinguish between words and things." In this connection, discuss the following episode in which a small child is talking to her mother: "Mommy! I'm scared of *death.* I don't like to hear that word. It frightens me! If only it were called something else, like *looma.*" What in your opinion would happen if the word were changed?

2.   Evans makes the point that words must be defined for communication to be effective. As a writer you will often need to define and the more precise your definitions, the more clearly you will communicate. One way of defining a term is to place it in a class of similar items and then to show how it is different from the other items in that class. For example,

Word	Class	Characteristics
a *watch*	is a *mechanical device*	*for telling time and is usually carried or worn*
semantics	is an *area of linguistics*	*concerned with the study of the meaning of words.*

Certainly such definitions are not complete, and one could write an entire paragraph, essay, or book to define these terms more fully. This process, however, is useful for both thinking and writing.

Place each of the following terms in a class and then write a statement differentiating each term:

paper clip
pamphlet
anxiety
freedom

NOTE: Writing assignments for "Discovering Language" appear on p. 18.

WRITING ASSIGNMENTS FOR "DISCOVERING LANGUAGE"

1. Like Malcolm X, each of us can tell of an experience that has been unusually significant for us. Think about your own experiences, identify one incident that has been especially important for you, and write an essay about it. In preparing to write, you will find it helpful to ask yourself such questions as these: Why is the incident important for you? What aspects of the incident might interest someone else? What details will help you re-create the incident in the most engaging way? How can your narrative of the incident be most effectively organized?

2. Bergen Evans stresses the need for clarity and precision in writing. How clear and precise is your writing? As a test of your skills, study the following diagrams:

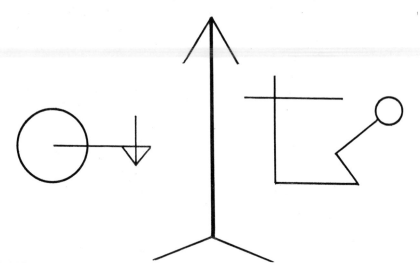

Next, produce a diagram of your own of comparable difficulty. Write a precise description of your diagram. Give your description (but not your diagram) to another member of your class and ask that person to draw the figure you have described. Compare your original drawing with your classmate's drawing based on your description. Discuss the reasons for any discrepancies that exist.

NOTE: Suggested topics for research papers appear on p. 293.

NOTABLE QUOTATIONS

The following quotations are drawn from the articles in this section. They are presented as additional topics for classroom discussion or for writing assignments.

"I saw that the best thing I could do was get hold of a dictionary—to study, to learn some words."   *Malcolm X*

"No, you just can't trust the English language."   *Lamar*

"Words are one of our chief means of adjusting to all the situations of life."   *Evans*

"A vocabulary is a tool which one uses in formulating the important questions of life, the questions which must be asked before they can be answered."   *Evans*

"Man has been defined as a tool-using animal, but his most important tool, the one that distinguishes him from all other animals, is his speech."   *Evans*

II
Politics and Doublespeak

1
Politics and the English Language

GEORGE ORWELL

Occasionally an essay becomes a classic, usually because it makes an important statement about some subject with unusual effectiveness. Such is the case with this essay, written in the 1940s. Here George Orwell, author of 1984, *discusses the condition of the English language and the ways in which it has seriously deteriorated. He concludes by suggesting a number of remedies to help restore the language to a healthier state.*

Most people who bother with the matter at all would admit that the English language is in a bad way, but it is generally assumed that we cannot by conscious action do anything about it. Our civilization is decadent and our language—so the argument runs—must inevitably share in the general collapse. It follows that any struggle against the abuse of language is a sentimental archaism, like preferring candles to electric light or hansom cabs to aeroplanes. Underneath this lies the half-conscious belief that language is a natural growth and not an instrument which we shape for our own purposes.

Now, it is clear that the decline of a language must ultimately have political and economic causes: it is not due simply to the bad influence of this or that individual writer. But an effect can become a cause, reinforcing the original cause and producing the same effect in an intensified form, and so on indefinitely. A man may take to drink because he feels himself to be a failure, and then fail all the more completely because he drinks. It is rather the same thing that is happening to the English language. It becomes ugly and inaccurate because our thoughts are foolish, but the slovenliness of our language makes it easier for us to have foolish thoughts. The point is that the process is reversible. Modern English, especially written English, is full of bad habits which spread by imitation and which can be avoided if one is willing to take the necessary trouble. If one gets rid of these habits one can think more clearly, and to think clearly is a necessary first step towards political regeneration: so that the fight against bad English is not frivolous and is not the exclusive concern of professional writers. I will come back to this presently, and I hope that by that time the meaning of what I have said here will have become clearer. Meanwhile here are five specimens of the English language as it is now habitually written.

These five passages have not been picked out because they are   3 especially bad—I could have quoted far worse if I had chosen—but because they illustrate various of the mental vices from which we now suffer. They are a little below the average, but are fairly representative samples. I number them so that I can refer back to them when necessary:

(1) I am not, indeed, sure whether it is not true to say that the Milton who once seemed not unlike a seventeenth-century Shelley had not become, out of an experience ever more bitter in each year, more alien [sic] to the founder of that Jesuit sect which nothing could induce him to tolerate.

> Professor Harold Laski (Essay in *Freedom of Expression*).

(2) Above all, we cannot play ducks and drakes with a native battery of idioms which prescribes such egregious collocations of vocables as the Basic *put up with* for *tolerate* or *put at a loss* for *bewilder.*

> Professor Lancelot Hogben (*Interglossa*).

(3) On the one side we have the free personality: by definition it is not neurotic, for it has neither conflict nor dream. Its desires, such as they are, are transparent, for they are just what institutional approval keeps in the forefront of consciousness; another institutional pattern would alter their number and intensity; there is little in them that is natural, irreducible, or culturally dangerous. But *on the other side,* the social bond itself is nothing but the mutual reflection of these self-secure integrities. Recall the definition of love. Is not this the very picture of a small academic? Where is there a place in this hall of mirrors for either personality or fraternity?

> Essay on psychology in *Politics* (New York).

(4) All the "best people" from the gentlemen's clubs, and all the frantic fascist captains, united in common hatred of Socialism and bestial horror of the rising tide of the mass revolutionary movement, have turned to acts of provocation, to foul incendiarism, to medieval legends of poisoned wells, to legalize their own destruction of proletarian organizations, and rouse the agitated petty-bourgeoisie to chauvinistic fervor on behalf of the fight against the revolutionary way out of the crisis.

> Communist pamphlet.

(5) If a new spirit *is* to be infused into this old country, there is one thorny and contentious reform which must be tackled, and that is the

humanization and galvanization of the B.B.C. Timidity here will bespeak canker and atrophy of the soul. The heart of Britain may be sound and of strong beat, for instance, but the British lion's roar at present is like that of Bottom in Shakespeare's *Midsummer Night's Dream*—as gentle as any sucking dove. A virile new Britain cannot continue indefinitely to be traduced in the eyes or rather ears, of the world by the effete languors of Langham Place, brazenly masquerading as "standard English." When the voice of Britain is heard at nine o'clock, better far and infinitely less ludicrous to hear aitches honestly dropped than the present priggish, inflated, inhibited, school-ma'amish arch braying of blameless bashful mewing maidens!

Letter in *Tribune.*

Each of these passages has faults of its own, but, quite apart   4 from avoidable ugliness, two qualities are common to all of them. The first is staleness of imagery; the other is lack of precision. The writer either has a meaning and cannot express it, or he inadvertently says something else, or he is almost indifferent as to whether his words mean anything or not. This mixture of vagueness and sheer incompetence is the most marked characteristic of modern English prose, and especially of any kind of political writing. As soon as certain topics are raised, the concrete melts into the abstract and no one seems able to think of turns of speech that are not hackneyed: prose consists less and less of *words* chosen for the sake of their meaning, and more and more of *phrases* tacked together like the sections of a prefabricated hen-house. I list below, with notes and examples, various of the tricks by means of which the work of prose-construction is habitually dodged:

DYING METAPHORS

A newly invented metaphor assists thought by evoking a visual   5 image, while on the other hand a metaphor which is technically "dead" (e.g., *iron resolution*) has in effect reverted to being an ordinary word and can generally be used without loss of vividness. But in between these two classes there is a huge dump of worn-out metaphors which have lost all evocative power and are merely used because they save people the trouble of inventing phrases for themselves. Examples are: *Ring the changes on, take up the cudgels for, toe the line, ride roughshod over, stand shoulder to shoulder with, play into the hands of, no axe to grind, grist to the mill, fishing in troubled waters, on the order of the day, Achilles' heel, swan song, hotbed.* Many of these are used without knowledge of their meaning (what is a "rift," for instance?), and incompatible metaphors are frequently mixed, a sure sign that the writer is not interested in what he is saying. Some metaphors now current have been twisted out of their original meaning without those who use them even being aware of the fact. For example, *toe the line* is sometimes written *tow the line*. Another example is the *hammer and the anvil*, now always used with the implication that the anvil gets the worst of it. In real life it is always the anvil that breaks the hammer, never the other way about: a writer who stopped to think what he was saying would be aware of this, and would avoid perverting the original phrase.

OPERATORS OR VERBAL FALSE LIMBS

These save the trouble of picking out appropriate verbs and nouns, and at the same time pad each sentence with extra syllables which give it an appearance of symmetry. Characteristic phrases are *render inoperative, militate against, make contact with, be subjected to, give rise to, give grounds for, have the effect of, play a leading part (role) in, make itself felt, take effect, exhibit a tendency to, serve the purpose of, etc., etc.* The keynote is the elimination of simple verbs. Instead of being a single word, such as *break, stop, spoil, mend, kill,* a verb becomes a *phrase*, made up of a noun or adjective tacked on to some general-purposes verb such as *prove, serve, form, play, render.* In addition, the passive voice is wherever possible used in preference to the active, and noun constructions are used instead of gerunds (*by examination of* instead of *by examining*). The range of verbs is further cut down by means of the *-ize* and *de-* formations, and the banal statements are given an appearance of profundity by means of the *not un-* formation. Simple conjunctions and prepositions are replaced by such phrases as *with respect to, having regard to, the fact that, by dint of, in view of, in the interests of, on the hypothesis that*; and the ends of sentences are saved from anticlimax by such resounding common-places as *greatly to be desired, cannot be left out of account, a development to be expected in the near future, deserving of serious consideration, brought to a satisfactory conclusion*, and so on and so forth.

PRETENTIOUS DICTION

Words like *phenomenon, element, individual* (as noun), *objective, categorical, effective, virtual, basic, primary, promote, constitute, exhibit, exploit, utilize, eliminate, liquidate*, are used to dress up simple statements and give an air of scientific impartiality to biased judgments. Adjectives like *epoch-making, epic, historic, unforgettable, triumphant, age-old, inevitable, inexorable, veritable,* are used to dignify the sordid processes of international politics, while writing that aims at glorifying war usually takes on an archaic color, its characteristic words being: *realm, throne, chariot, mailed fist, trident, sword, shield, buckler, banner, jackboot, clarion.* Foreign words and expressions such as *cul de sac, ancien régime, deus ex machina, mutatis mutandis, status quo, gleichschaltung, weltanschauung,* are used to give an air of culture and elegance. Except for the useful abbreviations *i.e., e.g.,* and *etc.,* there is no real need for any of the hundreds of foreign phrases now current in English. Bad writers, and especially scientific, political and sociological writers, are nearly always haunted by the notion that Latin or Greek words are grander than Saxon ones, and unnecessary words like *expedite, ameliorate, predict, extraneous, deracinated, clandestine, subaqueous* and hundreds of others constantly gain ground from their Anglo-Saxon opposite numbers.[1] The jargon peculiar to Marxist writing (*hyena, hangman, cannibal, petty bourgeois, these gentry, lacquey, flunkey, mad dog, White Guard,* etc.) consists largely of words and phrases translated from Russian, German or French; but the normal way of coining a new word is to use a Latin or Greek root with the appropriate affix and, where necessary, the -*ize* formation. It is often easier to make up words of this kind (*deregionalize, impermissible, extramarital, non-fragmentary* and so forth) than to think up the English words that will cover one's meaning. The result, in general, is an increase in slovenliness and vagueness.

MEANINGLESS WORDS

In certain kinds of writing, particularly in art criticism and literary criticism, it is normal to come across long passages which are almost completely lacking in meaning.[2] Words like *romantic, plastic, values, human, dead, sentimental, natural, vitality,* as used in art criti-

[1] An interesting illustration of this is the way in which the English flower names which were in use till very recently are being ousted by Greek ones, *snapdragon* becoming *antirrhinum, forget-me-not* becoming *myosotis,* etc. It is hard to see any practical reason for this change of fashion: it is probably due to an instinctive turning-away from the more homely word and a vague feeling that the Greek word is scientific.

[2] Example: "Comfort's catholicity of perception and image, strangely Whitmanesque in range, almost the exact opposite in aesthetic compulsion, continues to evoke that trembling atmospheric accumulative hinting at a cruel, an inexorably serene timelessness. . . . Wrey Gardiner scores by aiming at simple bull's-eyes with precision. Only they are not so simple, and through this contented sadness runs more than the surface bittersweet of resignation." (*Poetry Quarterly.*)

cism, are strictly meaningless, in the sense that they not only do not point to any discoverable object, but are hardly ever expected to do so by the reader. When one critic writes, "The outstanding feature of Mr. X's work is its living quality," while another writes, "The immediately striking thing about Mr. X's work is its peculiar deadness," the reader accepts this as a simple difference of opinion. If words like *black* and *white* were involved, instead of the jargon words *dead* and *living,* he would see at once that language was being used in an improper way. Many political words are similarly abused. The word *Fascism* has now no meaning except in so far as it signifies "something not desirable." The words *democracy, freedom, patriotic, realistic, justice,* have each of them several different meanings which cannot be reconciled with one another. In the case of a word like *democracy,* not only is there no agreed definition, but the attempt to make one is resisted from all sides. It is almost universally felt that when we call a country democratic we are praising it: consequently the defenders of every kind of regime claim that it is a democracy, and fear that they might have to stop using the word if it were tied down to any one meaning. Words of this kind are often used in a consciously dishonest way. That is, the person who uses them has his own private definition, but allows his hearer to think he means something quite different. Statements like, *Marshal Pétain was a true patriot, The Soviet Press is the freest in the world, The Catholic Church is opposed to persecution,* are almost always made with intent to deceive. Other words used in variable meanings, in most cases more or less dishonestly, are: *class, totalitarian, science, progressive, reactionary, bourgeois, equality.*

Now that I have made this catalogue of swindles and perversions, let me give another example of the kind of writing that they lead to. This time it must of its nature be an imaginary one. I am going to translate a passage of good English into modern English of the worst sort. Here is a well-known verse from *Ecclesiastes*:   9

> I returned and saw under the sun, that the race is not to the swift, nor the battle to the strong, neither yet bread to the wise, nor yet riches to men of understanding, nor yet favour to men of skill; but time and chance happeneth to them all.

Here it is in modern English: 10

> Objective consideration of contemporary phenomena compels the conclusion that success or failure in competitive activities exhibits no tendency to be commensurate with innate capacity, but that a considerable element of the unpredictable must invariably be taken into account.

This is a parody, but not a very gross one. Exhibit (3), above, for   11
instance, contains several patches of the same kind of English. It
will be seen that I have not made a full translation. The beginning
and ending of the sentence follow the original meaning fairly
closely, but in the middle the concrete illustrations—race, battle,
bread—dissolve into the vague phrase "success or failure in competitive activities." This had to be so, because no modern writer of
the kind I am discussing—no one capable of using phrases like
"objective consideration of contemporary phenomena"—would
ever tabulate his thoughts in that precise and detailed way. The
whole tendency of modern prose is away from concreteness. Now
analyse these two sentences a little more closely. The first contains
forty-nine words but only sixty syllables, and all its words are those
of everyday life. The second contains thirty-eight words of ninety
syllables: eighteen of its words are from Latin roots, and one from
Greek. The first sentence contains six vivid images, and only one
phrase ("time and chance") that could be called vague. The second
contains not a single fresh, arresting phrase, and in spite of its ninety
syllables it gives only a shortened version of the meaning contained
in the first. Yet without a doubt it is the second kind of sentence that
is gaining ground in modern English. I do not want to exaggerate.
This kind of writing is not yet universal, and outcrops of simplicity
will occur here and there in the worst-written page. Still, if you or I
were told to write a few lines on the uncertainty of human fortunes,
we should probably come much nearer to my imaginary sentence
than to the one from *Ecclesiastes.*

As I have tried to show, modern writing at its worst does not   12
consist in picking out words for the sake of their meaning and inventing images in order to make the meaning clearer. It consists in
gumming together long strips of words which have already been set
in order by someone else, and making the results presentable by
sheer humbug. The attraction of this way of writing is that it is easy.
It is easier—even quicker, once you have the habit—to say *In my
opinion it is not an unjustifiable assumption that* than to say *I think.*
If you use ready-made phrases, you not only don't have to hunt
about for words; you also don't have to bother with the rhythms of
your sentences, since these phrases are generally so arranged as to
be more or less euphonious. When you are composing in a hurry—
when you are dictating to a stenographer, for instance, or making a
public speech—it is natural to fall into a pretentious, Latinized style.
Tags like *a consideration which we should do well to bear in mind* or
a conclusion to which all of us would readily assent will save many a
sentence from coming down with a bump. By using stale metaphors,

similes and idioms, you save much mental effort, at the cost of leaving your meaning vague, not only for your reader but for yourself. This is the significance of mixed metaphors. The sole aim of a metaphor is to call up a visual image. When these images clash—as in *The Fascist octopus has sung its swan song, the jackboot is thrown into the melting pot*—it can be taken as certain that the writer is not seeing a mental image of the objects he is naming; in other words he is not really thinking. Look again at the examples I gave at the beginning of this essay. Professor Laski (1) uses five negatives in fifty-three words. One of these is superfluous, making nonsense of the whole passage, and in addition there is the slip *alien* for akin, making further nonsense, and several avoidable pieces of clumsiness which increase the general vagueness. Professor Hogben (2) plays ducks and drakes with a battery which is able to write prescriptions, and, while disapproving of the everyday phrase *put up with*, is unwilling to look *egregious* up in the dictionary and see what it means; (3), if one takes an uncharitable attitude towards it, is simply meaningless: probably one could work out its intended meaning by reading the whole of the article in which it occurs. In (4), the writer knows more or less what he wants to say, but an accumulation of stale phrases chokes him like tea leaves blocking a sink. In (5), words and meaning have almost parted company. People who write in this manner usually have a general emotional meaning— they dislike one thing and want to express solidarity with another— but they are not interested in the detail of what they are saying. A scrupulous writer, in every sentence that he writes, will ask himself at least four questions, thus: What am I trying to say? What words will express it? What image or idiom will make it clearer? Is this image fresh enough to have an effect? And he will probably ask himself two more: Could I put it more shortly? Have I said anything that is avoidably ugly? But you are not obliged to go to all this trouble. You can shirk it by simply throwing your mind open and letting the ready-made phrases come crowding in. They will construct your sentences for you—even think your thoughts for you, to a certain extent—and at need they will perform the important service of partially concealing your meaning even from yourself. It is at this point that the special connection between politics and the debasement of language becomes clear.

In our time it is broadly true that political writing is bad writing.   13
Where it is not true, it will generally be found that the writer is some kind of rebel, expressing his private opinions and not a "party line." Orthodoxy, of whatever color, seems to demand a lifeless, imitative style. The political dialects to be found in pamphlets, leading arti-

cles, manifestos, White Papers and the speeches of under-secretaries do, of course, vary from party to party, but they are all alike in that one almost never finds in them a fresh, vivid, home-made turn of speech. When one watches some tired hack on the platform mechanically repeating the familiar phrases—*bestial atrocities, iron heel, bloodstained tyranny, free peoples of the world, stand shoulder to shoulder*—one often has a curious feeling that one is not watching a live human being but some kind of dummy: a feeling which suddenly becomes stronger at moments when the light catches the speaker's spectacles and turns them into blank discs which seem to have no eyes behind them. And this is not altogether fanciful. A speaker who uses that kind of phraseology has gone some distance towards turning himself into a machine. The appropriate noises are coming out of his larynx, but his brain is not involved as it would be if he were choosing his words for himself. If the speech he is making is one that he is accustomed to make over and over again, he may be almost unconscious of what he is saying, as one is when one utters the responses in church. And this reduced state of consciousness, if not indispensable, is at any rate favorable to political conformity.

In our time, political speech and writing are largely the defence   14
of the indefensible. Things like the continuance of British rule in India, the Russian purges and deportations, the dropping of the atom bombs on Japan, can indeed be defended, but only by arguments which are too brutal for most people to face, and which do not square with the professed aims of political parties. Thus political language has to consist largely of euphemism, question-begging and sheer cloudy vagueness. Defenceless villages are bombarded from the air, the inhabitants driven out into the countryside, the cattle machine-gunned, the huts set on fire with incendiary bullets: this is called *pacification*. Millions of peasants are robbed of their farms and sent trudging along the roads with no more than they can carry: this is called *transfer of population* or *rectification of frontiers*. People are imprisoned for years without trial, or shot in the back of the neck or sent to die of scurvy in Arctic lumber camps: this is called *elimination of unreliable elements*. Such phraseology is needed if one wants to name things without calling up mental pictures of them. Consider for instance some comfortable English professor defending Russian totalitarianism. He cannot say outright, "I believe in killing off your opponents when you can get good results by doing so." Probably, therefore, he will say something like this:

"While freely conceding that the Soviet régime exhibits certain   15
features which the humanitarian may be inclined to deplore, we

must, I think, agree that a certain curtailment of the right to political opposition is an unavoidable concomitant of transitional periods, and that the rigors which the Russian people have been called upon to undergo have been amply justified in the sphere of concrete achievement.''

The inflated style is itself a kind of euphemism. A mass of Latin words falls upon the facts like soft snow, blurring the outlines and covering up all the details. The great enemy of clear language is insincerity. When there is a gap between one's real and one's declared aims, one turns as it were instinctively to long words and exhausted idioms, like a cuttlefish squirting out ink. In our age there is no such thing as "keeping out of politics." All issues are political issues, and politics itself is a mass of lies, evasions, folly, hatred and schizophrenia. When the general atmosphere is bad, language must suffer. I should expect to find—this is a guess which I have not sufficient knowledge to verify—that the German, Russian and Italian languages have all deteriorated in the last ten or fifteen years, as a result of dictatorship. 16

But if thought corrupts language, language can also corrupt thought. A bad usage can spread by tradition and imitation, even among people who should and do know better. The debased language that I have been discussing is in some ways very convenient. Phrases like *a not unjustifiable assumption, leaves much to be desired, would serve no good purpose, a consideration which we should do well to bear in mind,* are a continuous temptation, a packet of aspirins always at one's elbow. Look back through this essay, and for certain you will find that I have again and again committed the very faults I am protesting against. By this morning's post I have received a pamphlet dealing with conditions in Germany. The author tells me that he "felt impelled" to write it. I open it at random, and here is almost the first sentence that I see: "[The Allies] have an opportunity not only of achieving a radical transformation of Germany's social and political structure in such a way as to avoid a nationalistic reaction in Germany itself, but at the same time of laying the foundations of a cooperative and unified Europe." You see, he "feels impelled" to write—feels, presumably, that he has something new to say—and yet his words, like cavalry horses answering the bugle, group themselves automatically into the familiar dreary pattern. The invasion of one's mind by ready-made phrases (*lay the foundations, achieve a radical transformation*) can only be prevented if one is constantly on guard against them, and every such phrase anaesthetizes a portion of one's brain. 17

I said earlier that the decadence of our language is probably 18 curable. Those who deny this would argue, if they produced an argument at all, that language merely reflects existing social conditions, and that we cannot influence its development by any direct tinkering with words and constructions. So far as the general tone or spirit of a language goes, this may be true, but it is not true in detail. Silly words and expressions have often disappeared, not through any evolutionary process but owing to the conscious action of a minority. Two recent examples were *explore every avenue* and *leave no stone unturned,* which were killed by the jeers of a few journalists. There is a long list of flyblown metaphors which could similarly be got rid of if enough people would interest themselves in the job; and it should also be possible to laugh the *not un-* formation out of existence,[3] to reduce the amount of Latin and Greek in the average sentence, to drive out foreign phrases and strayed scientific words, and, in general, to make pretentiousness unfashionable. But all these are minor points. The defence of the English language implies more than this, and perhaps it is best to start by saying what it does *not* imply.

To begin with, it has nothing to do with archaism, with the salvaging of obsolete words and turns of speech, or with the setting up of a "standard English" which must never be departed from. On the contrary, it is especially concerned with the scrapping of every word or idiom which has outworn its usefulness. It has nothing to do with correct grammar and syntax, which are of no importance so long as one makes one's meaning clear, or with the avoidance of Americanisms, or with having what is called a "good prose style." On the other hand it is not concerned with fake simplicity and the attempt to make written English colloquial. Nor does it even imply in every case preferring the Saxon word to the Latin one, though it does imply using the fewest and shortest words that will cover one's meaning. What is above all needed is to let the meaning choose the word, and not the other way about. In prose, the worst thing one can do with words is to surrender to them. When you think of a concrete object, you think wordlessly, and then, if you want to describe the thing you have been visualizing you probably hunt about till you find the exact words that seem to fit it. When you think of something abstract you are more inclined to use words from the start, and unless you make a conscious effort to prevent it, the existing dialect will come rushing in and do the job for you, at the expense of blurring or even changing your meaning. Probably it is better to put off using words as long as possible and get one's meaning as clear as

[3] One can cure oneself of the *not un-* formation by memorizing this sentence: *A not unblack dog was chasing a not unsmall rabbit across a not ungreen field.*

one can through pictures or sensations. Afterwards one can choose —not simply *accept*—the phrases that will best cover the meaning, and then switch round and decide what impression one's words are likely to make on another person. This last effort of the mind cuts out all stale or mixed images, all prefabricated phrases, needless repetitions, and humbug and vagueness generally. But one can often be in doubt about the effect of a word or a phrase, and one needs rules that one can rely on when instinct fails. I think the following rules will cover most cases:

1. Never use a metaphor, simile, or other figure of speech which you are used to seeing in print.
2. Never use a long word where a short one will do.
3. If it is possible to cut a word out, always cut it out.
4. Never use the passive where you can use the active.
5. Never use a foreign phrase, a scientific word or a jargon word if you can think of an everyday English equivalent.
6. Break any of these rules sooner than say anything outright barbarous.

These rules sound elementary, and so they are, but they demand a deep change of attitude in anyone who has grown used to writing in the style now fashionable. One could keep all of them and still write bad English, but one could not write the kind of stuff that I quoted in those five specimens at the beginning of this article.

I have not here been considering the literary use of language, but merely language as an instrument for expressing and not for concealing or preventing thought. Stuart Chase and others have come near to claiming that all abstract words are meaningless, and have used this as a pretext for advocating a kind of political quietism. Since you don't know what Fascism is, how can you struggle against Fascism? One need not swallow such absurdities as this, but one ought to recognize that the present political chaos is connected with the decay of language, and that one can probably bring about some improvement by starting at the verbal end. If you simplify your English, you are freed from the worst follies of orthodoxy. You cannot speak any of the necessary dialects, and when you make a stupid remark its stupidity will be obvious, even to yourself. Political language—and with variations this is true of all political parties, from Conservatives to Anarchists—is designed to make lies sound truthful and murder respectable, and to give an appearance of solidity to pure wind. One cannot change this all in a moment, but one can at least change one's own habits, and from time to time one can even, if one jeers loudly enough, send some worn-out and useless

20

phrase—some *jackboot, Achilles' heel, hotbed, melting pot, acid test, veritable inferno* or other lump of verbal refuse—into the dustbin where it belongs.

QUESTIONS ON CONTENT

1. In your own words, summarize Orwell's argument in this essay.

2. It is often said that "mixed metaphors" (e.g., "politicians who have their heads in the sand are leading the country over the precipice") are undesirable in either speech or writing because they are inaccurate. For Orwell, a mixed metaphor is symptomatic of a greater problem. What is that problem?

3. Study paragraph 2 of the essay. What, according to Orwell, is the nature of cause-and-effect relationships?

4. Our world is becoming increasingly prefabricated. What does the concept of prefabrication have to do with Orwell's argument concerning the prevalence of the habitual and hackneyed phrase?

5. Orwell states that he himself in this essay is guilty of some of the errors he is pointing out. Can you detect any of them?

6. According to Orwell, what are four important prewriting questions a scrupulous writer will ask himself or herself?

7. Orwell says that one of the evils of political language is "begging the question." What does he mean? Why, according to Orwell, has political language deteriorated? Do you agree with him that "the decadence of our language is probably curable"? Explain.

QUESTIONS ON RHETORIC

1. Why does Orwell present the "five specimens of the English language as it is now habitually written"? What use does he make of these five passages later in his essay?

2. Following are some of the metaphors and similes that Orwell uses in his essay. Account for the effectiveness of each.
   a. . . . prose consists less . . . of *words* chosen for the sake of their meaning, and more . . . of *phrases* tacked together like the sections of a prefabricated hen-house (paragraph 4).
   b. But in between these two classes there is a huge dump of worn-out metaphors which have lost all evocative power . . . (paragraph 5).
   c. . . . the writer knows . . . what he wants to say, but an accumulation of stale phrases chokes him like tea leaves blocking a sink (paragraph 12).

d. A mass of Latin words falls upon the facts like soft snow, blurring the outlines and covering up all the details (paragraph 16).

e. When there is a gap between one's real and one's declared aims, one turns . . . instinctively to long words and exhausted idioms, like a cuttlefish squirting out ink (paragraph 16).

f. . . . he . . . feels, presumably, that he has something new to say—and yet his words, like cavalry horses answering the bugle, group themselves automatically into the familiar dreary pattern (paragraph 17).

3. At the end of paragraph 4 Orwell speaks of "the tricks by means of which the work of prose-construction is habitually dodged" and he then goes on to classify them. Why is his classification helpful?

4. In what respect is Orwell's use of "habit" and "mental vices" to refer to language abuse consistent with his thesis?

VOCABULARY

decadent	impartiality	scrupulous
frivolous	biased	humanitarian
inadvertently	reconciled	evolutionary
implication	pretentious	

CLASSROOM ACTIVITIES

1. Orwell suggests that you should never use the passive voice when you can use the active voice. Consider the following example:

Passive: It is expected that the welfare budget will be cut by Congress.
Active: We expect Congress to cut the welfare budget.

Not only is the active version shorter, but it is more precise in that it properly emphasizes "Congress" as the doer of the action. Rewrite each of the following sentences in the active voice.

a. The line-drive single was hit by John.

b. Two eggs and one stick of butter should be added to the other ingredients.

c. Information of a confidential nature cannot be released by doctors.

d. Figures showing that the cost of living rose sharply during the past twelve months were released by the administration today.

e. It was decided that a meeting would be held on each Monday.

Are there any situations in which the passive voice is more appropriate than the active? Explain. What conclusions can you draw about the active and passive voices?

2. Orwell says, "As soon as certain topics are raised, the concrete melts in the abstract." One such topic has always been war. Compare the following two war prayers, the first from a Catholic missal and the second by Mark Twain:

O Lord, graciously regard the sacrifice which we offer up: that it may deliver us from all the evil of war, and establish us under Thy sure protection. Through our Lord Jesus Christ, Thy Son, who liveth and reigneth with Thee in the unity of the Holy Ghost.

Oh Lord our God, help us to tear their soldiers to bloody shreds with our shells; help us to cover their smiling fields with their patriot dead; help us to lay waste their humble homes with a hurricane of fire; help us to wring the hearts of their unoffending widows with unavailing grief; help us to turn them out roofless with their little children to wander un-friended the wastes of their desolated land in rags and hunger and thirst. Lord, blast their hopes, blight their lives, protract their bitter pilgrim-age, make heavy their steps, water their way with their tears. We ask it, in the spirit of love, of Him Who is the Source of Love, and who is the ever-faithful refuge and friend of all that are sore beset and seek his aid.

How would you characterize the very different effects of these two war prayers? Specifically, how do you account for the differences in effect?

NOTE: Writing assignments for "Politics and Doublespeak" appear on p. 64.

2
Gobbledygook

STUART CHASE

Stuart Chase, well-known commentator on the dynamics of our language and author of The Power of Words *and* The Tyranny of Words, *examines the world of obscure language, or gobbledygook, as it has come to be called. According to Chase, "gobbledygook not only flourishes in government bureaus but grows wild and lush in the law, the universities, and sometimes among the literati."*

Said Franklin Roosevelt, in one of his early presidential speeches: 1 "I see one-third of a nation ill-housed, ill-clad, ill-nourished." Translated into standard bureaucratic prose his statement would read:

> It is evident that a substantial number of persons within the Continental boundaries of the United States have inadequate financial resources with which to purchase the products of agricultural communities and industrial establishments. It would appear that for a considerable segment of the population, possibly as much as 33.3333* of the total, there are inadequate housing facilities, and an equally significant proportion is deprived of the proper types of clothing and nutriment.

This rousing satire on gobbledygook—or talk among the bureau- 2 crats—is adapted from a report[1] prepared by the Federal Security Agency in an attempt to break out of the verbal squirrel cage. "Gobbledygook" was coined by an exasperated Congressman, Maury Maverick of Texas, and means using two, or three, or ten words in the place of one, or using a five-syllable word where a single syllable would suffice. Maverick was censuring the forbidding prose of executive departments in Washington, but the term has now spread to windy and pretentious language in general.

"Gobbledygook" itself is a good example of the way a language 3 grows. There was no word for the event before Maverick's inven-

---
* Not carried beyond four places.
[1] This and succeeding quotations from F.S.A. report by special permission of the author, Milton Hall.

tion; one had to say: "You know, that terrible, involved, polysyllabic language those government people use down in Washington." Now one word takes the place of a dozen.

A British member of Parliament, A. P. Herbert, also exasperated   4
with bureaucratic jargon, translated Nelson's immortal phrase, "England expects every man to do his duty":

> England anticipates that, as regards the current emergency, personnel will face up to the issues, and exercise appropriately the functions allocated to their respective occupational groups.

A New Zealand official made the following report after surveying   5
a plot of ground for an athletic field:[2]

> It is obvious from the difference in elevation with relation to the short depth of the property that the contour is such as to preclude any reasonable developmental potential for active recreation.

Seems the plot was too steep.

An office manager sent this memo to his chief: 6

> Verbal contact with Mr. Blank regarding the attached notification of promotion has elicited the attached representation intimating that he prefers to decline the assignment.

Seems Mr. Blank didn't want the job.

> A doctor testified at an English trial that one of the parties was suffering   7
> from "circumorbital haematoma."

Seems the party had a black eye.

> In August 1952 the U.S. Department of Agriculture put out a pamphlet   8
> entitled: "Cultural and Pathogenic Variability in Single-Condial and Hyphaltip Isolates of Hemlin-Thosporium Turcicum Pass."

Seems it was about corn leaf disease.

On reaching the top of the Finsteraarhorn in 1845, M. Dollfus-   9
Ausset, when he got his breath, exclaimed:

> The soul communes in the infinite with those icy peaks which seem to have their roots in the bowels of eternity.

Seems he enjoyed the view.

A governmental department announced: 10

> Voucherable expenditures necessary to provide adequate dental treatment required as adjunct to medical treatment being rendered a pay

[2] This item and the next two are from the piece on gobbledygook by W. E. Farbstein, *New York Times*, March 29, 1953.

patient in in-patient status may be incurred as required at the expense of the Public Health Service.

Seems you can charge your dentist bill to the Public Health Service. Or can you?

LEGAL TALK

Gobbledygook not only flourishes in government bureaus but grows   11
wild and lush in the law, the universities, and sometimes among the literati. Mr. Micawber was a master of gobbledygook, which he hoped would improve his fortunes. It is almost always found in offices too big for face-to-face talk. Gobbledygook can be defined as squandering words, packing a message with excess baggage and so introducing semantic "noise." Or it can be scrambling words in a message so that meaning does not come through. The directions on cans, bottles, and packages for putting the contents to use are often a good illustration. Gobbledygook must not be confused with double talk, however, for the intentions of the sender are usually honest.

I offer you a round fruit and say, "Have an orange." Not so an   12
expert in legal phraseology, as parodied by editors of *Labor*:

> I hereby give and convey to you, all and singular, my estate and inter-
> ests, right, title, claim and advantages of and in said orange, together
> with all rind, juice, pulp, and pits, and all rights and advantages therein
> . . . anything hereinbefore or hereinafter or in any other deed or deeds,
> instrument or instruments of whatever nature or kind whatsoever, to the
> contrary, in any wise, notwithstanding.

The state of Ohio, after five years of work, has redrafted its legal   13
code in modern English, eliminating 4,500 sections and doubtless a blizzard of "whereases" and "hereinafters." Legal terms of necessity must be closely tied to their referents, but the early solons tried to do this the hard way, by adding synonyms. They hoped to trap the physical event in a net of words, but instead they created a mumbo-jumbo beyond the power of the layman, and even many a lawyer, to translate. Legal talk is studded with tautologies, such as "cease and desist," "give and convey," "irrelevant, incompetent, and imma-terial." Furthermore, legal jargon is a dead language; it is not spo-ken and it is not growing. An official of one of the big insurance companies calls their branch of it "bafflegab." Here is a sample from his collection:[3]

[3]Interview with Clifford B. Reeves by Sylvia F. Porter, *New York Evening Post*, March 14, 1952.

One-half to his mother, if living, if not to his father, and one-half to his mother-in-law, if living, if not to his mother, if living, if not to his father. Thereafter payment is to be made in a single sum to his brothers. On the one-half payable to his mother, if living, if not to his father, he does not bring in his mother-in-law as the next payee to receive, although on the one-half to his mother-in-law, he does bring in the mother or father.

You apply for an insurance policy, pass the tests, and instead of   14
a straightforward "here is your policy," you receive something like this:

This policy is issued in consideration of the application therefor, copy of which application is attached hereto and made part hereof, and of the payment for said insurance on the life of the above-named insured.

ACADEMIC TALK

The pedagogues may be less repetitious than the lawyers, but many   15
use even longer words. It is a symbol of their calling to prefer Greek and Latin derivatives to Anglo-Saxon. Thus instead of saying: "I like short clear words," many a professor would think it more seemly to say: "I prefer an abbreviated phraseology, distinguished for its lucidity." Your professor is sometimes right, the longer word may carry the meaning better—but not because it is long. Allen Upward in his book *The New Word* warmly advocates Anglo-Saxon English as against what he calls "Mediterranean" English, with its polysyllables built up like a skyscraper.

Professional pedagogy, still alternating between the Middle Ages   16
and modern science, can produce what Henshaw Ward once called the most repellent prose known to man. It takes an iron will to read as much as a page of it. Here is a sample of what is known in some quarters as "pedageese":

Realization has grown that the curriculum or the experiences of learners change and improve only as those who are most directly involved examine their goals, improve their understandings and increase their skill in performing the tasks necessary to reach newly defined goals. This places the focus upon teacher, lay citizen and learner as partners in curricular improvement and as the individuals who must change, if there is to be curriculum change.

I think there is an idea concealed here somewhere. I think it   17
means: "If we are going to change the curriculum, teacher, parent, and student must all help." The reader is invited to get out his semantic decoder and check on my translation. Observe there is no

technical language in this gem of pedageese, beyond possibly the word "curriculum." It is just a simple idea heavily ververbalized.

In another kind of academic talk the author may display his   18
learning to conceal a lack of ideas. A bright instructor, for instance, in need of prestige may select a common sense proposition for the subject of a learned monograph—say, "Modern cities are hard to live in" and adorn it with imposing polysyllables: "Urban existence in the perpendicular declivities of megalopolis . . ." et cetera. He coins some new terms to transfix the reader—"mega-decibel" or "strato-cosmopolis"—and works them vigorously. He is careful to add a page or two of differential equations to show the "scatter." And then he publishes, with 147 footnotes and a bibliography to knock your eye out. If the authorities are dozing, it can be worth an associate professorship.

While we are on the campus, however, we must not forget that   19
the technical language of the natural sciences and some terms in the social sciences, forbidding as they may sound to the layman, are quite necessary. Without them, specialists could not communicate what they find. Trouble arises when experts expect the uninitiated to understand the words; when they tell the jury, for instance, that the defendant is suffering from "circumorbital haematoma."

Here are two authentic quotations. Which was written by a dis-   20
tinguished modern author, and which by a patient in a mental hospital? You will find the answer at the end of this essay.

> 1. Have just been to supper. Did not knowing what the woodchuck sent me here. How when the blue blue blue on the said anyone can do it that tries. Such is the presidential candidate.

> 2. No history of a family to close with those and close. Never shall he be alone to be alone to be alone to be alone to be alone to lend a hand and leave it left and wasted.

REDUCING THE GOBBLE

As government and business offices grow larger, the need for doing   21
something about gobbledygook increases. Fortunately the biggest office in the world is working hard to reduce it. The Federal Security Agency in Washington,[4] with nearly 100 million clients on its books, began analyzing its communication lines some years ago, with gratifying results. Surveys find trouble in three main areas: correspond-

[4] Now the Department of Health, Education, and Welfare.

ence with clients about their social security problems, office memos, official reports.

Clarity and brevity, as well as common humanity, are urgently   22
needed in this vast establishment which deals with disability, old age, and unemployment. The surveys found instead many cases of long-windedness, foggy meanings, clichés, and singsong phrases, and gross neglect of the reader's point of view. Rather than talking to a real person, the writer was talking to himself. "We often write like a man walking on stilts."

Here is a typical case of long-windedness: 23

> *Gobbledygook as found:* "We are wondering if sufficient time has passed so that you are in a postion to indicate whether favorable action may now be taken on our recommendation for the reclassification of Mrs. Blank, junior clerk-stenographer, CAF 2, to assistant clerk-stenographer, CAF 3?"

> *Suggested improvement:* "Have you yet been able to act on our recommendation to reclassify Mrs. Blank?"

Another case:

> Although the Central Efficiency Rating Committee recognizes that there are many desirable changes that could be made in the present efficiency rating system in order to make it more realistic and more workable than it now is, this committee is of the opinion that no further change should be made in the present system during the current year. Because of conditions prevailing throughout the country and the resultant turnover in personnel, and difficulty in administering the Federal programs, further mechanical improvement in the present rating system would require staff retraining and other administrative expense which would seem best withheld until the official termination of hostilities, and until restoration of regular operations.

The F.S.A. invites us to squeeze the gobbledygook out of this   24
statement. Here is my attempt:

> The Central Efficiency Rating Committee recognizes that desirable changes could be made in the present system. We believe, however, that no change should be attempted until the war is over.

This cuts the statement from 111 to 30 words, about one-quarter   25
of the original, but perhaps the reader can do still better. What of importance have I left out?

Sometimes in a book which I am reading for information—not   26
for literary pleasure—I run a pencil through the surplus words. Often I can cut a section to half its length with an improvement in

clarity. Magazines like *The Reader's Digest* have reduced this process to an art. Are long-windedness and obscurity a cultural lag from the days when writing was reserved for priests and cloistered scholars? The more words and the deeper the mystery, the greater their prestige and the firmer the hold on their jobs. And the better the candidate's chance today to have his doctoral thesis accepted.

The F.S.A. surveys found that a great deal of writing was obscure although not necessarily prolix. Here is a letter sent to more than 100,000 inquirers, a classic example of murky prose. To clarify it, one needs to *add* words, not cut them: 27

> In order to be fully insured, an individual must have earned $50 or more in covered employment for as many quarters of coverage as half the calendar quarters elapsing between 1936 and the quarter in which he reaches age 65 or dies, whichever first occurs.

Probably no one without the technical jargon of the office could translate this: nevertheless, it was sent out to drive clients mad for seven years. One poor fellow wrote back: "I am no longer in covered employment. I have an outside job now."

Many words and phrases in officialese seem to come out automatically, as if from lower centers of the brain. In this standardized prose people never *get jobs,* they "secure employment"; *before* and *after* become "prior to" and "subsequent to"; one does not *do,* one "performs"; nobody *knows* a thing, he is "fully cognizant"; one never *says,* he "indicates."' A great favorite at present is "implement."   28

Some charming boners occur in this talking-in-one's-sleep. For instance: 29

> The problem of extending coverage to all employees, regardless of size, is not as simple as surface appearances indicate.
> Though the proportions of all males and females in ages 16–45 are essentially the same . . .
> Dairy cattle, usually and commonly embraced in dairying . . .

In its manual to employees, the F.S.A. suggests the following: 30

Instead of	Use
give consideration to	consider
make inquiry regarding	inquire
is of the opinion	believes
comes into conflict with	conflicts
information which is of a confidential nature	confidential information

Professional or office gobbledygook often arises from using the   31 passive rather than the active voice. Instead of looking you in the eye, as it were, and writing "This act requires . . ." the office worker looks out of the window and writes: "It is required by this statute that . . ." When the bureau chief says, "We expect Congress to cut your budget," the message is only too clear; but usually he says, "It is expected that the departmental budget estimates will be reduced by Congress."

> *Gobbled:* "All letters prepared for the signature of the Administrator will be single spaced."
> *Ungobbled:* "Single space all letters for the Administrator."
> (Thus cutting 13 words to 7.)

ONLY PEOPLE CAN READ

The F.S.A. surveys pick up the point that human communication involves a listener as well as a speaker. Only people can read, though a lot of writing seems to be addressed to beings in outer space. To whom are you talking? The sender of the officialese message often forgets the chap on the other end of the line. [32]

A woman with two small children wrote the F.S.A. asking what she should do about payments, as her husband had lost his memory. "If he never gets able to work," she said, "and stays in an institution would I be able to draw any benefits? . . . I don't know how I am going to live and raise my children since he is disable to work. Please give me some information. . . ." [33]

To this human appeal, she received a shattering blast of gobbledygook, beginning, "State unemployment compensation laws do not provide any benefits for sick or disabled individuals . . . in order to qualify an individual must have a certain number of quarters of coverage . . ." et cetera, et cetera. Certainly if the writer had been thinking about the poor woman he would not have dragged in unessential material about old-age insurance. If he had pictured a mother without means to care for her children, he would have told her where she might get help—from the local office which handles aid to dependent children, for instance. [34]

Gobbledygook of this kind would largely evaporate if we thought of our messages as two way—in the above case, if we pictured ourselves talking on the doorstep of a shabby house to a woman with two children tugging at her skirts, who in her distress does not know which way to turn. [35]

RESULTS OF THE SURVEY

The F.S.A. survey showed that office documents could be cut 20 to   36
50 per cent, with an improvement in clarity and a great saving to
taxpayers in paper and payrolls.

A handbook was prepared and distributed to key officials.[5] They   37
read it, thought about it, and presently began calling section meetings to discuss gobbledygook. More booklets were ordered, and the
local output of documents began to improve. A Correspondence
Review Section was established as a kind of laboratory to test
murky messages. A supervisor could send up samples for analysis
and suggestions. The handbook is now used for training new members; and many employees keep it on their desks along with the
dictionary. . . .

The handbook makes clear the enormous amount of gobbledy-   38
gook which automatically spreads in any large office, together with
ways and means to keep it under control. I would guess that at least
half of all the words circulating around the bureaus of the world are
"irrelevant, incompetent, and immaterial"—to use a favorite legal-
ism; or are just plain "unnecessary"—to ungobble it.

My favorite story of removing the gobble from gobbledygook   39
concerns the Bureau of Standards at Washington. I have told it
before but perhaps the reader will forgive the repetition. A New
York plumber wrote the Bureau that he had found hydrochloric acid
fine for cleaning drains, and was it harmless? Washington replied:
"The efficacy of hydrochloric acid is indisputable, but the chlorine
residue is incompatible with metallic permanence."

The plumber wrote back that he was mighty glad the Bureau   40
agreed with him. The Bureau replied with a note of alarm: "We
cannot assume responsibility for the production of toxic and nox-
ious residues with hydrochloric acid, and suggest that you use an
alternate procedure." The plumber was happy to learn that the Bureau still agreed with him.

Whereupon Washington exploded: "Don't use hydrochloric   41
acid; it eats hell out of the pipes!"

NOTE: The second quotation on p. 42 comes from Gertrude Stein's *Lucy Church
Amiably*.

QUESTIONS ON CONTENT

1. What is gobbledygook? Give three examples of gobbledygook
not mentioned by Chase. Why does Chase object to gobbledygook?

[5] By Milton Hall.

What does he mean when he says, "Gobbledygook . . . would largely evaporate if we thought of our messages as two way"?

2. Why do bureaucrats, lawyers, and professors, among others, use gobbledygook? Is its use ever justified? Explain.

3. Do you agree with Chase's paraphrases or translations of bureaucratic jargon in paragraphs 4–10? Rewrite these passages differently from the way Chase has.

4. Review Orwell's list of questions that you should ask yourself before you begin to write (Orwell, end of paragraph 12) and his list of rules for writing (Orwell, end of paragraph 19). Having read Chase's essay, can you add anything to Orwell's lists?

5. Chase's statement "It is almost always found in offices too big for face-to-face talk" emphasizes that gobbledygook goes hand in hand with the dehumanizing character of most of our institutions. What is the connection between this statement and Orwell's recommendation to use concrete terms when writing?

QUESTIONS ON RHETORIC

1. What methods does Chase use to define gobbledygook? Why is it important for him to establish a definition for the term? What does Chase see as the main distinction between gobbledygook and double-talk (sometimes also referred to as *doublespeak*)?

2. What is the function of the many examples and quotations that Chase uses? Why are they important?

VOCABULARY

pretentious	tautologies	murky
immortal	advocates	clients
squandering	proposition	

CLASSROOM ACTIVITIES

1. In his essay "The Marks of an Educated Man" (*Context,* Spring 1961), Alan Simpson presents the following example of inflated prose, or, as he aptly dubs it, "verbal smog."

> It is inherent to motivational phenomena that there is a drive for more gratification than is realistically possible, on any level or in any type of personality organization. Likewise it is inherent to the world of objects that not all potentially desirable opportunities can be realized within a human life span. Therefore, any personality must involve an organiza-

tion that allocates opportunities for gratifications, that systematizes precedence relative to the limited possibilities. The possibilities of gratification, simultaneously or sequentially, of all need dispositions are severely limited by the structure of the object system and by the intrasystemic incompatibility of the consequences of gratifying them all.

What is the author of this passage trying to say? Rewrite the paragraph eliminating the unnecessary verbiage.

NOTE: Writing assignments for "Politics and Doublespeak" appear on p. 64.

3
Public Doublespeak:
On Beholding and Becoming

TERENCE P. MORAN

In 1971 the National Council of Teachers of English passed a resolution to "find means to study dishonest and inhumane uses of language and literature by advertisers, to bring offenses to public attention, to propose classroom techniques for preparing children to cope with commercial propaganda." To carry out this resolution and a related resolution about political propaganda, the NCTE established the Committee on Public Doublespeak of which Terence P. Moran is a member. In the following article Moran, director of the Media Ecology Program at New York University, examines the way language is manipulated by the Army, dentists, the funeral industry, and college teachers and administrators.

According to a report by the Roper Organization,[1] Americans have increased their reliance on television as the source of their information from 51% in 1959 to 64% in 1972; in addition the percentage who listed television news as "most believable" increased from 29% in 1959 to 48% in 1972. Other sources of information included newspapers, radio, and magazines. What this means is that we are living in a world increasingly bounded by mass media, a world in which symbols have more meaning than reality, a world in which we have no way to check secondhand reports with firsthand observations. In such a world, symbols—especially language—play a major role in structuring our "reality" and in shaping what we are becoming.

The artificiality of mass media creates a number of illusions. Some illusions are relatively harmless and humorous: for example, many people think that Johnny Carson actually "visits" their homes. Indeed, television performers frequently refer to the view-

[1] "What People Think of Television and Other Mass Media, 1959-1972," *A Report by the Roper Organization* (New York: Television Information Office, May 1973).

49

ers as "friends" and thank them for "allowing us to come into your homes." This illusion of friendship and visiting by the television performer carries over to real life, so that fans (and let us not forget that the word is short for fanatics) think nothing of stopping in to visit Mr. Carson when they are in California. Carol Burnett tells of the time when some fans visited her: "One day we had a family walk right into the kitchen and demand a tour of the house. When my daughter asked them to leave, they got very huffy. 'We certainly will not,' they said, 'We came all the way from Ohio to see this.' "[2] After so many years of being "so glad we had this time together" Carol should not have been surprised by the Ohio family's business; after all, they were "friends," and "friends" do expect to be accorded hospitality when they come to "visit." When Andy Williams found four fans swimming in his pool and asked them to leave, they rightly objected to his behavior by saying, "You're not as nice as you seem on TV!"[3] Exactly. Life is not what it seems on television but how are we viewers to know that when our experiences are so bounded by media?

Television, however, is not the only place in which confusion is created. Consider this language use from the program for a convention of the Law Enforcement Intelligence Unit in which something labeled "cultural enrichment" occurs every day from 6 to 8 p.m. and which turns out to be the daily cocktail party. Actually "cocktail party" is itself a euphemism for what H. L. Mencken liked to call "boozing." Such pollution of the semantic environment may be relatively harmless but one notes a rising level of pollutants, many of which are far from trivial. Probably no one, except for the many aspiring writers who go unpublished, is really hurt if the *Ladies' Home Journal* pays Spiro Agnew a reputed $100,000 for the rights to his first novel; as Lenore Hershey, the editor of the *Journal* explained, "We always like to encourage new writers."[4] Some encouragement. Some new writer. . . .

The following is an invitation published in numerous national magazines:

Take the Army's 16-Month Tour of Europe

Right out of high school.
In today's Army you can enlist for European duty that guarantees at least 16 months with one of seven crack outfits stationed in Germany.

[2]Jeanie Kasindorf, "Rand McNally Move Over," *TV GUIDE*, Vol. 22, No. 22 (June 1, 1974), p. 32.
[3]*Ibid.*, p. 33.
[4]*New York Times* (February 6, 1974).

France, Denmark and Switzerland are just across the border. Within easy reach of any free weekend. Italy and the Riviera are just a few hours away. Just waiting for you on some of that 30 days paid vacation you earn each year in the Army.

This is your chance of a lifetime. To live and work in Europe. To get to know places like no tourist ever can. To get to know the people. Pick up the language.

If you want to live and work where tourists only visit, drop us the coupon. Or talk to your nearby Army representative about enlisting in the Army for European duty.

Today's Army Wants to Join You

Perhaps "today's Army" wants to join you at home. Notice how the supposed "defense" purposes of having an American Army in Western Europe are not even mentioned. From this it might be concluded that our Army is in Europe to provide travel and vacation for recent high school graduates. Some vacation. Some invitation. . . .

Attempts at controlling and limiting our semantic world abound   5
in our society. Dentists are given lists of phrases to say and phrases to avoid in dealing with patients:

Do Say	Don't Say
Reception room	Waiting room
Treatment room	Operatory
Consultation room	Private
Case discussion	Case presentation
Necessary x-rays	Full-mouth series
Diagnostic models	Study models
Complete dentistry	Rehabilitation
Treatment or dentistry	Work
Considerable (or small amount of) decay	Cavities, areas or surfaces
Restoration	Filling
Sedative dressing or medicinal restoration	Temporary filling
Removal	Extraction
Follow-up visit or preventive program	Recall
Prepare the tooth	Grind the tooth
Partial denture	Partials
Primary or foundation teeth	Baby teeth
My assistant	My girl
Fee	Bill
How did you plan	Would you like
Take care of	Pay for

Payment arrangements	Financial arrangements
Agreement	Contract or note
Investment	Cost
Did you want to take care of this by cash or check?	That will be ten dollars
Three twenty-seven	Three hundred twenty-seven
I recommend	I suggest
The Doctor recommends	Doctor would like
Bookkeeper's allowance	Discount
Professional courtesy	Professional discount
Thorough examination	Check up
Mrs. Scott, Doctor is ready to see you now	Would you like to come in?
Uncomplicated	Simple
Dr. Adams is with a patient right now. This is Ann, Doctor's secretary. How may I help you?	Who's calling please? Doctor is busy. May I help you?
Do you prefer mornings or afternoons?	When would you like to come in?
Doctor's schedule is filled for today. However, he can see you . . .	He's all booked up. He can't see you until . . .

In *The American Way of Death,* Jessica Mitford examines the   6
semantic environment of the funeral industry and finds:

> . . . a whole new terminology, as ornately shoddy as the satin rayon
> casket liner, has been invented by the funeral industry to replace the
> direct and serviceable vocabulary of former times. Undertaker has been
> supplanted by "funeral director" or "mortician." (Even the classified
> section of the telephone directory gives recognition to this; in its pages
> you will find "Undertakers—see Funeral Directors.") Coffins are
> "caskets"; hearses are "coaches" or "professional cars"; flowers are
> "floral tributes"; corpses generally are "loved ones," but mortuary
> etiquette dictates that a specific corpse be referred to by name only—as
> "Mr. Jones"; cremated ashes are "cremains." Euphemisms such as
> "slumber room," "reposing room," and "calcination—the *kindlier*
> heat" abound in the funeral business.[5]

According to Mitford, "funeral director" is being replaced by "grief
therapist," a further debasing of the language. . . .

Another contributor to the polluting of our semantic environ-   7
ment can be found in college catalogs. A small business college in
Ohio offers six points for "Communications I, II" which is de-

[5]New York: Simon and Schuster, 1963, pp. 18-19.

scribed as "A review for the mature student of the rules and the conventions governing punctuation." So much for communication. Under "Special Courses" are offered these two:

> *Personal Development* (for Women)   1¹/₂ credits
>   Training in selecting styles of dress, grooming, and general physical appearance consistent with life-style and the demands of the occasion. Special emphasis is placed on the expanded and emancipated roles open to women in a changing society.
>
> *Personal Development* (for Men)   1¹/₂ credits
>   Training in the art and science of achieving success in the business world without sacrificing human values or life-style options. Course includes grooming essentials, dress options, effective communication skills, and the prerequisites of poise.

A great urban university offers degrees, including the doctor of philosophy, in "Leisure Studies," with a course in "Values in Leisure" that promises "Emphasis is on studying changing concepts of work and leisure; value of leisure and its contribution to the quality of life; and resources for leisure pursuits." Evidently, in our society we must learn how to deal with our leisure time; one more indication of our immersion in a world bounded more by media than by reality. Any college bulletin offers a wealth of data on the deterioration of the English language. And the products of the colleges and universities frequently wind up teaching others. Consider, for example, the following recommendations given to the faculty of an elementary school in Brooklyn: [8]

FOR PARENT INTERVIEWS AND REPORT CARDS

Harsh Expression (Avoid)	Euphemism
1. Does all right if pushed	Accomplishes tasks when interest is stimulated.
2. Too free with fists	Resorts to physical means of winning his point or attracting attention.
3. Lies (Dishonest)	Shows difficulty in distinguishing between imaginary and factual material.
4. Cheats	Needs help in learning to adhere to rules and standards of fair play.
5. Steals	Needs help in learning to respect the property rights of others.
6. Noisy	Needs to develop quieter habits of communication.
7. Lazy	Needs ample supervision in order to work well.

8. Is a bully	Has qualities of leadership but needs help in learning to use them democratically.
9. Associates with "Gangs"	Seems to feel secure only in group situations; needs to develop a sense of independence.
10. Disliked by other children	Needs help in learning to form lasting friendships.

Whatever such changes may mean to the improvement of inter-   9
personal relations among teachers, students, and parents, they offer
little hope for communicating ideas between people. Whatever the
speaker or writer may mean by the suggested euphemism is open to
various interpretations by the listeners or readers; what results is
not communication but pseudocommunication, an illusion that
meaning has passed from speaker to listener.

Such pseudocommunication (doublespeak) is not limited to the   10
orthodox. The Esalen Institute, for example, offers a weekend
workshop called "Tennis Flow" that promises to ". . . integrate
principles of body awareness, movement, dance, music, and meditation with traditional methods of tennis instruction and practice."
As far as I can determine anything concrete from all this, it would
seem that they are going to play tennis, a bit pretentiously, but
tennis nonetheless. For those who spend their "leisure time" with
golf, Esalen offers a workshop entitled "Golf, Energy Awareness,
and Video Feedback" which offers meditation and video feedback
as approaches to improving one's golf game with ". . . sessions for
practicing energy awareness and integrating these approaches by
working on the golf swing at the local driving range." A swimming
class becomes "Knowing Your Body in Water" or "A Reunion with
the Sea."

Another unorthodox approach to education is offered by "Open   11
Space" a "free curriculum" at New York University. Among the
offerings for Spring 1974 we find "Astrology," . . . "Scrabble
Theory," "Bicycle Repair," "Introduction to Go," "Folk-Rock
Guitar," "Beginning and Advanced Chess," "Tibetan Buddhist
Art," "Juggling," "Leathercraft," "Consciousness III" (which offers the "geodesic dome, ekistics, arcologies, floating cities, the
world game, the limits to growth, futuristics, design initiative,
spaceship earth, alternative futures, cybernetics, recycling, postin-
dustrial society, technotronic age, neoluddites, communes and uto-
pias, dysutopias, Poujadisme, prognostics-diagnostics-agnostics-
synnostics. . . ."); all in four one-hour sessions. Perhaps the most
interestingly worded offering is one called "Thoroughbred
Thought." Here is the full description:

The exciting world of horse racing reaches its pinnacle every May with the running of the Kentucky Derby. This course is designed to teach a basic understanding in handicapping the well-bred horses that run in this type of race. Lectures cover training techniques and a discussion of breeding.

The class is not geared for everyday gambling, but rather a patient view of the sport, with an occasional investment when the right circumstances arise. Two field trips to Aqueduct Race Track and a tour of the Belmont Park training facilities and stable area.

Tuesdays 7-8:30 p.m.   6 sessions
                               Plus field trips

April 2-May 7 $7.00

Playing the ponies has taken on an academic facade. With the new Off-Track Betting in New York State, perhaps the course could be an at-home study offering. And, if successful, this course might be the answer to the continuing money problems besetting most private colleges and universities in America. . . .

A word of caution: one person's trivia and trivialities frequently are another's relevance and passion. The offerings, both orthodox and unorthodox, are open equally to examination and criticism. It is not the individual items that should concern us but the overall pattern of collective uncritical thinking. . . .

In examining what our students are beholding in the world bounded by television, magazines, newspapers, radio, advertisements, college catalogues, and all the other components of the semantic environment, and in monitoring the products of their languaging, we begin to see what they, and all of us, are becoming. It is not that some sinister force (the omnipotent and unseen *they*) is imposing such uncritical languaging on us, but that our semantic environment is suffering from a tendency for the system to swamp the users: we are self-polluters living in a world of semantic garbage, both offender and victim. In the writings examined here we can readily see the use of the easy phrase, the meaningless platitude, the uncritical commonplace; in short we witness not communication, but pseudocommunication, not language but "duckspeak," quacking made to appear like speech.

Orwell, however, believed that such decay of our language is curable. His advice is simple and pointed:

> If you can simplify your English, you are freed from the worst follies of orthodoxy. You cannot speak any of the necessary dialects, and when you make a stupid remark its stupidity will be obvious, even to yourself.[6]

[6]"Politics and the English Language." *The Orwell Reader* (New York: A Harvest Book, Harcourt, Brace and Company, 1956), p. 366.

Of course it may be that our media-bounded world is far too   15
symbol-oriented for us to reverse the trend. It may well be that what
we have beheld and are beholding will so structure what we are
becoming that some form of "newspeak," where sincerity counts
for more than verification and where being yourself supersedes all
else, will become our language. But if we are to attempt to follow
Orwell's advice to stop this trend, then we have to begin somewhere. And that somewhere lies, in Ray Bradbury's fine phrase,
"between the left ear and the right."

QUESTIONS ON CONTENT

1. What conclusions does Moran draw from the statistics in the
report by the Roper Organization? What does he mean when he says
that "we are living in . . . a world in which symbols have more
meaning than reality"?

2. What is Moran's attitude toward euphemisms?

3. Why does Moran find fault with the army's invitation to enlist
(paragraph 4)?

4. What differences in meaning do you see in the following terms:
undertaker, funeral director, and *grief therapist*? Is *grief therapist,* as
Moran suggests, really "a further debasing of the language"?
Explain.

5. What word of caution concerning Public Doublespeak does
Moran offer?

QUESTIONS ON RHETORIC

1. What is the controlling idea of paragraph 2? How does Moran
support this idea?

2. Moran ends paragraphs 3 and 4 with short sentence fragments.
What does he achieve by ending his paragraphs this way?

3. By what means does Moran define *pseudocommunication* (paragraphs 9, 10, and 13)? What examples does he use to illustrate this
concept?

VOCABULARY

reliance	artificiality	trivia
symbols	deterioration	sinister

role   orthodox   verification

CLASSROOM ACTIVITIES

1. Examine Moran's "list of phrases to say and phrases to avoid in dealing with patients" (paragraph 5). Discuss with other members of your class the semantic differences between the "Do Say" and "Don't Say" expressions. What general conclusions can you draw about the language dentists are being encouraged to use with their patients?

2. The following excerpt from Benjamin Lee Whorf's *Language, Thought and Reality* suggests that language acts as a filter for our experience and as such helps shape reality for us:

> We have the same word for falling snow, snow on the ground, snow packed hard like ice, slushy snow, wind-driven flying snow—whatever the situation may be. To an Eskimo, this all-inclusive word would be almost unthinkable: he would say that falling snow, slushy snow, and so on, are sensually and operationally different, different things to contend with; he uses different words for them and for other kinds of snow. The Aztecs go even farther than we in the opposite direction with "cold," "ice," and "snow" all represented by the same basic word. . . .

Discuss with your classmates several incidents from your own experience that clearly exemplify the shaping power of language. For example, consider some of the recent purchases you have made. Have any of them been influenced by brand names, advertisements, or language used by salesmen? Did you ever find yourself taking or avoiding a course primarily because of its name?

NOTE: Writing assignments for "Politics and Doublespeak" appear on p. 64.

4

The Euphemism:
Telling It Like
It Isn't

TIME

Many Americans feel that nothing is taboo anymore—that anything that can be imagined can be said or filmed or printed. The editors of Time, *however, make clear in this essay that the euphemism is prevalent in America precisely because people often do not want to "tell it like it is." The euphemisms themselves and the aspects of life to which they are applied may change, but the euphemism shows no signs of disappearing.*

Modern American speech, while not always clear or correct or   1
turned with much style, is supposed to be uncommonly frank. Witness the current explosion of four-letter words and the explicit discussion of sexual topics. In fact, gobbledygook and nice-Nellyism
still extend as far as the ear can hear. Housewives on television may
chat about their sex lives in terms that a decade ago would have
made gynecologists blush; more often than not, these emancipated
women still speak about their children's "going to the potty." Government spokesmen talk about "redeployment" of American
troops; they mean withdrawal. When sociologists refer to blacks
living in slums, they are likely to mumble about "nonwhites" in a
"culturally deprived environment." The CIA may never have used
the expression "to terminate with extreme prejudice" when it
wanted a spy rubbed out. But in the context of a war in which
"pacification of the enemy infrastructure" is the military mode of
reference to blasting the Viet Cong out of a village, the phrase
sounded so plausible that millions readily accepted it as accurate.

The image of a generation blessed with a swinging, liberated   2
language is largely an illusion. Despite its swaggering sexual candor,
much contemporary speech still hides behind that traditional enemy
of plain talk, the euphemism.

From a Greek word meaning "to use words of good omen," 3 euphemism is the substitution of a pleasant term for a blunt one— telling it like it isn't. Euphemism has probably existed since the beginning of language. As long as there have been things of which men thought the less said the better, there have been better ways of saying less. In everday conversation the euphemism is, at worst, a necessary evil; at its best, it is a handy verbal tool to avoid making enemies needlessly, or shocking friends. Language purists and the blunt-spoken may wince when a young woman at a party coyly asks for direction to "the powder room," but to most people this kind of familiar euphemism is probably no more harmful or annoying than, say, a split infinitive.

On a larger scale, though, the persistent growth of euphemism in 4 a language represents a danger to thought and action, since its fundamental intent is to deceive. As linguist Benjamin Lee Whorf has pointed out, the structure of a given language determines, in part, how the society that speaks it views reality. If "substandard housing" makes rotting slums appear more livable or inevitable to some people, then their view of American cities has been distorted and their ability to assess the significance of poverty has been reduced. Perhaps the most chilling example of euphemism's destructive power took place in Hitler's Germany. The wholesale corruption of the language under Nazism, notes critic George Steiner, is symbolized by the phrase *endgültige Lösung* (final solution), which "came to signify the death of 6,000,000 human beings in gas ovens."

No one could argue that American English is under siege from 5 linguistic falsehood, but euphemisms today have the nagging persistence of a headache. Despite the increasing use of nudity and sexual innuendo in advertising, Madison Avenue is still the great exponent of talking to "the average person of good upbringing"—as one TV executive has euphemistically described the ordinary American—in ways that won't offend him. Although this is like fooling half the people none of the time, it has produced a handsome bouquet of roses by other names. Thus there is "facial-quality tissue" that is not intended for use on faces, and "rinses" or "tints" for women who might be unsettled to think they dye their hair. In the world of deodorants, people never sweat or smell; they simply "offend." False teeth sound truer when known as "dentures."

Admen and packagers, of course, are not the only euphemizers. 6 Almost any way of earning a salary above the level of ditchdigging is known as a profession rather than a job. Janitors for several years have been elevated by image-conscious unions to the status of "custodians"; nowadays, a teen-age rock guitarist with three chords to his credit can class himself with Horowitz as a "recording artist." Cadillac dealers refer to autos as "preowned" rather than "second-hand." Government researchers concerned with old people call them "senior citizens." Ads for bank credit cards and department stores refer to "convenient terms"—meaning 18% annual interest rates payable at the convenience of the creditor.

Jargon, the sublanguage peculiar to any trade, contributes to   7 euphemism when its terms seep into general use. The student New Left, which shares a taste for six-syllable words with Government bureaucracy, has concocted a collection of substitute terms for use in politics. To "liberate," in the context of campus uproars, means to capture and occupy. Four people in agreement form a "coalition." In addition to "participatory democracy," which in practice is often a description of anarchy, the university radicals have half seriously given the world "anticipatory Communism," which means to steal. The New Left, though, still has a long way to go before it can equal the euphemism-creating ability of Government officials. Who else but a Washington economist would invent the phrase "negative saver" to describe someone who spends more money than he makes?

A persistent source of modern euphemisms is the feeling, in-   8 spired by the prestige of science, that certain words contain implicit subjective judgments, and thus ought to be replaced with more "objective" terms. To speak of "morals" sounds both superior and arbitrary, as though the speaker were indirectly questioning those of the listener. By substituting "values," the concept is miraculously turned into a condition, like humidity or mass, that can be safely measured from a distance. To call someone "poor," in the modern way of thinking, is to speak pejoratively of his condition, while the substitution of "disadvantaged" or "underprivileged," indicates that poverty wasn't his fault. Indeed, says linguist Mario Pei, by using "underprivileged," we are "made to feel that it is all our fault." The modern reluctance to judge makes it more offensive than ever before to call a man a liar; thus there is a "credibility gap" instead.

The liberalization of language in regard to sex involves the use of   9 perhaps a dozen words. The fact of their currency in what was once known as polite conversation raises some unanswered linguistic questions. Which, really, is the rose, and which the other name? Are the old forbidden obscenities really the crude bedrock on which softer and shyer expressions have been built? Or are they simply coarser ways of expressing physical actions and parts of the human anatomy that are more accurately described in less explicit terms? It remains to be seen whether the so-called forbidden words will contribute anything to the honesty and openness of sexual discussion. Perhaps their real value lies in the power to shock, which is inevitably diminished by overexposure. Perhaps the Victorians, who preferred these words unspoken and unprinted, will prove to have had a point after all.

For all their prudery, the Victorians were considerably more   10 willing than modern men to discuss ideas—such as social distinctions, morality and death—that have become almost unmentionable. Nineteenth-century gentlewomen whose daughters had "limbs" instead of suggestive "legs" did not find it necessary to call their maids "housekeepers," nor did they bridle at referring to "upper" or "lower" classes within society. Rightly or wrongly, the Victorian could talk without embarrassment about "sin," a word that today few but clerics use with frequency or ease. It is even becoming difficult to find a doctor, clergyman or undertaker (known as a "mortician") who will admit that a man has died rather than "expired" or "passed away." Death has not lost its sting; the words for it have.

There is little if any hope that euphemisms will ever be excised   11 from mankind's endless struggle with words that, as T. S. Eliot lamented, bend, break and crack under pressure. For one thing, certain kinds of everyday euphemisms have proved their psychological necessity. The uncertain morale of an awkward teen-ager may be momentarily buoyed if he thinks of himself as being afflicted by facial "blemishes" rather than "pimples" The label "For motion discomfort" that airlines place on paper containers undoubtedly helps the squeamish passenger keep control of his stomach in bumpy weather better than if they were called "vomit bags." Other forms of self-deception may not be beneficial, but may still be emotionally necessary. A girl may tolerate herself more readily if she thinks of herself as a "swinger" rather than as "promiscuous." Voyeurs can salve their guilt feelings when they buy tickets for certain "adult entertainments" on the ground that they are implicitly supporting "freedom of artistic expression."

Lexicographer Bergen Evans of Northwestern University be-   12 lieves that euphemisms persist because "lying is an indispensable part of making life tolerable." It is virtuous, but a bit beside the point, to contend that lies are deplorable. So they are; but they cannot be moralized or legislated away, any more than euphemisms can be. Verbal miasma, when it deliberately obscures truth, is an offense to reason. But the inclination to speak of certain things in uncertain terms is a reminder that there will always be areas of life that humanity considers too private, or too close to feelings of guilt, to speak about directly. Like stammers or tears, euphemisms will be created whenever men doubt, or fear, or do not know. The instinct is not wholly unhealthy; there is a measure of wisdom in the familiar saying that a man who calls a spade a spade is fit only to use one.

QUESTIONS ON CONTENT

1. What is a euphemism?

2. People use euphemisms when they want to avoid talking directly about subjects that make them uncomfortable, although what makes people uncomfortable changes. For example, we have been able to talk about "legs" and "breasts" for quite a while, and "venereal disease" for a shorter time; but many people still avoid the words "die" and "death." Identify some other subjects for which euphemisms are still prevalent and list several euphemisms for each. Do you use the same euphemisms as your parents? As your grandparents?

3. Linguist Benjamin Lee Whorf has pointed out that "the structure of a given language determines, in part, how the society that speaks it views reality" (paragraph 4). Explain how our use of euphemisms affects both our behavior and our opinion of our behavior. Consider, for example, the following expressions and the euphemisms for them:

> refugee camp ("new life hamlet")
> typist ("information processor")
> air raid ("limited duration protective reaction strike")
> assassination team ("health alteration committee")
> defoliation ("resources control program")

List other euphemisms used by government and big business. How may the use of such euphemisms influence behavior?

4. Do you agree with the editors of *Time* that "despite its swaggering sexual candor, much contemporary speech still hides behind that traditional enemy of plain talk, the euphemism"? Explain.

5. What does *Time* mean by the "psychological necessity" of euphemisms?

QUESTIONS ON RHETORIC

1. What is the thesis of this essay and where is it stated?

2. In your opinion, why doesn't the definition of euphemism come earlier than paragraph 3 of the essay? Explain.

VOCABULARY

frank	prestige	obscures
deprived	pejoratively	
illusion	tolerate	

CLASSROOM ACTIVITIES

1. Study the following list of euphemisms:
   rest room
   john
   lavatory
   men's room
   ladies' room
   powder room
   bathroom

What does the widespread use of these euphemisms suggest about our culture?

WRITING ASSIGNMENTS FOR "POLITICS AND DOUBLESPEAK"

1. Some of our most pressing social issues depend for their solutions upon the precise definition of critical terms. The Karen Quinlan case, for example, brought worldwide attention to the legal and medical definitions of the word *death*. Debates continue about the meaning of other controversial words, such as *morality, minority* (ethnic), *alcoholism, life* (as in the abortion issue), *pornography, kidnapping, drug, censorship, remedial, insanity, monopoly* (business), and *literacy*. Select one of these words and write a 300–500-word essay in which you discuss the problems associated with the definition of the term.

2. Argue either that the euphemism is "a handy verbal tool to avoid making enemies needlessly, or shocking friends," or that it is "a danger to thought and action, since its fundamental intent is to deceive."

3. In his book *The Second Sin,* psychiatrist Thomas Szasz makes the following observations:
   a. The prevention of parenthood is called "planned parenthood."
   b. Policemen receive bribes; politicians receive campaign contributions.
   c. Homicide by physicians is called "euthanasia."
   d. Marijuana and heroin are sold by pushers; cigarettes and alcohol are sold by businessmen.
   e. Imprisonment by psychiatrists is called "mental hospitalization."

Using Szasz's observations or similar ones of your own, write an essay in which you discuss the way people manipulate words and meanings to suit their particular needs.

NOTE: Suggested topics for research papers appear on p. 293.

NOTABLE QUOTATIONS

The following quotations are drawn from the articles in this section. They are presented as additional topics for classroom discussion or for writing assignments.

"But if thought corrupts language, language can also corrupt thought." *Orwell*

"The inflated style is itself a kind of euphemism." *Orwell*

"In our time, political speech and writing are largely the defense of the indefensible." *Orwell*

"Most people who bother with the matter at all would admit that the English language is in a bad way, but it is generally assumed that we cannot by conscious action do anything about it." *Orwell*

"Many words and phrases in official use seem to come out automatically, as if from lower centers of the brain." *Chase*

"Professional or office gobbledygook often arises from using the passive rather than the active voice." *Chase*

"Symbols—especially language—play a major role in structuring our 'reality' and in shaping what we are becoming." *Moran*

"In short, we witness not communication, but pseudocommunication, not language but 'duckspeak,' quacking made to appear like speech." *Moran*

"The image of a generation blessed with a swinging, liberated language is largely an illusion." *Time*

"Verbal miasma, when it deliberately obscures truth, is an offense to reason." *Time*

"Like stammers or tears, euphemisms will be created whenever men doubt, fear, or do not know." *Time*

III
The Language of Advertising

1
Bugs Bunny Says They're Yummy

DAWN ANN KURTH

In 1972, eleven-year-old Dawn Ann Kurth, a fifth-grader at Meadowlane Elementary School in Melbourne, Florida, was a surprise witness at a Senate subcommittee hearing on television advertising. She believes that TV commercials, especially those shown on Saturday-morning television, take unfair advantage of children. The following is a transcript of her testimony to the committee.

Mr. Chairman:

My name is Dawn Ann Kurth. I am 11 years old and in the fifth grade at Meadowlane Elementary School in Melbourne, Florida. This year I was one of the 36 students chosen by the teachers out of 20,000 5th-through-8th graders to do a project in the Talented Student Program in Brevard County. We were allowed to choose a project in any field we wanted. It was difficult to decide. There seem to be so many problems in the world today. What could I do?

A small family crisis solved my problem. My sister Martha, who is 7, had asked my mother to buy a box of Post Raisin Bran so that she could get the free record that was on the back of the box. It had been advertised several times on Saturday morning cartoon shows. My mother bought the cereal, and we all (there are four children in our family) helped Martha eat it so she could get the record. It was after the cereal was eaten and she had the record that the crisis occurred. There was no way the record would work.

Martha was very upset and began crying and I was angry too. It just didn't seem right to me that something could be shown on TV that worked fine and people were listening and dancing to the record and when you bought the cereal, instead of laughing and dancing, we were crying and angry. Then I realized that perhaps here was a problem I could do something about or, if I couldn't change things,

1

2

3

at least I could make others aware of deceptive advertising practices to children.

To begin my project I decided to keep a record of the number of commercials shown on typical Saturday morning TV shows. There were 25 commercial messages during one hour, from 8 to 9 A.M., not counting ads for shows coming up or public service ads. I found there were only 10 to 12 commercials during shows my parents like to watch. For the first time, I really began to think about what the commercials were saying. I had always listened before and many times asked my mother to buy certain products I had seen advertised, but now I was listening and really thinking about what was being said. Millions of kids are being told:

"Make friends with Kool-Aid. Kool-Aid makes good friends."

"People who love kids have to buy Fritos."

"Hershey chocolate makes milk taste like a chocolate bar." Why should milk taste like a chocolate bar anyway?

"Cheerios make you feel groovy all day long." I eat them sometimes and I don't feel any different.

"Libby frozen dinners have fun in them." Nothing is said about the food in them.

"Cocoa Krispies taste like a chocolate milk shake only they are crunchy."

"Lucky Charms are magically delicious with sweet surprises inside." Those sweet surprises are marshmallow candy.

I think the commercials I just mentioned are examples of deceptive advertising practices.

Another type of commercial advertises a free bonus gift if you buy a certain product. The whole commercial tells about the bonus gift and says nothing about the product they want you to buy. Many times, as in the case of the record, the bonus gift appears to be worthless junk or isn't in the package. I wrote to the TV networks and found it costs about $4,000 for a 30-second commercial. Many of those ads appeared four times in each hour. I wonder why any company would spend $15,000 or $20,000 an hour to advertise worthless junk.

The ads that I have mentioned I consider deceptive. However, I've found others I feel are dangerous.

Bugs Bunny vitamin ads say their vitamins "taste yummy" and taste good.

Chocolate Zestabs says their product is "delicious" and compare taking it with eating a chocolate cookie.

If my mother were to buy those vitamins, and my little sister got to the bottles, I'm sure she would eat them just as if they were candy.

I do not know a lot about nutrition, but I do know that my mother   18
tries to keep our family from eating so many sweets. She says they are bad for our teeth. Our dentist says so too. If they are bad, why are companies allowed to make children want them by advertising on TV? Almost all of the ads I have seen during children's programs are for candy, or sugar-coated cereal, or even sugar-coated cereal with candy in it.

I know people who make these commercials are not bad. I know   19
the commercials pay for TV shows and I like to watch TV. I just think that it would be as easy to produce a good commercial as a bad one. If there is nothing good that can be said about a product that is the truth, perhaps the product should not be sold to kids on TV in the first place.

I do not know all the ways to write a good commercial, but I   20
think commercials would be good if they taught kids something that was true. They could teach about good health, and also about where food is grown. If my 3-year-old sister can learn to sing, "It takes two hands to handle a whopper 'cause the burgers are better at Burger King," from a commercial, couldn't a commercial also teach her to recognize the letters of the alphabet, numbers, and colors? I am sure that people who write commercials are much smarter than I and they should be able to think of many ways to write a commercial that tells the truth about a product without telling kids they should eat it because it is sweeter or "shaped like fun" (what shape *is* fun, anyway?) or because Tony Tiger says so.

I also think kids should not be bribed to buy a product by com-   21
mercials telling of the wonderful free bonus gift inside.

I think kids should not be told to eat a certain product because a   22
well-known hero does. If this is a reason to eat something, then, when a well-known person uses drugs, should kids try drugs for the same reason?

Last of all, I think vitamin companies should never, never be   23
allowed to advertise their product as being delicious, yummy, or in any way make children think they are candy. Perhaps these commercials could teach children the dangers of taking drugs or teach children that, if they do find a bottle of pills, or if the medicine closet is open, they should run and tell a grown-up, and never, never eat the medicine.

I want to thank the Committee for letting me appear. When I   24
leave Washington, the thing that I will remember for the rest of my

life is that some people *do* care what kids think. I know I could have led a protest about commercials through our shopping center and people would have laughed at me or thought I needed a good spanking or wondered what kind of parents I had that would let me run around in the streets protesting. I decided to gather my information and write letters to anyone I thought would listen. Many of them didn't listen, but some did. That is why I am here today. Because some people cared about what I thought. I hope now that I can tell every kid in America that when they see a wrong, they shouldn't just try to forget about it and hope it will go away. They should begin to do what they can to change it.

People will listen. I know, because you're here listening to me.   25

QUESTIONS ON CONTENT

1. Why do you think there are more than twice as many commercial messages during children's shows as during shows intended for adults?

2. Kurth feels that the ads for Kool-Aid, Fritos, Hershey chocolate, Cheerios, Libby frozen dinners, Cocoa Krispies, and Lucky Charms are "examples of deceptive advertising practices." What exactly is deceptive about each ad?

3. What ads does Kurth feel are dangerous? Why?

4. If, as Kurth says, "it would be as easy to produce a good commercial as a bad one," why are there not more good ads on television?

QUESTIONS ON RHETORIC

1. Kurth prepared this statement to be read at a Senate subcommittee hearing in Washington. How does the style of the statement identify it as a speech rather than an essay?

2. What was Kurth's purpose in pursuing a project on advertisements directed at children, and where does she state her purpose?

3. Why does Kurth narrate the incident about her sister Martha and the Post Raisin Bran record?

4. Where is Kurth's argument summarized? What is the function of the last two paragraphs?

VOCABULARY

deceptive   nutrition
bonus   bribed

CLASSROOM ACTIVITIES

1. You are preparing for a school vacation and you are short of cash. You have decided to sell some of your possessions. Write an ad for the dorm bulletin board or school newspaper (seventy-five-word limit) that will bring you the best possible price for one of the following: stereo amp, guitar, bicycle, skis, '54 Ford.

NOTE: Writing assignments for "The Language of Advertising" appear on p. 103.

2
Weasel Words: God's Little Helpers

PAUL STEVENS

Commercials are a very real part of our daily lives. As a recent television critic reported in TV Guide, *the show "came on at 11 A.M. and was interrupted as follows: at 11:03 for two 30-second spots, at 11:12 for four 30s, at 11:18 for a one-minute network promo, 11:26 for two 30s and at 11:28 for a close-out with nearly a minute more of network blurbs and two 30s and a 10-second spot." In his book* I Can Sell You Anything, *Paul Stevens, a writer of television commercials, reveals the secrets of successful advertising. Advertisers really don't have to substantiate their claims since they make you, the consumer, hear things that aren't being said.*

First of all, you know what a weasel is, right? It's a small, slimy animal that eats small birds and other animals, and is especially fond of devouring vermin. Now, consider for a moment the kind of winning personality he must have. I mean, what kind of a guy would get his jollies eating rats and mice? Would you invite him to a party? Take him home to meet your mother? This is one of the slyest and most cunning of all creatures; sneaky, slippery, and thoroughly obnoxious. And so it is with great and warm personal regard for these attributes that we humbly award this King of All Devious the honor of bestowing his name upon our golden sword: the weasel word.

A weasel word is "a word used in order to evade or retreat from a direct or forthright statement or position" (Webster). In other words, if we can't say it, we'll weasel it. And, in fact, a weasel word has become more than just an evasion or retreat. We've trained our weasels. They can do anything. They can make you hear things that aren't being said, accept as truths things that have only been implied, and believe things that have only been suggested. Come to think of it, not only do we have our weasels trained, but they, in turn, have got you trained. When *you* hear a weasel word, you automatically hear the implication. Not the real meaning, but the

74

meaning *it* wants *you* to hear. So if you're ready for a little re-education, let's take a good look under a strong light at the two kinds of weasel words.

WORDS THAT MEAN THINGS THEY REALLY DON'T MEAN

Help

That's it. "Help." It means "aid" or "assist." Nothing more. Yet, "help" is the one single word which, in all the annals of advertising, has done the most to say something that couldn't be said. Because "help" is the great qualifier; once you say it, you can say almost anything after it. In short, "help" has helped help us the most.

> Helps keep you young
> Helps prevent cavities
> Help keep your house germ-free

"Help" qualifies everything. You've never heard anyone say, "This product will keep you young," or "This toothpaste will positively prevent cavities for all time." Obviously, we can't say anything like that, because there aren't any products like that made. But by adding that one little word, "help," in front, we can use the strongest language possible afterward. And the most fascinating part of it is, you are immune to the word. You literally don't hear the word "help." You only hear what comes after it. And why not? That's strong language, and likely to be much more important to you than the silly little word at the front end.

I would guess that 75 percent of all advertising uses the word "help." Think, for a minute, about how many times each day you hear these phrases:

> Helps stop . . .
> Helps prevent . . .
> Helps fight . . .
> Helps overcome . . .
> Helps you feel . . .
> Helps you look . . .

I could go on and on, but so could you. Just as a simple exercise, call it homework if you wish, tonight when you plop down in front of the boob tube for your customary three and a half hours of violence and/or situation comedies, take a pad and pencil, and keep score. See if you can count how many times the word "help" comes up during the commercials. Instead of going to the bathroom during the pause before Marcus Welby operates, or raiding the refrigerator prior to witnessing the Mod Squad wipe out a nest of dope pushers, stick with it. Count the "helps," and discover just how dirty a four-letter word can be.

Like

Coming in second, but only losing by a nose, is the word "like," used in comparison. Watch:

> It's like getting one bar free
> Cleans like a white tornado
> It's like taking a trip to Portugal

Okay. "Like" is a qualifier, and is used in much the same way as "help." But "like" is also a comparative element, with a very specific purpose; we use "like" to get you to stop thinking about the product per se, and to get you thinking about something that is bigger or better or different from the product we're selling. In other words, we can make you believe that the product is more than it is by likening it to something else.

Take a look at that first phrase, straight out of recent Ivory Soap advertising. On the surface of it, they tell you that four bars of Ivory cost about the same as three bars of most other soaps. So, if you're going to spend a certain amount of money on soap, you can buy four bars instead of three. Therefore, it's like getting one bar free. Now, the question you have to ask yourself is, "Why the weasel? Why do they say 'like'? Why don't they just come out and say, 'You get one bar free'?" The answer is, of course, that for one reason or another, you really don't. Here are two possible reasons. One: sure, you get four bars, but in terms of the actual amount of soap that you get, it may very well be the same as in three bars of another brand. Remember, Ivory has a lot of air in it—that's what makes it float. And air takes up room. Room that could otherwise be occupied by more soap. So, in terms of pure product, the amount of actual soap in four bars of Ivory may be only as much as the actual amount of soap in three bars of most others. That's why we can't—or won't—come out with a straightforward declaration such as, "You get 25 percent more soap," or "Buy three bars, and get the fourth one free."

Reason number two: the actual cost and value of the product. Did it ever occur to you that Ivory may simply be a cheaper soap to make and, therefore, a cheaper soap to sell? After all, it doesn't have any perfume or hexachlorophene, or other additives that can raise the cost of manufacturing. It's plain, simple, cheap soap, and so it can be sold for less money while still maintaining a profit margin as great as more expensive soaps. By way of illustrating this, suppose you were trying to decide whether to buy a Mercedes-Benz or a Ford. Let's say the Mercedes cost $7,000, and the Ford $3,500. Now the Ford salesman comes up to you with this deal: as long as you're considering spending $7,000 on a car, buy my Ford for $7,000 and I'll give you a second Ford, free! Well, the same principle can apply to Ivory: as long as you're considering spending 35 cents on soap, buy my cheaper soap, and I'll give you more of it.

I'm sure there are other reasons why Ivory uses the weasel "like." Perhaps you've thought of one or two yourself. That's good. You're starting to think.   10

Now, what about that wonderful white tornado? Ajax pulled that one out of the hat some eight years ago, and you're still buying it. It's a classic example of the use of the word "like" in which we can force you to think, not about the product itself, but about something bigger, more exciting, certainly more powerful than a bottle of fancy ammonia. The word "like" is used here as a transfer word, which gets you away from the obvious—the odious job of getting down on your hands and knees and scrubbing your kitchen floor—and into the world of fantasy, where we can imply that this little bottle of miracles will supply all the elbow grease you need. Isn't that the name of the game? The whirlwind activity of the tornado replacing the whirlwind motion of your arm? Think about the swirling of the tornado, and all the work it will save you. Think about the power of that devastating windstorm; able to lift houses, overturn cars, and now, pick the dirt up off your floor. And we get the license to do it simply by using the word "like."   11

It's a copywriter's dream, because we don't have to substantiate anything. When we compare our product to "another leading brand," we'd better be able to prove what we say. But how can you compare ammonia to a windstorm? It's ludicrous. It can't be done. The whole statement is so ridiculous it couldn't be challenged by the government or the networks. So it went on the air, and it worked. Because the little word "like" let us take you out of the world of reality, and into your own fantasies.   12

Speaking of fantasies, how about that trip to Portugal? Mateus Rosé is actually trying to tell you that you will be transported clear across the Atlantic Ocean merely by sipping their wine. "Oh, come on," you say. "You don't expect me to believe that." Actually, we don't expect you to believe it. But we do expect you to get our meaning. This is called "romancing the product," and it is made possible by the dear little "like." In this case, we deliberately bring   13 attention to the word, and we ask you to join us in setting reality aside for a moment. We take your hand and gently lead you down the path of moonlit nights, graceful dancers, and mysterious women. Are we saying that these things are all contained inside our wine? Of course not. But what we mean is, our wine is part of all this, and with a little help from "like," we'll get you to feel that way, too. So don't think of us as a bunch of peasants squashing a bunch of grapes. As a matter of fact, don't think of us at all. Feel with us.

"Like" is a virus that kills. You'd better get immune to it.   14

Other Weasels

"Help" and "like" are the two weasels so powerful that they can   15
stand on their own. There are countless other words, not quite so potent, but equally effective when used in conjunction with our two basic weasels, or with each other. Let me show you a few.

VIRTUAL *or* VIRTUALLY. How many times have you responded to an ad that said:

> Virtually trouble-free . . .
> Virtually foolproof . . .
> Virtually never needs service . . .

Ever remember what "virtual" means? It means in essence or effect, but not in fact." Important—"but not in fact." Yet today the word "virtually" is interpreted by you as meaning "almost or just about the same as. . . ." Well, gang, it just isn't true. "Not," in fact, means not, in fact. I was scanning, rather longingly I must confess, through the brochure Chevrolet publishes for its Corvette, and I came to this phrase: "The seats in the 1972 Corvette are virtually handmade." They had me, for a minute. I almost took the bait of that lovely little weasel. I almost decided that those seats were just about completely handmade. And then I remembered. Those seats were not, *in fact,* handmade. Remember, "virtually" means "not, in fact," or you will, in fact, get sold down the river.

ACTS *or* WORKS. These two action words are rarely used alone,   17
and are generally accompanied by "like." They need help to work, mostly because they are verbs, but their implied meaning is deadly, nonetheless. Here are the key phrases:

> Acts like . . .
> Acts against . . .
> Works like . . .

Works against . . .
Works to prevent (or help prevent) . . .

You see what happens? "Acts" or "works" brings an action to the product that might not otherwise be there. When we say that a certain cough syrup "acts on the cough control center," the implication is that the syrup goes to this mysterious organ and immediately makes it better. But the implication here far exceeds what the truthful promise should be. An act is simply a deed. So the claim "acts on" simply means it performs a deed on. What that deed is, we may never know.

The rule of thumb is this: if we can't say "cures" or "fixes" or   18
use any other positive word, we'll nail you with "acts like" or "works against," and get you thinking about something else. Don't.

Miscellaneous Weasels

CAN BE. This is for comparison, and what we do is to find an announ-   19
cer who can really make it sound positive. But keep your ears open. "Crest can be of significant value when used in . . .," etc., is indicative of an ideal situation, and most of us don't live in ideal situations.

UP TO. Here's another way of expressing an ideal situation. Remem-   20
ber the cigarette that said it was aged, or "cured for up to eight long, lazy weeks"? Well, that could, and should, be interpreted as meaning that the tobaccos used were cured anywhere from one hour to eight weeks. We like to glamorize the ideal situation; it's up to you to bring it back to reality.

AS MUCH AS. More of the same. "As much as 20 percent greater   21
mileage" with our gasoline again promises the ideal, but qualifies it.

REFRESHES, COMFORTS, TACKLES, FIGHTS, COMES ON. Just a handful   22
of the same action weasels, in the same category as "acts" and "works," though not as frequently used. The way to complete the thought here is to ask the simple question, "How?" Usually, you won't get an answer. That's because, usually, the weasel will run and hide.

FEEL or THE FEEL OF. This is the first of our subjective weasels.   23
When we deal with a subjective word, it is simply a matter of opinion. In our opinion, Naugahyde has the feel of real leather. So we can say it. And, indeed, if you were to touch leather, and then touch Naugahyde, you may very well agree with us. But that doesn't mean it is real leather, only that it feels the same. The best way to handle subjective weasels is to complete the thought yourself, by simply

saying, "But it isn't." At least that way you can remain grounded in reality.

THE LOOK OF *or* LOOKS LIKE. "Look" is the same as "feel," our subjective opinion. Did you ever walk into a Woolworth's and see those $29.95 masterpieces hanging in their "Art Gallery"? "The look of a real oil painting," it will say. "But it isn't," you will now reply. And probably be $29.95 richer for it.

WORDS THAT HAVE NO SPECIFIC MEANING

If you have kids, then you have all kinds of breakfast cereals in the house. When I was a kid, it was Rice Krispies, the breakfast cereal that went snap, crackle, and pop. (One hell of a claim for a product that is supposed to offer nutritional benefits.) Or Wheaties, the breakfast of champions, whatever that means. Nowadays, we're forced to a confrontation with Quisp, Quake, Lucky-Stars, Cocoa-Puffs, Clunkers, Blooies, Snarkles and Razzmatazz. And they all have one thing in common: they're all "fortified." Some are simply "fortified with vitamins," while others are specifically "fortified with vitamin D," or some other letter. But what does it all mean?

"Fortified" means "added on to." But "fortified," like so many other weasel words of indefinite meaning, simply doesn't tell us enough. If, for instance, a cereal were to contain one unit of vitamin D, and the manufacturers added some chemical which would produce two units of vitamin D, they could then claim that the cereal was "fortified with twice as much vitamin D." So what? It would still be about as nutritional as sawdust.

The point is, weasel words with no specific meaning don't tell us enough, but we have come to accept them as factual statements closely associated with something good that has been done to the product. Here's another example.

Enriched

We use this one when we have a product that starts out with nothing. You mostly find it in bread, where the bleaching process combined with the chemicals used as preservatives renders the loaves totally void of anything but filler. So the manufacturer puts a couple of drops of vitamins into the batter, and presto! It's enriched. Sounds great when you say it. Looks great when you read it. But what you have to determine is, is it really great? Figure out what information is missing, and then try to supply that information. The odds are, you won't. Even the breakfast cereals that are playing it straight, like Kellogg's Special K, leave something to be desired. They tell you what vitamins you get, and how much of each in one serving. The catch is, what constitutes a serving? They say, one ounce. So now you have to whip out your baby scale and weigh one serving. Do you have any idea how much that is? Maybe you do. Maybe you don't care. Okay, so you polish off this mound of dried stuff, and now what? You have ostensibly received the minimum, repeat, minimum dosage of certain vitamins for the day. One day. And you still have to go find the vitamins you didn't get. Try looking it up on a box of frozen peas. Bet you won't find it. But do be alert to "fortified" and "enriched." Asking the right questions will prove beneficial.

Did you buy that last sentence? Too bad, because I weaseled   29
you, with the word "beneficial." Think about it.

Flavor and Taste

These are two totally subjective words that allow us to claim mar-   30
velous things about products that are edible. Every cigarette in the world has claimed the best taste. Every supermarket has advertised the most flavorful meat. And let's not forget "aroma," a subdivision of this category. Wouldn't you like to have a nickel for every time a room freshener (a weasel in itself) told you it would make your home "smell fresh as all outdoors"? Well, they can say it, because smell, like taste and flavor, is a subjective thing. And, incidentally, there are no less than three weasels in that phrase. "Smell" is the first. Then, there's "as" (a substitute for the ever-popular "like"), and, finally, "fresh," which, in context, is a subjective comparison, rather than the primary definition of "new."

Now we can use an unlimited number of combinations of these   31
weasels for added impact. "Fresher-smelling clothes." "Fresher-tasting tobacco." "Tastes like grandma used to make." Unfortunately, there's no sure way of bringing these weasels down to size, simply because you can't define them accurately. Trying to ascertain the meaning of "taste" in any context is like trying to push a rope up a hill. All you can do is be aware that these words are subjective, and represent only one opinion—usually that of the manufacturer.

Style and Good Looks

Anyone for buying a new car? Okay, which is the one with the good   32
looks? The smart new styling? What's that you say? All of them?
Well, you're right. Because this is another group of subjective opinions. And it is the subjective and collective opinion of both Detroit
and Madison Avenue that the following cars have "bold new styling": Buick Riviera, Plymouth Satellite, Dodge Monaco, Mercury
Brougham, and you can fill in the spaces for the rest. Subjectively,
you have to decide on which bold new styling is, indeed, bold new
styling. Then, you might spend a minute or two trying to determine
what's going on under that styling. The rest I leave to Ralph Nader.

Different, Special, and Exclusive

To be different, you have to be not the same as. Here, you must rely   33
on your own good judgment and common sense. Exclusive formulas
and special combinations of ingredients are coming at you every
day, in every way. You must constantly assure yourself that, basically, all products in any given category are the same. So when you
hear "special," "exclusive," or "different," you have to establish
two things: on what basis are they different, and is that difference an
important one? Let me give you a hypothetical example.

All so-called "permanent" antifreeze is basically the same. It is   34
made from a liquid known as ethylene glycol, which has two amazing properties: It has a lower freezing point than water, and a higher
boiling point than water. It does not break down (lose its properties),
nor will it boil away. And every permanent antifreeze starts with it
as a base. Also, just about every antifreeze has now got antileak
ingredients, as well as antirust and anticorrosion ingredients. Now,
let's suppose that, in formulating the product, one of the companies
comes up with a solution that is pink in color, as opposed to all the
others, which are blue. Presto—an exclusivity claim. "Nothing else
looks like it, nothing else performs like it." Or how about, "Look at
ours, and look at anyone else's. You can see the difference our
exclusive formula makes." Granted, I'm exaggerating. But did I
prove a point?

A Few More Goodies

At Phillips 66, it's performance that counts   35
Wisk puts its strength where the dirt is

At Bird's Eye, we've got quality in our corner
Delicious and long-lasting, too

Very quickly now, let's deflate those four lines. First, what the hell does "performance" mean? It means that this product will do what any other product in its category will do. Kind of a back-handed reassurance that this gasoline will function properly in your car. That's it, and nothing more. To perform means to function at a standard consistent with the rest of the industry. All products in a category are basically the same.

Second line: What does "strength" or "strong" mean? Does it mean "not weak"? Or "superior in power"? No, it means consistent with·the norms of the business. You can bet your first-born that if Wisk were superior in power to other detergents, they'd be saying it, loud and clear. So strength is merely a description of a property inherent in all similar products in its class. If you really want to poke a pin in a bubble, substitute the word "ingredients" for the word "strength." That'll do it every time.

Third line: The old "quality" claim, and you fell for it. "Quality" is not a comparison. In order to do that, we'd have to say, "We've got better quality in our corner than any other frozen food." Quality relates only to the subjective opinion that Bird's Eye has of its own products, and to which it is entitled. The word "quality" is what we call a "parity" statement; that is, it tells you that it is as good as any other. Want a substitute? Try "equals," meaning "the same as."

Fourth line: How delicious is delicious? About the same as good-tasting is good-tasting, or fresher-smelling is fresher-smelling. A subjective opinion regarding taste, which you can either accept or reject. More fun, though, is "long-lasting." You might want to consider writing a note to Mr. Wrigley, inquiring as to the standard length of time which a piece of gum is supposed to last. Surely there must be a guideline covering it. The longest lasting piece of gum I ever encountered lasted just over four hours, which is the amount of time it took me to get it off the sole of my shoe. Try expressing the line this way: "It has a definite taste, and you may chew it as long as you wish." Does that place it in perspective?

There are two other aspects of weasel words that I should mention here. The first one represents the pinnacle of the copywriter's craft, and I call it the "Weasel of Omission." Let me demonstrate:

Of America's best-tasting gums, Trident is sugar-free

Disregard, for a moment, the obvious subjective weasel "best-tasting." Look again at the line. Something has been left out. Omitted very deliberately. Do you know what that word is? The word that's missing is the word "only," which should come right before the name of the product. But it doesn't. It's gone. Left out. And the question is, why? The answer is, the government wouldn't let them. You see, they start out by making a subjective judgment, that their gum is among the best-tasting. That's fine, as far as it goes. That's their opinion, but it is also the opinion of every other maker of sugar-free gum that his product is also among the best-tasting. And, since both of their opinions must be regarded as having equal value, neither one is allowed the superiority claim, which is what the word "only" would do. So Trident left it out. But the sentence is so brilliantly constructed, the word "only" is so heavily implied, that most people hear it, even though it hasn't been said. That's the Weasel of Omission. Constructing a set of words that forces you to a conclusion that otherwise could not have been drawn. Be on the lookout for what isn't said, and try to fill the gaps realistically.

The other aspect of weasels is the use of all those great, groovy, 41 swinging, wonderful, fantastic, exciting and fun-filled words known as adjectives. Your eyes, ears, mind, and soul have been bombarded by adjectives for so long that you are probably numb to most of them by now. If I were to give you a list of adjectives to look out for, it would require the next five hundred pages, and it wouldn't do you any good, anyway. More important is to bear in mind what adjectives do, and then to be able to sweep them aside and distinguish only the facts.

An adjective modifies a noun, and is generally used to denote the 42 quality or a quality of the thing named. And that's our grammar lesson for today. Realistically, an adjective enhances or makes more of the product being discussed. It's the difference between "Come visit Copenhagen," and "Come visit beautiful Copenhagen." Adjectives are used so freely these days that we feel almost naked, robbed, if we don't get at least a couple. Try speaking without adjectives. Try describing something; you can't do it. The words are too stark, too bare-boned, too factual. And that's the key to judging advertising. There is a direct, inverse proportion between the number of adjectives and the number of facts. To put it succinctly, the more adjectives we use, the less we have to say.

You can almost make a scale, based on that simple mathematical 43 premise. At one end you have cosmetics, soft drinks, cigarettes, products that have little or nothing of any value to say. So we get them all dressed up with lavish word and thought images, and present you with thirty or sixty seconds of adjectival puffery. The other end of the scale is much harder to find. Usually, it will be occupied by a new product that is truly new or different. . . . Our craving for adjectives has become so overriding that we simply cannot listen to what is known as "nuts and bolts" advertising. The rest falls somewhere in the middle; a combination of adjectives, weasels, and semitruths. All I can tell you is, try to brush the description aside, and see what's really at the bottom.

QUESTIONS ON CONTENT

1. What are "weasel words"? Why do advertisers find them useful? Why is it important for the average American to know about weasel words?

2. What does Stevens mean by "qualifiers"?

3. Why has Stevens chosen the weasel to describe certain types of advertising language; that is, what characteristics does a weasel have that make this association appropriate? Explain.

4. Weasel words help make advertising the fine art of deception. In weasels like "fortified" and "enriched," the advertisers try to convince us they give us something "extra." Is this true? What happens in the process of bleaching flour for "white" bread?

QUESTIONS ON RHETORIC

1. What is the function of the questions Stevens asks in paragraph 1?

2. How does Stevens organize his classification of weasel words? What is the purpose of the classification?

3. Advertisers often create similes, direct comparisons using *like* or *as*: "Ajax cleans *like* a white tornado." What, according to Stevens, is the advertisers' intent in using the simile? Outside of the advertising world, similes are not normally used to deceive. What value do similes have for you as a student of composition?

4. Stevens has consciously adopted an informal tone in this essay; he wishes to create the impression that he is talking to you, his reader. What devices does Stevens use to establish this informal tone? And how does his choice of words contribute to this informality?

VOCABULARY

obnoxious   ludricrous   hypothetical

| odious | edible | perspective |
| substantiate | ascertain | succinctly |

CLASSROOM ACTIVITIES

1. Using the phrase "adjectival puffery," Stevens claims that "our craving for adjectives has become so overriding that we simply cannot listen to what is known as 'nuts and bolts' advertising." Examine several written advertisements with a substantial amount of text for examples of adjectival puffery, weasel words, and semi-truths. Is Stevens' claim valid?

2. As Stevens suggests, "tonight when you plop down in front of the boob tube for your customary three and a half hours of violence and/or situation comedies, take a pad and pencil, and keep score." List the weasels that come up during the commercials. Compare your list with those made by others in your class.

NOTE: Writing assignments for "The Language of Advertising" appear on p. 103.

3
Intensify/Downplay

HUGH RANK

Hugh Rank, professor of literature at Governors State University in Park Forest, Illínois, is a member of the Committee on Public Doublespeak (National Council of Teachers of English). His schema "Intensify/Downplay" was developed to help people deal with public persuasion. As Rank explains, " 'Intensify/Downplay' *is a pattern useful to analyze communication, persuasion, and propaganda. All people* intensify *(commonly by* repetition, association, composition*) and* downplay *(commonly by* omission, diversion, confusion*) as they communicate in words, gestures, numbers, etc. But,* 'professional persuaders' *have more training, technology, money, and media access than the average citizen. Individuals can better cope with organized persuasion by recognizing the common ways how communication is intensified or downplayed, and by considering* who is saying what to whom, with what intent and what results."

The Committee on Public Doublespeak gave Rank's schema the George Orwell Award for 1976.

INTENSIFY

INTENSIFY/DOWNPLAY is a pattern useful to analyze communication, persuasion and propaganda. All people *intensify* (commonly by *repetition, association, composition*) and *downplay* (commonly by *omission, diversion, confusion*) as they communicate in words, gestures, numbers, etc. But, "professional persuaders" have more training, technology, money and media access than the average citizen. Individuals can better cope with organized persuasion by recognizing the common ways *how* communication is intensified or downplayed, and by considering *who is saying what to whom, with what intent and what result.*

Repetition

Intensifying by repetition is an easy, simple, and effective way to persuade. People are comfortable with the *known*, the *familiar*. As children, we love to hear the same stories repeated; later, we have "favorite" songs, TV programs, etc. All cultures have chants, prayers, rituals, dances based on repetition. Advertising slogans, brand names, logos, and signs are common. Much education, training, indoctrination is based on repetition to imprint on *memory* of the receiver to identify, recognize, and *respond*.

Association

Intensifying by linking (1) the idea or product with (2) something *already loved/desired by–or hated/feared by* (3) the intended audience. Thus, need for **audience analysis**: surveys, polls, "market research," "consumer behavior," psychological and sociological studies. Associate by *direct* assertions or *indirect* ways: metaphoric language, allusions, backgrounds, contexts, etc. Terms describing common *subject matters* used to link: *Flag-Waving, God-on-Our Side, Plain Folks, Band-Wagon, Testimonials, Tribal Pride, Heritage, Progress*, etc.

Composition

Intensifying by pattern and arrangement uses *design, variations in sequence* and *in proportion* to add to the force of words, images, movements, etc. How we put together, or compose, is important: e.g. in verbal communication the choice of words, their level of abstraction, their patterns within sentences, the strategy of longer messages. **Logic**, inductive and deductive, puts ideas together systematically. **Non-verbal** compositions involve *visuals* (color, shape, size); *aural* (music); *mathematics* (quantities, relationships) *time* and *space* patterns.

Omission

Downplaying by omission is common since the basic selection/omission process *necessarily omits* more than can be presented. All communication is limited, is edited, is slanted or biased to include and exclude items. But omission can also be used as a *deliberate* way of concealing, hiding. Half-truths, quotes out of context, etc. are very hard to detect or find. Political examples include *cover-ups, censorship, book-burning, managed news, secret police activities.* Receivers, too, can omit: can "filter out" or be closed minded, prejudiced.

Diversion

Downplaying by distracting focus, diverting attention away from key issues or important things; usually by intensifying the side-issues, the non-related, the trivial. Common variations include: *"hairsplitting," "nit-picking," "attacking a straw man," "red herring";* also, those emotional attacks and appeals *(ad hominem, ad populum),* plus things which drain the energy of others: *"busy work," legal harassment,* etc. Humor and entertainment *("bread and circuses")* are used as pleasant ways to divert attention from major issues.

Confusion

Downplaying issues by making things so complex, so chaotic, that people "give up," get weary, "overloaded." This is dangerous when people are unable to understand, comprehend, or make reasonable decisions. Chaos can be the accidental result of a disorganized mind, or the deliberate flim-flam of a *con man,* or the political *demagogue* (who then offers a "simple solution" to the confused.) Confusion can result from *faulty logic, equivocation, circumlocution, contradictions, multiple diversions, inconsistencies, jargon* or anything which blurs clarity or understanding.

© 1976 by Hugh Rank. Permission to reprint for educational purposes hereby granted, *pro bono publico.* Endorsed by the Committee on Public Doublespeak, National Council of Teachers of English (NCTE).

DOWNPLAY

QUESTIONS ON CONTENT

1. What does Rank mean by "professional persuaders"?

2. What types of public persuasion is each of us confronted with daily?

3. Explain the three ways by which persuaders intensify and the three ways they downplay.

4. Is it possible for someone to intensify and downplay at the same time? Explain.

VOCABULARY

cultures	indoctrination	slanted
rituals	inductive	context
slogans	deductive	

CLASSROOM ACTIVITIES

1. Choose one of the advertisements on pp. 91–93 and analyze it using "Intensify/Downplay." What insights have you gained as a result of your analysis? Explain.

2. Real estate advertisements are often deliberately designed to manipulate potential buyers. For example, one language analyst noted that in his home town "adorable" meant "small," "eat-in kitchen" meant "no dining room," "handyman's special" meant "portion of building still standing," "by appointment only" meant "expensive," and "starter home" meant "cheap." Analyze the language used in the real estate advertisements in your local newspaper. Does the real estate that one company offers sound better to you than that offered by another company? Do any realtors have their own special vocabulary?

3. Does Rank's "Intensify/Downplay" schema work to analyze news writing as well? Take an editorial and analyze its slant through Rank's method.

NOTE: Writing assignments for "The Language of Advertising" appear on p. 103.

DRIVE A CAR THAT IMPRESSES PEOPLE WHO AREN'T EASILY IMPRESSED.

A lot of cars will impress your neighbors.
But when you buy a Volvo, you'll own a car that impresses a more impressive group of people.

THE U.S. GOVERNMENT

The U.S. government recently bought 24 Volvos. All 24 are being tested in high-speed collisions.
Out of the wreckage will emerge information which the government will use to help establish
safety standards for cars in the future.
It was no accident that the government selected Volvo for this safety program.
Of all the cars involved in preliminary crash-testing, Volvo showed significantly greater potential
for occupant protection than any car in its class.

G.M. AND FORD

Between them, G.M. and Ford have bought 13 Volvos to study and analyze.
After years of following the "bigger is better" philosophy, they're introducing "trim, sensibly-sized" cars.
Maybe they feel there's something to be learned
from a company that's been making trim, sensibly-sized cars for 50 years.

THE STATE OF CALIFORNIA

California has the strictest automobile emissions requirements in the nation.
And they get stricter all the time.
While some car makers were loudly protesting that these requirements could not be met,
Volvo was quietly working on a new type of emissions control system that would not only meet these
standards, but exceed them.
This system, called "Lambda Sond," will be on every 1977 Volvo 240 series car sold in California.
The California Air Resources Board is very impressed. They've called it "virtually pollution free...
the most significant step ever made in the battle to develop clean automobiles."

VOLVO OWNERS

The ultimate test of any car is how the owner feels about it.
Volvo owners seem to be happier than the owners of other cars.
In fact, when new Volvo owners were asked in a recent nationwide survey how they felt about their cars,
more of them said they were "completely satisfied" or "very satisfied"
than did the owners of any car made by G.M., Ford, Chrysler or American Motors.
Now that you know who's impressed with Volvos, you can take a test drive and impress the most
important person of all: yourself.

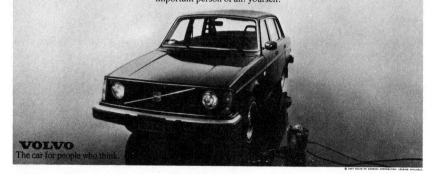

VOLVO
The car for people who think.

© 1977 VOLVO OF AMERICA CORPORATION. LEASING AVAILABLE.

This advertisement prepared by: SCALI, McCABE, SLOVES INC.
                                  Volvo of America/P-VAC-77-2697
                                  Wall Street Journal - June 24, 1977
                                  800 lines - B/W - 4 col x 200 lines

Too many people believe business doesn't give a damn about the public.

Minds are tough to change.

Times *do* change, though. And business is changing. Faster than a lot of people's attitudes toward business.

American business invests more money every year in strenuous efforts to communicate the benefits of competitive enterprise. (Including ads like this one.)

Yet survey after survey shows that public sentiment is against big business.

This suggests to us a communications problem. And a credibility problem.

It also suggests some possible corrective steps toward more effective communications with the public.

First, let's stop talking mostly to ourselves.

Let's stop resorting to one-sided arguments that thoughtful adults are no longer willing to accept on faith.

Let's stop pretending that there aren't any flaws at all in our system, and the way it works.

Instead, let's face up to our mistakes, and correct them. Admit that we're not perfect. And engage in open discourse instead of arm-twisting diatribes.

Since public opinion is ultimately the controlling force in our democracy, an informed public is really one of the costs of staying in business.

Thus there may be only one way for business to restore its credibility. And that's to tell it like it is.

It's definitely worth a try.

(Why not try these thoughts out on somebody who's turned off by business?)

Pennwalt Corporation, Three Parkway, Philadelphia, Pa. 19102.

For 126 years we've been making things people need—including profits.

PENNWALT
CHEMICALS ■ EQUIPMENT
HEALTH PRODUCTS

People invest for one reason: to make money.

The three key factors in making money are
- premier quality investment advice
- order executions that save you money
- investing through a financially
    dependable firm

For seventy-three years, E. F. Hutton has
been helping people make money.

When E.F. Hutton talks, people listen.

4

Correspondence with the Ford Motor Company

MARIANNE MOORE

In 1955 the American poet Marianne Moore (1887–1972) received a letter from David Wallace, a Ford Motor Company executive, entreating her to submit some names for a very important new car Ford was about to market. Thus began a delightful exchange of letters in which Moore suggested a series of names, humorously stretching believability in order to reveal the very essence of the naming process.

OCTOBER 19, 1955

Miss Marianne Moore
Cumberland Street
Brooklyn 5, New York

Dear Miss Moore:

This is a morning we find ourselves with a problem which, strangely enough, is more in the field of words and the fragile meaning of words than in car-making. And we just wonder whether you might be intrigued with it sufficiently to lend us a hand.

Our dilemma is a name for a rather important new series of cars.

We should like this name to be more than a label. Specifically, we should like it to have a compelling quality in itself and by itself. To convey, through association or other conjuration, some visceral feeling of elegance, fleetness, advanced features and design. A name, in short, that flashes a dramatically desirable picture in people's minds. (Another "Thunderbird" would be fine.)

Over the past few weeks this office has confected a list of three hundred-odd candidates which, it pains me to relate, are characterized by an embarrassing pedestrianism. We are miles short of our ambition. And so we are seeking the help of one who knows more about this sort of magic than we.

As to how we might go about this matter, I have no idea. But, in any event, all would depend on whether you find this overture of some challenge and interest.

Should we be so fortunate as to have piqued your fancy, we will be pleased to write more fully. And, of course, it is expected that our relations will be on a fee basis of an impeccably dignified kind.

Respectfully,

DAVID WALLACE

Special Products Division

OCTOBER 21, 1955

Let me take it under advisement, Mr. Wallace. I am complimented to be recruited in this high matter.

I have seen and admired "Thunderbird" as a Ford designation. It would be hard to match; but let me, the coming week, talk with my brother, who would bring ardor and imagination to bear on the quest.

Sincerely yours,

MARIANNE MOORE

OCTOBER 27, 1955

DEAR MR. WALLACE:

My brother thought most of the names I had considered suggesting to you for your new series too learned or too labored, but thinks I might ask if any of the following approximate the requirements:

THE FORD SILVER SWORD

This plant, of which the flower is a silver sword, I believe grows only on the Hawaiian Island Maui, on Mount Haleakala (House of the Sun); found at an altitude of from 9,500 to 10,000 feet. (The leaves—silver-white—surrounding the individual blossoms—have a pebbled texture that feels like Italian-twist backstitch allover embroidery.)

My first thought was of a bird series—the swallow species—Hirundo, or, phonetically, Aerundo. Malvina Hoffman is designing a device for the radiator of a made-to-order Cadillac, and said in her opinion the only term surpassing Thunderbird would be hurricane; and I then thought Hurricane Hirundo might be the first of a series such as Hurricane Aquila (eagle), Hurricane Accipiter (hawk), and so on. A species that takes its dinner on the wing ("swifts").

If these suggestions are not in character with the car, perhaps you could give me a sketch of its general appearance, or hint as to

some of its exciting potentialities—though my brother reminds me
that such information is highly confidential.

Sincerely yours,

MARIANNE MOORE

NOVEMBER 4, 1955

DEAR MISS MOORE:

I'm delighted that your note implies that you are interested in
helping us in our naming problem.

This being so, procedures in this rigorous business world dictate
that we on this end at least document a formal arrangement with
provision for a suitable fee or honorarium before pursuing the problem further.

One way might be for you to suggest a figure which could be
considered for mutual acceptance. Once this is squared away, we
will look forward to having you join us in the continuation of our
fascinating search.

Sincerely,

DAVID WALLACE

Special Products Division

NOVEMBER 7, 1955

DEAR MR. WALLACE:

It is handsome of you to consider remuneration for service
merely enlisted. My fancy would be inhibited, however, by acknowledgment in advance of performance. If I could be of specific
assistance, we could no doubt agree on some kind of honorarium for
the service rendered.

I seem to exact participation; but if you could tell me how the
suggestions submitted strayed—if obviously—from the ideal, I
could then perhaps proceed more nearly in keeping with the Company's objective.

Sincerely yours,

MARIANNE MOORE

NOVEMBER 11, 1955

DEAR MISS MOORE:

Our office philodendron has just benefited from an extra measure
of water as, pacing about, I have sought words to respond to your

recent generous note. Let me state my quandary thus. It is unspeakably contrary to procedure to accept counsel—even needed counsel —without a firm prior agreement of conditions (and, indeed, to follow the letter of things, without a Purchase Notice in quadruplicate and three Competitive Bids). But then, seldom has the auto business had occasion to indulge in so ethereal a matter as this. So, if you will risk a mutually satisfactory outcome with us, we should like to honor your wish for a fancy unencumbered.

As to wherein your earlier suggestions may have "strayed," as you put it—they did not at all. Shipment No. 1 was fine, and we would like to luxuriate in more of same—even those your brother regarded as overlearned or labored. For us to impose an ideal on your efforts would, I fear, merely defeat our purpose. We have sought your help to get an approach quite different from our own. In short, we should like suggestions that we ourselves would not have arrived at. And, in sober fact, have not.

Now we on this end must help you by sending some tangible representation of what we are talking about. Perhaps the enclosed sketches will serve the purpose. They are not IT, but they convey the feeling. At the very least, they may give you a sense of participation should your friend Malvina Hoffman break into brisk conversation on radiator caps.

Sincerely yours,
DAVID WALLACE
Special Products Division

NOVEMBER 13, 1955
DEAR MR. WALLACE:

The sketches. They are indeed exciting; they have quality, and the toucan tones lend tremendous allure—confirmed by the wheels. Half the magic—sustaining effects of this kind. Looked at upside down, furthermore, there is a sense of fish buoyancy. Immediately your word "impeccable" sprang to mind. Might it be a possibility? The Impeccable. In any case, the baguette lapidary glamour you have achieved certainly spurs the imagination. Car-innovation is like launching a ship—"drama."

I am by no means sure that I can help you to the right thing, but performance with elegance casts a spell. Let me do some thinking in the direction of impeccable, symmechromatic, thunderblender. . . . (The exotics, if I can shape them a little.) Dearborn might come into one.

If the sketches should be returned at once, let me know. Otherwise, let me dwell on them for a time. I am, may I say, a trusty confidante.

I thank you for realizing that under contract esprit could not flower. You owe me nothing, specific or moral.

Sincerely,
MARIANNE MOORE

NOVEMBER 19, 1955

Some other suggestions, Mr. Wallace, for the phenomenon:

THE RESILIENT BULLET
or Intelligent Bullet
or Bullet Cloisonné or Bullet Lavolta

(I have always had a fancy for THE INTELLIGENT WHALE—the little first Navy submarine, shaped like a sweet potato; on view in our Brooklyn Yard.)

THE FORD FABERGÉ

(That there is also a perfume Fabergé seems to me to do no harm, for here allusion is to the original silversmith.)

THE ARC-EN-CIEL (the Rainbow) ARCENCIEL?

Please do not feel that memoranda from me need acknowledgment. I am not working day and night for you; I feel that etymological hits are partially accidental.

The bullet idea has possibilities, it seems to me, in connection with Mercury (with Hermes and Hermes Trismegistus) and magic (white magic).

Sincerely,
MARIANNE MOORE

NOVEMBER 28, 1955

DEAR MR. WALLACE:

MONGOOSE CIVIQUE
ANTICIPATOR
REGNA RACER (couronne à couronne) sovereign to sovereign
AEROTERRE
Fée Rapide (Aérofee, Aéro Faire, Fée Aiglette, Magi-faire) Comme Il
  Faire

Tonnerre Alifère (winged thunder)
Aliforme Alifère (wing-slender, a-wing)
TURBOTORC (used as an adjective by Plymouth)
THUNDERBIRD Allié (Cousin Thunderbird)
THUNDER CRESTER
DEARBORN Diamante
MAGIGRAVURE
PASTELOGRAM

I shall be returning the sketches very soon.

M.M.

DECEMBER 6, 1955

DEAR MR. WALLACE:

Regina-rex
Taper Racer   Taper Acer
Varsity Stroke
Angelastro
Astranaut
Chaparral
Tir a l'arc (bull's eye)
Cresta Lark
Triskelion (three legs running)
Pluma Piluma (hairfine, feather-foot)
Andante con Moto (description of a good motor?)

My findings thin, so I terminate them and am returning the sketches. Two principles I have not been able to capture: 1, the topknot of the peacock and topnotcher of speed. 2, the swivel-axis (emphasized elsewhere), like the Captain's bed on the whaleship, Charles Morgan—balanced so that it levelled whatever the slant of the ship.

If I stumble on a hit, you shall have it. Anything so far has been pastime. Do not ponder appreciation, Mr. Wallace. That was embodied in the sketches.

M.M.

I cannot resist the temptation to disobey my brother and submit TURCOTINGA (turquoise cotinga—the cotinga being a South American finch or sparrow) solid indigo.

(I have a three-volume treatise on flowers that might produce something but the impression given should certainly be unlabored.)

DECEMBER 8, 1955

MR. WALLACE:

May I submit UTOPIAN TURTLE-TOP? Do not trouble to answer unless you like it.

MARIANNE MOORE

DECEMBER 23, 1955

MERRY CHRISTMAS TO OUR FAVORITE TURTLETOPPER.

DAVID WALLACE

DECEMBER 26, 1955

DEAR MR. WALLACE:

An aspiring turtle is certain to glory in spiral eucalyptus, white pine straight from the forest, and innumerable scarlet roses almost too tall for close inspection. Of a temperament susceptible to shock though one may be, to be treated like royalty could not but induce sensations unprecedented august.

Please know that a carfancyer's allegiance to the Ford automotive turtle—extending from the Model T Dynasty to the Wallace Utopian Dynasty—can never waver; impersonal gratitude surely becoming infinite when made personal. Gratitude to unmiserly Mr. Wallace and his idealistic associates.

MARIANNE MOORE

NOVEMBER 8, 1956

DEAR MISS MOORE:

Because you were so kind to us in our early days of looking for a suitable name, I feel a deep obligation to report on events that have ensued.

And I feel I must do so before the public announcement of same come Monday, November 19.

We have chosen a name out of the more than six thousand-odd candidates that we gathered. It fails somewhat of the resonance, gaiety, and zest we were seeking. But it has a personal dignity and meaning to many of us here. Our name, dear Miss Moore, is— Edsel.

I hope you will understand.

Cordially,

DAVID WALLACE
Special Products Division

QUESTIONS ON CONTENT

1. Who was Marianne Moore, and why did the Ford Motor Company ask her to be a consultant?

2. What kind of name was Ford looking for? What kind of image did it want to project for its new car?

3. Why did Moore ask for a sketch of the new automobile?

4. Why, in your opinion, were Marianne Moore's names unacceptable?

5. Where did the name Edsel come from? Why did Ford use it if, as Wallace admits, "It fails somewhat of the resonance, gaiety, and zest we were seeking"? Do you think Moore "understood"?

QUESTIONS ON RHETORIC

1. How in his first letter does Wallace attempt to interest Marianne Moore in his project?

2. How would you characterize the tone of Moore's letters?

3. What is Moore's attitude toward the project? At what point in the correspondence does Wallace appear to be aware of this attitude? Explain.

4. How would you characterize Wallace's diction in each of his letters? Do you see any changes in his diction as the correspondence develops?

VOCABULARY

visceral	remuneration	innumerable
piqued	tangible	allegiance
impeccably	buoyancy	

CLASSROOM ACTIVITIES

1. As evidenced in the Moore-Wallace correspondence, businessmen are very conscious of the connotations of the names they give their products. Automobile manufacturers draw heavily on animal names—Impala, Pinto, Cougar, Mustang, Thunderbird, Jaguar, Cricket, Skylark, and Charger—to suggest the strength, size, and

speed of the various models. If an automobile can be named Cobra, why not Rattler or Sidewinder? Make up a brand name with unappealing connotations and write an advertisement of a paragraph or two for the product—for instance, the Buick Buffalo, Antelope, or Ostrich.

2. Many product names are chosen because of their connotative or suggestive value. For example, the name Tide for the detergent suggests the power of the ocean tides and the rhythmic surge of cleansing waters. Discuss how the connotations of the following brand names enhance the product's appeal: Atlas tires, Pride, Axion, Downy, Arrid, Love cosmetics, Ajax.

3. Our first impression of strangers is based on their physical appearance, the way they dress, how they talk, and their names. Sometimes our reaction to a person's name is personal. For example, perhaps our favorite aunt was named Gertrude, and we are favorably disposed to anyone we meet named Gertrude. Some reactions to names, however, are not personal but rather reflect expectations widely shared by Americans. Thus most people would find it difficult to think of Queen Lizzie instead of Queen Elizabeth. Test these statements by matching each occupation in the lefthand column with a name in the righthand column.

1. member of a teenage street gang	a. William L. Thompson
2. shortstop for the Boston Red Sox	b. W. Louis Thompson
3. novelist	c. Bill Thompson
4. financier	d. Lou Thompson
5. evangelist	e. Billy Lou Thompson
	f. Willie Thompson
	g. W. L. Thompson

WRITING ASSIGNMENTS FOR
"THE LANGUAGE OF ADVERTISING"

1. Think of a product that you like and want to use but one that has a dissatisfying or annoying feature or has failed to live up to advertising claims. Write and send a letter to the company explaining your complaint and offering constructive criticism.

2. Have you ever been victimized by the language of advertising? Write a narrative account of the incident. Be sure to analyze and describe how language was used to manipulate you.

3. You have just been hired by a local real estate firm as an advertising copywriter. Your first assignment is to describe this house:

Using the same house, describe it as though you were a bank appraiser evaluating the house for a possible mortgage loan.

4. Many advertisers seem to believe that by manipulating language they can make any product appeal to consumers. Here is how a very common item might be made to appear desirable by means of advertising:

NEW! CONVENIENT!
STRIKE-UPS

The latest scientific advance for smokers since the cigarette lighter. Inexpensive and lightweight, you'll never want to be caught without Strike-Ups.

Why tolerate heavy, expensive cigarette lighters? Why run the risk of soiling your clothes with dangerous lighter fluid? Why be hassled by the technicalities of replacing flints? Why be embarrassed by a lighter that fails when it means everything to you?

STRIKE-UPS HAS A BETTER WAY

Lightweight, 100% reliable, Strike-Ups gives 20, that's right 20, or more lights. Each booklet has its own handy striking surface, right where you need it—up front. A striking surface so large you'll be able to get quick and easy lights even in the darkest places. Strike-Ups comes with a handsome decorator cover. An added feature, at no extra cost, is the plain white surface inside the cover useful for phone numbers or doodling.

Once you use Strike-Ups, you'll agree, as many Americans have, that you simply can't do without them.

ASK FOR STRIKE-UPS AT ALL STORES WHERE
QUALITY SMOKING ACCESSORIES ARE SOLD.

Write an advertisement for any one of the items listed below; use as many of the advertising tricks or persuasive techniques as you can in order to sell your product.

paper clips
dental floss
toothpicks
rubber bands
salt shakers
staples
bottle caps

5. As more and more of our basic material needs are satisfied, the advertisers must create and push new "needs" so the buying process on which our consumer culture is based can continue. Many of these new "needs" are created by exploitative appeals to values we all cherish or even hold sacred. For example, the Gino's fast-food

chain uses the word *freedom* to sell its food: "Freedom of Choice—French Fries or Onion Rings." The word *love* is another highly exploited device of advertisers.

Jerry Rubin once said, "How can I say 'I love you' when 'Cars love Shell'?" Here are some other examples:

> "Canada Dry tastes like love."
>
> "Hello. I'm Catherine Denueve. When somebody loves me, I'm always surprised. But I don't want to be told. I prefer gestures. Like—Chanel No. 5."
>
> Olympic Gold Medal winner Mark Spitz: "You know what's a great feeling? Giving someone you love a gift. The Schick Flexamatic is a great gift."
>
> A beautiful woman in a trench coat stands alone in the fog on a waterfront. She says, "I like men. Even when they're unkind to me. But men are men. They need love. They need understanding. And they need English Leather."
>
> A good-looking man says, "I know what girls need. They need love. And love's a little color." A girl appears and the man starts applying makeup to her face. The announcer says, "Love's a Little Color isn't makeup. It's only a little color."
>
> "Love is being a nurse. Learn all about professional nursing by writing."

In each of these ads, a product is being sold by using the affective connotations of the word *love*—in other words, the word *love* (which ought to be sacred) is being exploited for profits.

Write a 500-word theme on the effects of debasing language by perverting the accepted meanings of a word for commercial purposes, focusing on the use of *love* in the ads listed above. Do you think it matters? If you do, how so? Can anything be done about it? What is the price we must pay for allowing our language to be so ill-used?

NOTE: Suggested topics for research papers appear on p. 293.

NOTABLE QUOTATIONS

The following quotations are drawn from the articles in this section. They are presented as additional topics for classroom discussion or for writing assignments.

"I had always listened before and many times asked my mother to buy certain products I had seen advertised, but now I was listening and really thinking about what was being said."   *Kurth*

"If there is nothing good that can be said about a product that is the truth, perhaps the product should not be sold to kids on TV in the first place." *Kurth*

"Adjectives are used so freely these days that we feel almost naked, robbed, if we don't get at least a couple." *Stevens*

"In advertising there is a direct, inverse proportion between the number of adjectives and the number of facts." *Stevens*

"All communication is limited, is edited, is slanted or biased to include or exclude items." *Rank*

"We should like this name to be more than a label. Specifically, we should like it to have a compelling quality in itself and by itself. To convey, through association or other conjuration, some visceral feeling of elegance, fleetness, advanced features and design. A name, in short, that flashes a dramatically desirable picture in people's minds." *Wallace* (in *Moore* selection)

IV

The Language of Radio, Television, and Newspapers

1

The Death
of Silence

ROBERT PAUL DYE

In "The Death of Silence," Robert Paul Dye of the University of Hawaii compares the way radio broadcasting used to be with the way it is now. Dye believes that the elimination of the artistic use of silence is the most important change that has occurred in radio broadcasting in recent years.

Radio's funniest moment occurred on the *Jack Benny* program   1
when a thief demanded from the great tightwad, "Your money or
your life." The long silence that followed was more violently hysterical than any of the quick retorts that are the stock in trade of most
comedians. Benny's use of silence, his great sense of timing, made
him one of the most popular comics of this century. Benny, of
course, was not the only radio artist who recognized that silence
could be more effective than sound: silence followed the crash of
Fibber McGee's closet, preceded McCarthy's responses to Bergen.
The chillers became more chilling when there were moments of
silence. Silence was used to make the romances erotic and the quiz
shows suspenseful.

Radio has changed. The cacophony of today's radio has been   2
dignified as "The Poetica of 'Top 40' "[1] by University of Oklahoma
professor Sherman P. Lawton. Dr. Lawton tells us to "Face up to
the fact that, like it or not, from the bowels of radio has come a new
art form." The practitioners of the new art are the managers of the
"screamer" stations, ". . . stations with an extreme foreground
treatment, playing only the top tunes, with breathless and witless
striplings making like carnival barkers."

[1] Sherman P. Lawton, "The Poetica of 'Top 40,' " *Journal of Broadcasting*, IX:2
(Spring 1965), 123-128.

The bible of the practitioners, Lawton tells us, is *The Nuts and* 3
Bolts of Radio, authored by George Skinner and published by the
Katz Agency. One of Mr. Skinner's prescriptions is that there
should be no silence longer than a fifth of a second, from sign-on to
sign-off *there shalt be continuous sound.* Lawton writes,

> On two stations, which I consider the prototypes of the new art, news
> headlines are proclaimed in a style which can best be described as one
> well suited to be the second Annunciation. Then, quick segue music,
> overlapping with the headline that follows. And then, Bam, we might
> get a roll of drums.

It is curious that the elimination of silence, so long in symbiosis 4
with sound, should be the major difference between the "new art"
and old time radio. It was silence which made radio visual, it gave
the listener time to imagine the faces, places and action suggested by
sound. Silence, like the white space between magazine articles, signalled conclusions and promised beginnings. Silence served as
comma, period and paragraph, just as those marks served to signal
silence.

Not all radio is continuous sound. Competing with the screamers 5
for popularity are the phone-in programs, an adaptation of two rural
America pastimes—listening in on the party line and speaking at the
town meeting. This is reactionary programming, an attempt to again
involve people in radio by providing a means for do-it-yourself programming. For the most part, the telephone programs are not
planned, they happen. They appear to serve as an antidote and as an
alternative to the screamers. However, on many stations the antidote and the alternative are more appearance than reality and Mr.
Skinner's prescription that there shalt be continuous sound is
obeyed.

The death of silence limits some types of aural communication, 6
in some cases eliminates them. The meaningful reporting of Ed
Murrow, the stirring rhetoric of Winston Churchill and the fireside
chats of Franklin Roosevelt would not have been possible if radio
had screamed in the Forties. When silence is prohibited so is drama
and poetry. Men like Orson Welles and Archibald MacLeish are
forever barred from using the "new art" for their art. Dialogue is
also impossible: people just don't speak to each other without so
much as a second of silence to signal meaning. Formerly, only ster-
eotyped, fictional creations spoke without pause.

The talkers Ring Lardner satirized would have envied the 7
screamers:

> Well girlie you see how busy I have been and am liable to keep right on

being busy as we are not going to let the grass grow under our feet but as soon as we have got this number placed we will get busy on another one as a couple like that will put me on Easy st. even if they don't go as big as we expect but even 25 grand is a big bunch of money and if a man could only turn out one hit a year and make that much out of it I would be on Easy st. and no more hammering on the old music box in some cabaret . . .[2]

But even Lardner's characters eventually had to breathe and lose the floor. The screamers, armed with years' worth of recorded sounds, instantly available and always repeatable, can chatter incessantly.

But unlike Ring Lardner, the screamers do not satirize monologue—they spoof it. They even spoof the commercials. Screamer stations have no sacred cows; at least they give that illusion. The screamers take nothing seriously, except themselves. What at first hearing appears to be pure play turns out to be pseudo-play and devoid of fun. What appears to be a playathon is really instant and constant spoof. Spoof is both the strength and the weakness of the screamers. It is a strength because spoofing is "in"—James Bond and his imitators. It is a weakness because spoofing is hypocritical.

Spoof is described by David Sonstroem[3] as "surgery with a rubber knife," as "a new kind of playful, ironic attitude toward the old conflict between good and evil." He says,

Spoof is not true to itself. It cheats at its own game. It only pretends to take life as a game, but then inadvertently lets earnest break in and govern it. Although pretending to be above and beyond it all, spoof cares, and cares very much. This unconscious hypocrisy lies at the root of all that I find objectionable in spoof, with its enchanting trick of protecting foolish fantasy by pretending to expose it.

The screamers are spoofers. They lack the courage to be moral and at the same time cannot deny the desire to be moral. The result is that the audience is cheated and deceived. It is neither shocked into moral consciousness, nor freed, for the moment, from moral considerations. It is mired in ambivalence, and the result is malaise.

Old time radio was not ambivalent, nor were its listeners. The residents of Allen's Alley did not spoof American society, they satirized it. The rise of Senator Claghorn hurried the demise of Senator Bilbo. And there was fun on old time radio, the kind of fun that comes from playing and results in laughter. The laughter from

[2] Quoted in Constance Rourke, *American Humor* (Garden City: Doubleday, n.d.), 228.
[3] David Sonstroem, "An Animadversion upon Spoof," *The Midwest Quarterly*, VIII (Spring 1967), 239-246.

old time radio was in the home, not merely the studio. There were belly laughs from the listeners, not merely self-conscious giggles from Lawton's "witless striplings."

Radio developed an art that quickened all the senses. The screamers have developed a technique of monopolizing a single sense. Radio once allowed the listener to participate. The screamers force him into the role of observer. Radio once took life seriously. The screamers take only themselves seriously. Spoof is a degenerate form. It is not true to itself, it prohibits participation. Art is true to itself, it causes participation. The screams from the bowels of today's radio are not the birth cries of a new art form, but the death rattle of an old art medium. The death of silence is the death of sound broadcasting.   12

QUESTIONS ON CONTENT

1. What, according to Dye, is the main difference between radio as it used to be and radio as it is today?

2. What is Dye's attitude toward today's radio? Does Dye agree with Dr. Sherman Lawton's assessment of radio broadcasting? Explain.

3. Why, in your opinion, has Dye labeled contemporary radio as the "screamers"? How have radio stations attempted to combat the "screamers"?

4. What is "spoof"? Why does Dye consider contemporary radio to be spoof rather than satire? What is the difference between "spoof" and "satire"? Explain.

QUESTIONS ON RHETORIC

1. What is Dye's thesis and where is it stated?

2. Carefully review paragraphs 1 and 4. What technique has Dye employed to make the use and meaning of silence in radio broadcasting understandable to the reader? Explain.

3. How has Dye emphasized the major differences between old-time and contemporary radio broadcasting in his last paragraph?

VOCABULARY

hysterical   incessantly   ambivalence

reactionary   ironic   monopolizing
antidote   inadvertently   degenerate

CLASSROOM ACTIVITIES

1. In his essay Dye discusses radio broadcasting as it once was and as it is today. His discussion, however, concerns only AM radio. Some interesting comparisons can be made between AM and FM radio broadcasting. In preparation for a classroom discussion of AM and FM radio broadcasting, listen to at least an hour of AM and FM radio, making notes of your observations and impressions. What significant differences and similarities do you find?

NOTE: Writing assignments for "The Language of Radio, Television, and Newspapers" appear on p. 153.

2

Bunkerisms: Archie's Suppository Remarks in "All in the Family"

ALFRED ROSA and PAUL ESCHHOLZ

Alfred Rosa and Paul Eschholz are both associate professors of English at the University of Vermont. Their analysis of Archie Bunker's language in the popular television series "All in the Family" first appeared in a different form in the Winter 1972 issue of the Journal of Popular Culture.

On January 12, 1971, American television viewers were first introduced to "All in the Family." It was not long before the Bunker family became an American institution. This award-winning show reaches an estimated fifty to one hundred million viewers weekly. It has spawned a huge commercial enterprise offering such items as sweatshirts, T-shirts, posters, ashtrays, beer mugs, and "Bunker Stickers." Another item in this commercial bonanza is *The Wit & Wisdom of Archie Bunker,* a book containing the most humorous lines and sequences from the show. Indeed, the book demonstrates that the humor of the show derives not only from the fact that it is a situational comedy but also from Archie's use of language. Archie's command of the language is "legionary"; viewers have witnessed him criticize Mike for reacting "on the sperm of the the moment," castigate Edith for taking things "out of contest," and tell his family that his prejudice is a "pigment of their imaginations." Archie's use of malapropisms and barbarisms, and especially of his unique creation, "Bunkerisms," deserves to be examined. These expressions are a major element in distinguishing "All in the Family" from other television situational comedies.

The malapropism—the inappropriate use of a word in place of   2
another that has some similarity to it— has a long tradition among
writers of comedy. Malapropisms indicate not only the ignorance
but also the vanity and affectation of the characters who speak
them. Shakespeare's Dogberry, for instance, states his belief that
"comparisons are odorous." Richard Sheridan's infamous Mrs.
Malaprop derives her name from this type of inappropriate usage.
One recalls that in *The Rivals* she implores Lydia to "promise to
forget this fellow—to illiterate him quite from [her] memory." In
"All in the Family," Archie uses many malapropisms:[1]

What is this, the United Nations? We gotta have a whole addenda?
I come home and tell you one o' the great antidotes of all times, an item
of real human interest, and you sit there like you're in a comma.
You sound like a regular Billie Sol Graham!
"Sorry" ain't-gonna clench my thirst.
. . . as one of your faithful constitutionals.
You gotta grab the bull by the corns and heave-ho.
This nation under God shall not diminish from the earth.
I don't need their whole Dun and Broadstreet.
We got a regular Edna St. Louis Millet here.
If he don't yell "pig" or none of them other epaulets, . . .
Ain't he took the exercise tax offa cars?
No, Edith. I was out expectin' the street lights.
How'd I know you had extensions to bein' an egghead?
We don't want people thinking we live in no pig's eye.
Let's take a look here and see what new subversion you got fermentin'
here.
He's comin' over to claim his pound of fish.
It's the survivor of the fitness!
Them eggs are starting to foment.
And position is nine-tenths of the law, right?
I received your leaflet at my home residence and the words "substantial
profit" fought my eye.
It ain't German to this conversation.
It's like looking for a needle in a hayride!
Call it a father's intermission . . . but I smell a rat.
No doubt about it there's somethin' broken off in there and it's ledged
between the nervous system and the brain.
Looking like it's straight outta Missile Impossible, . . .
Cold enough to freeze a witch's mitt.
It's some of that Morgan David wine.
You been standing on that phone like a pillow of salt.

[1] Examples used in this paper have been taken from *The Wit & Wisdom of Archie
Bunker* (Popular Library), the record "All in the Family" (Atlantic), and the television show itself.

... 'cause Cousin Oscar is leavin' here, in post and haste.
Rudy and me was as close as two peas in a pot.
I give ya the biggest build-up since Grant took Richard.
... right outta Science Friction.
For better or for worse, in secrets and in health till death do us part?
It's like trying to make a sow's purse outta silk!
Whoever sent 'em obviously wanted to remain unanimous.
I'll believe that when hell freezes under.

Several of the mistakes that Archie makes such as confusing   3
antidote and *anecdote* and *ferment* and *foment* excite nervous
laughter because we have all fallen into the trap at one time or
another. Archie's pendant for name dropping betrays his ignorance
and his inner desire to be more than the average American bread-
winner. Although he is very funny, much of his humor is the product
of dramatic irony; his use of clichés, humorous because of their
inaccuracies, displays his lack of true wit and imagination.

If Archie is a modern master of the malapropism, he is also a   4
prolific creator of barbarisms—made-up or malformed words produced by false analogy with other, legitimate words. Like malapropisms, barbarisms reflect ignorance and often pretentiousness on the
part of the person who uses them. Here are some of Archie's:

What am I, a clairavoyage or somethin'?
... what you call, connubible difficulties ...
It's gonna take a lotta thinkin' and it's gonna take all my consecretion.
One of these days I will probably dehead myself.
It was said under dupress.
... making you an excessity after the fact!
It's a regular facsamile of the Apollo 14.
Like the Presidential, the Senatorial, the Governororial, the Mayororo-
rial ...
These things ain't exactly hairlooms, you know.
What do you mean by that insinuendo?
Back to the groinocologist!
She's hangin' around my neck like an Albacross!
He had the infrontery to imply that ...
... what you might call a certain lack of drive—you know, personal
inititianative.
Make this meathead take the literaracy test.
I remember some of the beauties you hung around with, and they wasn't
exactly no "Madonises."
Now lay off the social menuneties.
He's a morphidite.
... nothin' but out in out *porna*graphy.
... some ground rules and some priorororities.

And then write yourself a little note—you know, like a reminderandum.
. . . you'd be layin' on that floor waitin' for Rigor Morris to set in.
I ain't saying' it's largesse, smallesse or no' kinda esse.
Redeeming socialness is where they do the same old pornagraphs but
they give ya some four-dollar words while they're doin' it.
You didn't go and do something unlegal, you big dumb Polack?
You've got a warfed sense of humor.

The analogies by which Archie creates these barbarisms are of   5
two kinds, conceptual and structural. In the conceptual analogy,
Archie remembers *accessory* because it is "something extra," and
so he creates *excessity; facsimile* because it is "the same as," and so
he creates *facsamile;* and *memorandum* because it "reminds," and
so he creates *reminderandum*. In the structural analogy, Archie in-
corporates erroneous prefixes, suffixes, or extra syllables that occur
legitimately in other words because of the way those words happen
to have developed historically. Thus he creates *dehead, Governororial, smallesse, socialness,* and *unlegal*. This structural analogy
process is commonly found among children who are trying to cope
with the complexities of the English language. Archie's usages are
funny because he is trying to apply logic where tradition holds sway.

As humorous as Archie's malapropisms and barbarisms are, the   6
comedy of "All in the Family" relies heavily on a third type of
expression—the Bunkerism. Although closely akin to the malapropisms and barbarisms we have been examining, Bunkerisms are
unique. More than just comical ignorance and pretentiousness is
involved in the Bunkerism. The essence of the Bunkerism is that it
both expresses and, because it is an absurd usage, simultaneously
undermines one or another of Archie's many prejudices. Expressions such as "Englebum Hunkerdunk," "dem bamboons," "like
the immaculate connection," "pushy imported ricans," "Welfare
incipients," and "a regular Marco Polish" are Bunkerisms. In *The
Wit & Wisdom of Archie Bunker,* Archie's comic usages are referred to as "Archieisms." While this label recognizes the unique
quality of Archie's speech, it does not effectively label his coinages.
After all, Archie is the arch-conservative and arch-debunker, and all
his remarks are in one way or another "suppository." In a conversation with Edith, Archie says:

> You think he's a nice boy after he did what he did? Comin' in here,
> makin' suppository remarks about our country. And calling me preju-
> diced, while I was singin' "God Bless America," a song written by a
> well-known and respected Jewish guy, Milton Berlin.

Although Archie is objecting to someone else's derogatory remarks, the comment in this context says more about Archie's own bigoted attitude.

Certain types of situations within the show give rise to the Bunkerism. When Archie is trapped by logic, usually by Mike, has an audience and wishes to appear as a "know-it-all," is embarrassed by or impatient with Edith, is nervous when confronted by a member of a minority group, or is forced to talk about taboo subjects, he loses control of the language and produces Bunkerisms. As we have noted, these are akin to either malapropisms or barbarisms. Here are some Bunkerisms of which Mrs. Malaprop could be proud:

It's a proven fact that Capital Punishment is a known detergent for crime.
Why don't you write a letter to dear Abie?
And who are you supposed to be—Blackberry Finn?
I personally don't agree with all the conflagration on the college campuses. . . .
Just who in hell are we entertaining here tonight? The Count of Monte Crisco?
Throwin' debriss at officers of the law . . . Desecrating on the American flag.
And you don't need to draw me any diaphragms neither!
. . . who weren't fortunate enough to be born with the same natural endorsements.
If tampering with the United States mail is a federal offense, so is excitement to riot.
We've got the world's grossest national product.
You coming here, a priest, hiding behind your hassock—. . .
I'll let you know when I—in my intimate wisdom—decide that the time has ripened.
You and that Reverend Bleedin' Heart Felcher up there in his ivory shower.
Don't take everything so liberally.
Look, I know you'se kids go by what you call this new mortality . . .
This political percussion is over as of here and now.
In them days Notre Dame was playing hardknocks football! No fat scholarships, none of them pet parties—. . .
Until then *I'm* king, the princess is upstairs, and you're the pheasant that has to keep her here!
Smells like a house of ill refute if ya ask me.
I call Chinese food chinks 'cause that what it is . . . chinks. There was no slurp intended against the Chinese.
The sexual submissiveness? It don't matter whatever time of day or night—well, that's your dismissive society.
Lady, you wanna stoop this conversation down to the gutter level, that's your derogative.

Bunkerisms that are akin to barbarisms—words made up or malformed by analogy with legitimate words—include the following:

> One religion. Until they started splitting 'em up 'til all them other denumerations.
> . . . and wouldn't be related to me for complexionary reasons.
> 'Cause if I hadda face that bum on a full stomach, I'd detergerate . . .
> He comes from the gretto.
> . . . the worst hypochondrijerk in the neighborhood . . .
> . . . infilterating into our own house, Edith.
> . . . insurruption of the campuses.
> If you two malinjerers want anything . . .
> Your mother ain't got no preconscrewed ideas.
> You ain't gonna sell me none of your pregressive pinko welfare ideas . . .
> The man don't have one regleaming feature.
> People like your mother gotta be unpartial 'cause they got no subconceived notions.
> In my day we used to keep things in their proper suspective.
> Don't you never read the papers about all them unflocked priests running around?

Laura Hobson in an article for *The New York Times* entitled "As I Listened to Archie Say 'Hebe' . . ." criticizes the show for its [8] implicit claims of complete and honest bigotry and what to her appears to be a very subtle manipulation of language. She claims that the show's producers have managed to make a distinction between "acceptable" terms of ethnic abuse and those which would be truly offensive. This, she contends, falsely permits Archie to be a lovable bigot and bigotry itself to be not so bad after all. Although Hobson recognizes the subtlety of the ethnic terms used on the show, she fails to see the full import of the self-debunking Bunkerism. There is a general impression that Archie is only "done out" in the waning moments of the show; however, the unintentional self-deprecating nature of the Bunkerism serves to undermine Archie's bigotry throughout the whole show. The writers have successfully employed age-old comic devices—together with a new creation, the Bunkerism—to fulfill their satiric intentions.

QUESTIONS ON CONTENT

1. According to Rosa and Eschholz, what accounts for the humor of "All in the Family"? How is this show distinguished from other comedy shows?

2. What is a malaproprism? What is a barbarism? How do they differ?

3. What are Bunkerisms, and how are they related to malapropisms and barbarisms?

4. What types of situations give rise to Archie's comic misuse of language?

5. In the concluding paragraph, the authors discuss Laura Hobson's charge that Archie's language is subtly manipulated to make bigotry seem, in their words, "not so bad after all." Rosa and Eschholz disagree with Hobson; they argue that "the unintentional self-deprecating nature of the Bunkerism serves to undermine Archie's bigotry throughout the whole show." Do you agree with Hobson, with Rosa and Eschholz, or with neither? Explain.

QUESTIONS ON RHETORIC

1. What functions are performed by paragraph 1?

2. What sentence in paragraph 1 controls the content of paragraphs 2–7?

3. How do the first sentences of paragraphs 4 and 6 provide links to the earlier paragraphs?

4. Into what main categories are Archie's expressions classified? Are any of these categories further subdivided? Give examples.

VOCABULARY

analogy	essence	implicit
affectation	derogatory	satiric
pretentiousness	bigoted	

CLASSROOM ACTIVITIES

1. Each of the following sentences contains one of Archie Bunker's misusages. Classify each one as either a malapropism, a barbarism, or a Bunkerism.

   a. There's no invading the issue.
   b. We're going to Florida as prederanged.
   c. It was a shrewd awakening for him.
   d. The Supreme Court should place a conjunction against those people.

e. They should make those meatheads take the literaracy test.
f. You can suspense with the hellos.
g. What you see here is a frigment of your imagination.
h. All I can say for that pinko is goodbye and good ribbons.
i. That's just an excuse for Commie infliteration.
j. He got rid of the exercise tax on cars.
k. He's got some big move up his sleeve that he can't revulge yet.
l. You're taking it out of contest.
m. Let 'em in and before you know it familyarity breeds content.

NOTE: Writing assignments for "The Language of Radio, Television, and Newspapers" appear on p. 153.

3
Fast as an Elephant, Strong as an Ant

BIL GILBERT

Bil Gilbert, a frequent contributor to Sports Illustrated, *feels that while the language of the sports page is vivid and energetic, its metaphors are inaccurate. He contends that tradition and haste of composition have forced the sportswriter and the rest of us into mindless habitual language patterns. His suggestion for improvement—"high-fidelity zoological metaphors," of course.*

One day recently I was reading a story about the San Diego Chargers when I came across the following sentence describing Mr. Ernie Ladd, a tackle who is said to be 6 feet 9 inches tall and to weigh 300 pounds. Ladd, the report stated, has "a body that a grizzly bear could be proud of." Now, this is an example of the falsely anthropomorphic and the factually inaccurate natural-history metaphor, a literary device widely used by sportswriters and one that I have long thought should be reported to authorities and stamped out.

The description of Ernie Ladd is objectionable on two counts. First, there is no evidence that bears take pride in their personal appearance, physical prowess or muscular development. Among animals, only men seem susceptible to narcissism. And even if grizzlies did have the emotions of a beach boy and sat about the woods admiring their physiques, no bear would be proud of having a body like that of Mr. Ladd.

According to my copy of *Mammals of the World* (Ernest P. Walker, The Johns Hopkins Press, 1964, page 1173), "Grizzlies 2.5 meters [about 8 feet] in length and 360 kg. [800 pounds] in weight have been recorded. . . ." In brief, Mr. Ladd is simply too puny to impress a grizzly even if grizzlies were impressionable in these matters.

I have never been one to criticize without offering constructive   4
alternatives. Additional reading of *Mammals of the World* has un-
covered some statistics that may prove useful in the future. Should
the need arise, one might accurately (though still anthropomorphi-
cally) write that Mr. Ernie Ladd has a body that a female gray seal
(150 kg., 2 meters) or a pygmy hippopotamus (160 kg., 1.9 meters,
counting tail) might be proud of.

It is not my purpose to embarrass or harass the man who wrote   5
the story. Rather, it is to point out that he is the inheritor, the victim,
of a bad journalistic tradition. Sportswriters have been comparing
such and such an athlete to this or that animal since the dawn of
sports. Many of these long-standing figures, metaphors, similes and
tropes are even more wildly inaccurate and ridiculous than the comparison of Mr. Ladd to a grizzly bear.

An example that comes quickly to mind is the expression "wild   6
as a hawk," used to describe either erratic performance (a baseball
pitcher who cannot throw the ball across the plate) or untamable
behavior (a fractious horse). In both senses the phrase is misleading.
As far as control goes, the birds of prey are the antithesis of wild-
ness (in the baseball use of the word). A duck hawk, for example,
flying a mile high in the sky, can suddenly turn, dive earthward at
175 mph and strike a tiny sandpiper flying just a few feet above the
ground. Sandy Koufax should be so accurate. As to being untamable, I, as a falconer, have often captured a feral adult hawk and in a
month had the bird flying free, returning to my hand in response to a
whistled command.

My own suggestion is that "wild as a heron" would better sug-   7
gest the kind of behavior that wild as a hawk is supposed to describe. In many situations herons appear uncoordinated, almost
spastic. Seeing a long-legged, gangly heron trying to land or take off
from the ground is an experience. Furthermore, herons are far
wilder (in the ferocious sense) than hawks. The most painful injury I
ever received from an animal was given me by an American bittern
(a heron type), who gouged a large hole in my wrist as I was attempt-
ing to free him from a fish trap.

"Loose as a goose" is an avian simile, supposedly suggesting   8
extreme suppleness. Actually, geese have rigid pinions and are more
or less bound like weight lifters by a heavy layer of pectoral muscle.
Straight as a goose, stiff as a goose, pompous as a goose would be all
right. But loose as a goose? Never. A better expression of the notion
would be: "Though Slats Slattern has been a stellar NBA performer
for 12 seasons, he remains young in spirit and loose as a mink." The
slim-bodied minks, as well as weasels, ferrets and otters, are de-

signed along the lines of a wet noodle. They look, and in fact are, far looser than a goose can possibly be.

Turning to mammals, an agility simile is "quick as a cat," often 9 used in connection with such athletes as shortstops and goalies. It is true that cats are quicker than some things—turtles, mice, goldfish in bowls, for example—but they are much less quick than many other creatures. Any wheezing old dog worth its salt can catch a cat. I once had a crow so quick that it could fly down and deliver three pecks between the eyes of a cat (which the crow despised) before the feline could raise a paw in self-defense. Not long ago I was watching a tame baboon which had the run of a yard in which was caged an ocelot. The baboon, even though working through bars, would reach into the cage and, while the ocelot was trying to get her reflexes in order, grab the cat by both her handsome tail and pointed ears. Baboon-quick is accurate and has a nice exotic ring to it.

Cats may not be the quickest animals, but at least one of the 10 family, the cheetah, is the swiftest mammal as far as straight-ahead sprinting goes. It would seem that "run like a cheetah" would be a natural simile for sportswriters, but what do we have? "Ziggy Zagowski, slashing left half for the Keokuk Kidneys, ran like a rabbit through the defending Sioux City Spleens." Now, for a few jumps a rabbit can move at a rate of 30 or 35 miles an hour, but 20 mph is its pace for a distance as great as 100 yards. This rate is about the same as—or a bit slower than—that of a journeyman human sprinter over the same course. The chances are that if old Zig could not outleg a bunny he would not have even made his high school team. If, however, he could run like a cheetah, it would be a different matter, since those cats can do the 440 at 71 mph.

Since an elephant can skip along as fast as 25 mph (a bit faster 11 than Bob Hayes or the average cottontail), it would be highly complimentary to say of an athlete that he runs like an elephant. However, the expression "elephantine" is actually used in sports as a term of derision, to twit a ponderous, slow-moving, clumsy performer. Actually, elephants are not only swift beasts but graceful ones. Despite their size, they are almost as quick as a baboon or as loose as a mink. They can slip quietly through the jungle, stand on a barrel or a ballerina at the behest of a ringmaster. "Horsine" would be a better term to designate a stumblebum. Horses are forever falling over small pebbles, ropes and their own feet. When a horse and rider start down even a gradual incline or up a path slightly narrower than the Pennsylvania Turnpike, the rider must dismount, and it is he who must lead, guide and, in general, prop up the horse.

Great strength has its place in sports, and it is traditional to 12 describe the athlete who possesses it as being "strong as an ox." As in the case of quick cats and fast rabbits, the simile is not completely false, only inadequate. In proportion to their bulk, oxen are relatively strong but not overpoweringly so. A team of oxen weighing 3,400 pounds can move a dead weight, say a block of granite, equal to about three times its own weight. This is a fair feat when compared to a 150-pound weight lifter who can dead-lift 300 pounds. However, it is a feeble effort when one considers the ant, which can pick up a load 50 times heavier than itself. To speak of a fullback as being strong as an ant would be high praise indeed, since it would signify that the player could, without undue strain, carry the entire opposing team not only across the goal line, but right up into Row E.

Held in high regard by coaches, reporters and fans is the athlete who works incessantly at mastering the fundamentals of his game. Often such persevering types are admired as "beavers." This, of course, is a contraction of the folksy expressions "to work like a beaver" or "to be as busy as a beaver," both of which are based upon a misunderstanding of the beaver's nature and misobservation of the animal's customary behavior. Unlike some animals that must travel many miles a day just to rustle up a square meal, beavers seldom forage more than a hundred yards from their home. Beavers construct their well-publicized dams and lodges only when it is absolutely impossible to find a suitable natural waterscape. The lowly mole, on the other hand, may dig several hundred yards of tunnel in a day in an incessant effort to keep body and soul together. "I like that boy, all spring long he's been moling away," would be an apt way for a coach to describe and praise industriousness.

Canines have a strong attraction for scribes looking for a vivid, if fallacious, phrase. There is, for example, the veteran who is a "sly, foxy" competitor. (If foxes are so sly, how come they never run down the hounds? Who ever heard of a hunt catching a skunk?) Then there is the prizefighter about to addle the brains of his opponent or the fast-ball pitcher poised to stick one in a batter's ear. These violent men, we are often told, have a "wolfish grin" on their faces.

One of the few naturalists who have been close enough long enough to *au naturel* wolves to observe their facial expressions is Farley Mowat, who spent a summer camped virtually on the den step of a family of Arctic wolves. Mowat in his delightful book, *Never Cry Wolf,* claims that *his* wolves were kindly, affectionate, tolerant animals who looked and acted more like diplomats than thugs. This stands to reason. Many creatures besides man are predatory, but hardly any species except man tries to do real violence to its own kind in play while contemplating the prospect with a grin. If such a premayhem facial expression as a "wolfish grin" actually exists, it is probably unique to man. If this peculiar look of violence must be compared to that of some other animal, I recommend the short-tailed shrew.

The short-tailed shrew is one of the commonest animals of North   16
America and one of the most perpetually predatory. Ounce for ounce (which is what a large shrew weighs), there is no busier killer in the world. Awake, the shrew is almost always preparing to kill, is killing or has just killed, and its victims include rodents, reptiles, birds and mammals several times its own size. The shrew, like almost all other mammals, does not kill out of capriciousness or playfulness, but rather because it has an extraordinarily high metabolic rate. It must daily consume the equivalent of its own body weight in order to keep the inner fires burning. (Eat like a shrew, rather than eat like a horse, would better describe the habits of a first baseman who is such a formidable trencherman that he can no longer bend down to scoop up low throws.) When a shrew closes in to kill something, say a white-footed mouse, it wears a really dreadful expression. A shrew is chinless, and its long mouth slashes across the underpart of its muzzle in a cruel, sharklike line. As the tiny killer closes in, its eyes glitter with excitement and two long brown fangs (which, incidentally, drip with a venomous saliva) are exposed. If Sonny Liston looked only half as wicked as a short-tailed shrew he might still be heavyweight champion of the world.

I fully realize that many of the criticisms and suggestions offered   17
here do violence to some of the most cherished traditions of sports journalism, but there is no holding back literary and scientific progress. Consider, for example, the manner in which the style I advocate, high-fidelity zoological metaphor, injects color as well as accuracy into the following interview with Sig Schock of the Pardy Pumas:

"Sig Schock, a big horsine man, grizzled as a Norway rat, leaned   18
back against the plywood bench, taking up a position so that the hot sun beat down on his ant-like shoulders. The eyes, old but still sharp as a barn owl's, flicked over the practice field, where the young Pumas cavorted as quick as so many baboons. 'I'll tell you,' Sig confided in his disconcertingly high, spring-peeperlike voice. 'These kids has got it. The most of them can run like elephants, a couple like cheetahs. And size. We finally got some. We got six boys with builds like a female gray seal's. Course, they're still young, some of them are wild as herons—that's O.K., they got the old desire. Every one of them is a snapping turtle or a raccoon. And I'll tell you

something,' the sly, skunky veteran added, lowering his squeaky voice. 'We'll chew 'em up and lay 'em out this season.' A shrewish grin spread across the battered old face.''

Leaving you with that, I remain pretty as a peacock, sassy as a jaybird, happy as a clam. 19

QUESTIONS ON CONTENT

1. What is a metaphor? What is a simile? Which of these figures of speech is used in the title of Gilbert's article? Which is used in the phrase "a body that a grizzly bear could be proud of"? Do you think that Gilbert's faulting of this last comparison is justified, or would it be effective for most readers?

2. Consider the alternative comparisons offered by Gilbert: "wild as a heron," for example, or "loose as a mink." Are these alternatives acceptable? Why or why not?

3. How seriously does Gilbert advocate "high-fidelity zoological metaphors"? How successful is his interview with Sig Schock in terms of "color," "accuracy," and "communication"?

QUESTIONS ON RHETORIC

1. What is Gilbert's thesis and where is it stated?

2. What is the purpose of paragraph 6?

3. Gilbert's tone in the essay is witty and ironic. Where specifically is his tone most clearly revealed?

4. What is the purpose of the last sentence?

VOCABULARY

prowess	gouged	fallacious
susceptible	agility	virtually
harass	exotic	perpetually
erratic	derision	formidable
	incessantly	

CLASSROOM ACTIVITIES

1. After reading Gilbert's article, what conclusions can you draw concerning the characteristics of effective metaphors and similes? Consider the effectiveness of the following literary metaphors and similes.

a. I wandered lonely as a cloud.
   William Wordsworth

b. That time of year thou mayst in me behold
   When yellow leaves, or none, or few, do hang
   Upon those boughs which shake against the cold,
   Bare ruined choirs where late the sweet birds sang.
   William Shakespeare

c. I saw eternity the other night
   Like a great ring of pure and endless light,
      All calm as it was bright;
   And round beneath it, time in hours, days, years,
      Driv'n by the spheres,
   Like a vast shadow moved, in which the world
      And all her train were hurled. . . .
   Henry Vaughan

d. Her feet beneath her petticoat,
   Like little mice stole in and out,
   As if they feared the light. . . .
   Sir John Suckling

e. Life, like a dome of many-colored glass,
   Stains the white radiance of Eternity.
   Percy Bysshe Shelley

f. He [the eagle] clasps the crag with crooked hands;
   Close to the sun in lonely lands,
   Ringed with the azure world, he stands.

   The wrinkled sea beneath him crawls;
   He watches from his mountain walls,
   And like a thunderbolt he falls.
   Alfred, Lord Tennyson

NOTE: Writing assignments for "The Language of Radio, Television, and Newspapers" appear on p. 153.

4
Football Verbiage

WILLIAM EBEN SCHULTZ

All of us at one time or another have tried to find fresh and more specific ways of describing commonplace events. Nowhere is this need more evident than on the sports pages of our newspapers. Here William Schultz presents an extensive list of the "action" verbs that sportswriters use to avoid trite- ness and brighten their reporting.

American speech is conceded to be energetic and picturesque, possibly as an expression or reflection of national activity and vari- ety. The sports pages of our newspapers, while often filled with a jargon not too desirable, and sometimes affected, help to illustrate this idea. Aside from the graphic names of athletic teams (not stud- ied in this article, but well known to the average reader—such as Titans, Trojans, and Tigers, along with a whole menagerie of other animals), there is no more outstanding characteristic of news stories rushed into print during the football season than the use of action verbs in the headlines. The following illustrations, arranged alpha- betically, have been gathered from week-end editions of a miscella- neous assortment of daily papers, ranging from small publications to the metropolitan press. . . .

Duke *annexes* victory
Lake Forest *baffles* Augustana
Iowa State *bags* tie with Mississippi
Ohio State *beats* Badgers
Lawrence *belts* Monmouth
Michigan Normal *blanks* Ball State
Illini *blast* Indiana
Gophers *bounce* Indiana
Oklahoma *bowls* over Nebraska
Gophers *bruise* Iowa
Tulane *bumps* Mississippi
Michigan *buries* Northwestern
Illinois *clips* Purdue

Millikin *clouts* Illinois College
Duke *conquers* North Carolina
Baylor *cops* close one
California *cracks* Washington
Huskies *crown* S.I.U.
Ohio *crushes* Minnesota
Cornell *douses* Columbia
Case *downs* Western Reserve
Illinois Wesleyan *drops* tough game to DePauw
Tulane *drowns* Navy
Anderson *drubs* McKendree
Notre Dame *dumps* Nebraska
Oklahoma *edges* Texas
Northwestern *explodes* Illinois Title
Illinois *grinds* out win
Yale *handed* defeat by Dartmouth
Navy *hangs* up victory
Georgia *halters* Boston College
Florida *halts* Vanderbilt
Eureka *humbles* McKendree
Colorado *jars* Aggies
Northwestern *jolts* Illinois
Western *laces* Shurtleff
Stanford *licks* Washington
Notre Dame *mauls* Indiana
Northwestern *nicks* Ohio
Oregon *nips* St. Mary's
U.S.C. *noses* out Stanford
Texas *nudges* Baylor
Texas Christian *outscrambles* Mississippi
Army *overwhelms* Lions
Normal *plasters* Western
Shurtleff *pops* Principia
St. Joseph *pounds* Mansfield
Drake *pummels* New Mexico
California *quells* U.S.C.
Tulane *races* to win
State Normal *racks* up win
Penn State *raps* Quakers
Oklahoma *rips* Colorado
Wesleyan *roars* to victory
Alabama *rolls* over Florida
Spartans *romp* over Cyclones
Ohio *routs* Northwestern
Tulane *shades* Auburn
Irish *shellack* Navy
Indiana *shocks* Pittsburgh

Pittsburgh *slaps* W. Virginia
Kansas State *smacks* Iowa
Yale *smashes* Harvard
Brown *smothers* Colgate
Michigan *snaps* Gopher streak
Wildcats *spank* Purdue
Flowers *sparks* Northwestern to victory
Cornell *spills* Navy
Wisconsin *squeezes* out decision over Illinois
Wake Forest *startles* Drake
Cyclones *stun* Illini
Texas *subdues* Oklahoma
Bucs *swamp* Pittsburgh
Notre Dame *tames* Iowa
Iowa *throttles* Wisconsin
Yale *thumps* Columbia
Washington *thwarts* Illinois Wesleyan
Iowa State *tips* Colorado
California *topples* Washington
Dartmouth *tops* Harvard
Wolverines *trample* Navy
Knox *trims* Beloit
Knox *trips* Monmouth
Mississippi *triumphs* over Tennessee
Princeton *tromps* Harvard
U.C.L.A. *trounces* Purdue
Louisiana State *upsets* North Carolina
Northwestern *wallops* Pittsburgh
Denver *whips* Wyoming
Iowa *yields* to Minnesota

There are many additional expressions for which I have saved no   2
definite references, like these: *batters, bows to, deals defeat, lashes,
outslickers, paces, shatters hopes, slashes, snares, squelches, swats,
whales.* I have not included common terms like *wins, loses, beats,
defeats, overcomes, outscores, takes game,* etc.

With such an expressive array of "verbiage," there seems to be   3
no danger that the sports editors will become stagnant, or that football as a game will lose its numerous and enthusiastic artists in the
field of athletic ballyhoo.

QUESTIONS ON CONTENT

1. Some writers claim that there are no exact synonyms in English,
no two words that have precisely the same meaning. The long list of

action verbs offered by Schultz provides an opportunity to test this claim, since all these verbs describe a situation in which one team wins and another team loses. Sort the verbs into two groups: those for winners and those for losers. Then compare the verbs in each group—for example, what exactly is the difference between "crushes" and "downs" or between "halts" and "humbles"? Are there any exact synonyms?

2. All of these headlines involve the use of figurative language. Explain the figures of speech and how they work in several of the headlines.

QUESTIONS ON RHETORIC

1. What is Schultz's thesis in this article?

2. What is the function of Schultz's extensive list of action verbs found in sportswriting?

VOCABULARY

conceded	jargon	array
picturesque	metropolitan	stagnant

CLASSROOM ACTIVITIES

1. Just as the sportswriter must repeatedly describe similar situations, so all of us talk about actions that we perform daily. If we were restricted to only one word for each of our activities, for example, our conversations would be repetitive and monotonous. List as many verbs as you can that mean "eat," "drink," "sleep," and "work." What denotative and connotative differences do you find in your list of alternatives?

NOTE: Writing assignments for "The Language of Radio, Television, and Newspapers" appear on p. 153.

5

A Vivacious Blonde
Was Fatally Shot Today
or How to Read a Tabloid

OTTO FRIEDRICH

In the following article, which appeared in American Scholar, *Otto Friedrich, author of* Going Crazy: An Inquiry into Madness in Our Time, *takes an inside look at the world of the tabloid newspaper. He examines tabloid prose ("the art of exaggerating without actually lying"), editorial policies, and the product—a newspaper that creates a kind of Shangri-la for the reader.*

There is a joke among newspapermen that if a woman is pretty, she is called "beautiful"; if she is plain, she is called "attractive"; and if she is hideous, she is called "vivacious." Half the joke is the exaggeration; the other half is that this is no exaggeration at all. In describing a woman involved in a murder or a robbery or a divorce case, the same technique is generally applied to every aspect of her appearance. If she is tall, she is "statuesque." If she is short, the word is "petite." Thin women are "slender," while fat ones are "curvaceous." Physical appearance is not so important in a man, and the emphasis shifts to financial appearance. "Socially prominent" is a popular description of any man who is murdered by his wife. Bookies and gigolos may be identified as "sportsmen." And one connoisseur has defined "socialite" as "a tabloid term meaning human being."

This form of wordmanship—the art of exaggerating without actually lying—is so common in tabloid newspapers that it may be termed tabloid prose, but it is by no means restricted to tabloids. Indeed, most newspapers and most wire services use it much of the time. Tabloid prose is not merely a corruption of the English language, however. Literary critics tell us that form cannot be disassociated from content, and since many writers of tabloid prose are intelligent and cultivated people, the reason for the use of a word such as "curvaceous" may be found in the mentality of the person for whom it is written. More accurately, the reason lies in the editor's concept of the mentality of the person who can be enticed by such words into surrendering his five or ten cents.

Despite all its pretenses of representing the public, the average 3 newspaper is simply a business enterprise that sells news and uses that lure to sell advertising space. It is scarcely different from enterprises selling shoes or grass seed. Like any other business, a newspaper obeys the law of supply and demand, and most newspapers have discovered that a sex murder attracts more readers than does a French cabinet crisis. Murder, however, is a fairly commonplace event—one a day is the average in New York alone—and the tabloid editor therefore makes distinctions between what are known as "classy cases" and "cheap cases."

It is commonly believed that a reader's interest is attracted by a 4 case with which he can identify himself—there but for the grace of God, et cetera. But if the average tabloid reader were murdered, his misfortune would not receive much coverage in the average tabloid. He would be a "cheap case." Essentially, a cheap case involves what tabloid editors consider to be cheap people. This includes all working-class people, such as factory hands, waitresses and the unemployed. It also includes farmers, usually brushed aside as "hillbilly stuff." Alcoholics, whose antics are sometimes extremely entertaining, come under the same ban. So do Negroes, Mexicans, Puerto Ricans and other "lesser breeds without the law." This causes some difficulties for the wire services since the current fashion is to delete any references to a criminal's race as "irrelevant." Thus an editor who might begin by showing great interest in a murder would cut the story down to a few paragraphs after learning that it involved a "Jig," but he would not publicly divulge the dread word that motivated his editing—and, of course, his editorial columns would continue to clamor for civil rights.

There is another subdivision of the cheap case that the editor 5 generally describes as "too gruesome." Onto his spike go the stories, more common than the average newspaper reader realizes, of children being raped or chopped to pieces, stories of burglars torturing their victims to make them reveal their cache. Both cheap and gruesome, in the minds of most editors, is the subject of homosexuality. A traveling salesman strangled by a boy he brought up to his room at the Y.M.C.A. would never deserve one-tenth the tabloid attention that he would attain if his assassin had been a girl.

Sadism, sodomy, tortures, drunken stabbings, certain adulteries   6
—these things happen every day, but in a kind of nether world that
lies beneath what the tabloids like to consider their dignity. In contrast to all this, there is the "classy case." What gives a murder
"class"? Rich men, beautiful women, yachts, racing stables—
everything, in short, that forms part of the dreamworld of the gum-
chewing tabloid reader. For the secret of the whole tabloid formula
is that the "classy" murder case is not one with which the reader
can identify himself but one with which he *would like* to identify
himself. *The New York Times* and the *Herald Tribune* provide society pages for social climbers to read; the tabloids provide society
columns for daydreaming shopgirls. The concept of class, in other
words, represents the Hollywood-fed all-American fantasy, and yet
the "news" about this dreamworld is always at least implicitly disastrous. The stockbroker is discovered in his "love nest"; the heiress is a "love slave"; the playboy is sued for "heart balm." Thus
the lower orders, in buying the news about the upper ones are given
satisfying accounts of their objects of envy committing depravities
and defalcations, of their imminent descent to the readers' own
level. Although reader-criminal identification may seem farfetched
here, one can assume that the tabloid reader would like to be in a
position to *have* a "love nest," even if it meant eventually being
"exposed."

Once in a decade there is a case like the shooting of Jim Fisk or   7
the kidnapping of the Lindbergh baby, a case in which all the rules
of the tabloid form fit into place and a famous story virtually writes
itself. But the tabloids are printed every day, and every day the
readers are hungry for a new taste of high-class sensations. That is
why the homely waitress strangled on the beach becomes a
"shapely blonde" (the favored term "blonde" can apply to almost
any color of hair, although obviously unblonde women are often
exoticized by terms such as "flame-haired" or "raven-tressed").
This is why the seedy sawbones who pinches his patients becomes a
"distinguished physician" living in "a luxurious home in the fashionable suburb of Blank." Indeed, tabloid prose often reads like the
same newspaper's real estate section for the simple reason that both
the tabloid writer and the advertising writer are trying to make the
shabby reality conform to the fantasy. Homes, in both cases, if not
luxurious, are then spacious. Suburbs are always fashionable.

And houses are always "homes," for all the idealizing forces   8
behind the tabloid writer require him to use the genteel euphemism
in every case where the unidiomatic word will provide "class."
Thus sons become heirs or scions. Doctors become physicians, car-

penters become contracting executives, and even the lowest of the species may be "socially prominent."

The tabloid distortions represent so ubiquitous a fantasy that the tabloid writer occasionally discovers one of his subjects really acting out the transformation of human being into socialite. A few years ago, a New York millionaire was shot to death by his wife, and the tabloids set up a hue and cry for every detail of the story. One of the gaps was the background of the wife, who had been generally thought to be the orphaned daughter of a colonel. It took a tabloid reporter a considerable amount of time to determine that the colonel had never existed, and that the actual father was still very much alive as a streetcar motorman in Detroit. When the father was finally interviewed about his daughter's misfortunes, he expressed surprise that she had married a New York millionaire. He remembered that she had changed her name to become a model, but for many years he had been under the impression that his daughter was a well-known Hollywood actress with a similar *nom de guerre*. Here is a tabloid creation in the flesh.

Sex, as is well known, combines with crime to provide the tabloids with their huge circulations. But sex is as strangely distorted as crime, as strangely twisted to fit the American fantasies. The same bans apply—drunks, Negroes, workers, homosexuals, all these have no sex life of any news value. And yet the lowest "starlet" in Hollywood has her casual affairs broadcast to millions under such wonderful disguises as "friends wonder if so-and-so is secretly married to so-and-so." Disguise is the essence of sex chronicles, for although sex sells newspapers, even the most lurid tabloid schizophrenically considers itself a "family newspaper." Although it may seem strange to a casual reader, the tabloid editor's desire to stimulate sales is handcuffed by a criterion known as "good taste." This criterion is so mysterious, so much a matter of "feel," that it can best be illustrated by an example.

An enterprising young lady once tried to achieve fame by going to a Cannes film festival, accosting a popular actor, stripping off all her clothes above the waist, and embracing the rather embarrassed actor while photographers frantically took pictures that could never be printed. From reporters' accounts of the scene, the girl achieved a certain small notoriety, enough to get her to Hollywood, where her misfortunes were usually reported as an excuse to run pictures of her. One day, this aspiring actress—or could it have been some other specimen of the familiar type?—appeared in a two-column picture, wearing a tiny crucifix that dangled down into a resting place between her luxurious breasts. The editor, who had been out of the office when the picture was first printed, returned to his desk and cried out in horror. At considerable expense, the picture was treated with an airbrush, which sprayed flesh-colored paint over the crucifix, so that a new engraving of the voluptuous bosom could be portrayed in the next edition without violating "good taste."

Perhaps one more incident would illustrate this strange concept further. A few years ago, a teen-age youth in a suburb of Boston murdered a girl with whom he had just had sexual intercourse on the front seat of an automobile. When the youth confessed to the police, he proudly repeated over and over the details of how he had become a man in the parked car, and the words he used to express that experience were: "Then I scored and then I scored again, that's where I scored." The childish boast embarrassed the same editors who normally want to emphasize every implication of sex, and when the story was finally printed the youth was quoted as saying that "intimacies had occurred" in the spotted front seat of the car.

Intimacies. This is the tabloid word for sex. It turns up over and over again. If any ingenuous tabloid writer tries to use a word like "sex," on the theory that an accurate term is always in better taste than a euphemism, the more experienced copy desk will change it to "intimacies." The reason for this involves the same fantasies that dominate Hollywood: Miss Blank, who has had three husbands, is cast as an ingénue stranded overnight on a mountain top with Mr. Blank, who has had three wives. There is much giggling as they pitch their separate tents, but at the end they will get married. The movie will be advertised with twenty-foot-high posters of Miss Blank lying panting on the mountain top in her chemise while Mr. Blank crouches nearby in the attitude of a neurotic gorilla. The movie-goer knows that he will not be actually shown anything that could offend the local archbishop, but he will be allowed his snicker. The snicker, the leer, that nervous substitute for the thwarted need, is the American emotional response to the so-called "popular culture."

Although the tabloids and the movies provide much the same outlet for the need to snicker, the tabloids push the whole process one step further than is possible in the movies. With an almost baroque stylization, the tabloids would take Mr. Blank and Miss Blank to the mountain top, and then, instead of fading out like a discreet movie camera, they would quote Miss Blank as saying that "intimacies occurred." Nor is that the only dainty disguise. Mr. Blank may also be said to have been "dallying" with Miss Blank, or maybe he was "romancing" her. He is her "sweetheart." No, says she, they are "just good friends," and everybody gets a good healthy snicker out of it.

Curiously enough, the chief trouble for the tabloid writer occurs   15
in supposed sex cases where no sex has been enjoyed, as far as can be determined. The problem arises, for instance, in the periodic story of the "nice" teen-age girl running off with a boy. The tabloid editors enjoy a vicarious thrill at the prospect of a young girl's availability, but the writer finds that everything he can say about the errant couple has already been tinged with the implications of past cases. Were they just "close friends"? Were they "intimate friends"? Had there been, all virginally, a "romance"? Every word revives echoes of the old euphemisms and the old snickers. Denials are accepted as lies. The English language has been wrung out.

Are the tabloids hopeless? Perhaps, but not on the grounds of   16
sensationalism. Having already become rich, they hunger nowadays after finer things, such as respectability and political influence. In New York, where the *Times* fills its half-size brothers with awe, the tabloids feel compelled to tell their uninterested readers about such portentous events as a Senate debate on farm parity, largely because the *Times* has or inevitably will do so. It is almost with shock that today's tabloid writer, looking back through clippings on the Lindbergh case,' finds Damon Runyon reporting the execution of Bruno Hauptmann in terms of near-hysteria: "The Wolf-man is dead." What amazement he feels, then, in looking at the old *Graphic*'s faked pictures of Peaches Browning in the bedroom with her aged husband, at the balloon that issues from Daddy's mouth and quotes him as quacking like a duck. To find such authentic trashiness now, one must leave America and take a look at the London *Mirror,* which is comparatively entertaining and consequently sells twice as many copies as its biggest New York counterpart. Although American tabloid circulations are in or near the millions, their sales are actually stagnant or declining, despite the increase in population. That is natural, however, when the popular touch has become the genteelism, when irreverence has given way to reverence, stuffiness, even pomposity.

One tabloid's saucy story about the preparations of a European   17
princeling's long-anticipated marriage to a celebrated beauty was killed on the strength of a new managerial directive that the wedding had been handled too impertinently and was henceforth to be treated "with dignity." And so for one solid week, it printed fifteen "romantic" but "dignified" manuscript pages per day on one of the

most laughable events of our time. The stories were laughable too, precisely because they accepted their subjects' social pretensions at face value. I wrote them myself.

QUESTIONS ON CONTENT

1. What is a tabloid newspaper? How does it differ from such non-tabloids as *The New York Times,* the *Christian Science Monitor,* and the *Wall Street Journal?*

2. What, according to Friedrich, characterizes "tabloid prose"? What reasons does he suggest for its use?

3. According to Friedrich, what does the reader of the "classy murder case" in a tabloid have in common with the reader of the society pages in papers such as *The New York Times?* Explain.

4. The tabloid editor, Friedrich says, is restricted by a mysterious code of "good taste." On the basis of the examples he gives in the article, try to explain what is involved here.

5. What does Friedrich see as the future of the tabloid?

QUESTIONS ON RHETORIC

1. How does Friedrich's opening paragraph capture the reader's attention? How is paragraph 1 related to paragraph 2?

2. What is Friedrich's purpose in writing this essay?

3. Examine the contrast Friedrich draws between a "cheap murder case" and a "classy murder case." On what basis does he contrast the two?

4. What is the function of the brief question that begins paragraph 16?

VOCABULARY

enticed	virtually	thwarted
pretenses	ubiquitous	portentous
	criterion	irreverence

CLASSROOM ACTIVITIES

1. The following newsstories about the Little League World Series appeared on November 11, 1974, in two very different newspapers. Carefully read each article, keeping in mind Friedrich's description of tabloid prose.

LITTLE LEAGUE SERIES BARS FOREIGNERS

By The Associated Press

WILLIAMSPORT, Pa., Nov. 11—The Little League will confine future world series to teams from the continental United States.

This was announced today at the headquarters of the national baseball organization. The effect was to exclude Taiwan, which won the series for boys 8 to 12 years old in the last four years, causing protests in this country. Japan won the two previous years, and Monterrey, Mexico, took the series in 1957 and 1958. The last United States winner was Wayne, N.J., in 1970.

The league said its board of directors had acted after a review of the competition. It said the regional championship series would be continued in Canada, the Far East, Europe and Latin America, and the playoffs for senior (ages 13 to 15) or big league (16 to 18) programs would not be affected.

A spokesman cited travel costs for foreign entries and the nationalistic approach taken abroad as reasons for the change. He described the United States programs as regional in make-up.

Since the Little League expanded in 1957 to include teams outside the continental United States, 20 foreign teams have competed. There are 9,000 teams in the United States.

Robert H. Stirrat, vice president and public relations director, would only say:

"We are standing by the board's resolution and will offer no further details."

The world series will be played next Aug. 19 to 23 at Williamsport, the birthplace of Little League baseball. Only four teams—the United States regional champions—will be entered. There were eight when foreign teams competed.

The ruling eliminates from world series competition children of American servicemen stationed in Europe because, a spokesman said, they are considered "foreign."

The first world series was played in 1947.

Last Aug. 24 Taiwan wrapped up its fourth straight world series with a 12–1 victory in the final over Red Bluff, Calif. The run was the first allowed by the Taiwanese in 46 innings, so completely did they dominate the series.

The team was led by Lin Wen-hsiung, a 12-year-old, right-handed pitcher, who hit two home runs and hurled a two-hitter in the final, striking out 15 of the 21 batters he faced.

The game was shown throughout Taiwan on television via satellite at 3 A.M., but many fans there considered the outcome such a foregone conclusion that they elected to go to sleep rather than watch.

Nevertheless, there were bursts of firecrackers before dawn to celebrate the victory.

So proficient have Taiwanese youngsters become at baseball that they have dominated not only Little League competition, but also divisions for older boys.

This year a Taiwanese team captured the Senior Little League world championship in Gary, Ind., for the third straight time, and the island's Big League team won the title at Fort Lauderdale, Fla., in its first attempt.

LITTLE LEAGUE BANS FOREIGNERS
No More Chinese HRs

Little League Shrinks Map
Limits World Series After Taiwan Romp

After watching Taiwan dominate the Little League World Series at Williamsport, Pa., for four years, the American sponsors found a way yesterday to end that victory streak: they banned foreign entries.

The ban, obviously, will do away with the so-called Chinese home run, a phrase New Yorkers learned about when the upper deck hung out over the playing field at the defunct Polo Grounds where the foul lines were short and homers were plentiful.

Peter J. McGovern, chief executive officer and board chairman of the Little League, said that the series would be restricted to the four regional U.S. champions from now on.

Robert H. Stirrat, vice president and public relations director for the league, said that the organization "is not nationalistic in its point of view." Stirrat said the group feels Little League is basically a community program and it intends returning to the original concept.

"The board took a long view of the international aspects of the program and decided a reassessment of the World Series competition for children aged 12 and under had to be regarded," Stirrat said. "It was their decision to limit the series from here on to the United States."

Stirrat also emphasized the ban on foreign clubs involves only the Little League series at Williamsport. He added that the senior league (13–15) and big league (16–18) are not affected. Those championships will still be waged on an international basis.

"The senior division is the world's largest baseball program," Stirrat said. "But they are unaffected by the decision." The seniors' finale will be played at Gary, Ind., with the big league finals at Fort Lauderdale, Fla.

Japanese Led the Parade

League officials deny the latest ruling was an effort to exclude Taiwan or any other non-U.S. squad. There are 9,000 little leagues in this country and since the Williamsport brass broadened its program in 1957 to include "outside" teams, 20 foreign clubs have competed.

An American team hasn't been the Little League champ since Wayne, N.J., in 1970. Since then, Japanese representatives won in 1968 and 1969, followed by Taiwan the past four years.

Regional championships will continue to be held in Canada, Latin America, Europe and the Far East, but those winners will not compete in Williamsport.

"The Little League is taken pretty much as a summertime activity for kids in the United States," Stirrat said, "and the World Series is sort of a natural finish of the season for them."

Now, with only four clubs contesting for the 1975 title, which will be decided Aug. 19-23 at Williamsport, Little League brass were undecided as to its new format. They must determine whether sudden-death or a double elimination series will be played.

In any event, the Little League World Series will be an all-American affair.

Which account do you think appeared in a tabloid? On what stylistic evidence did you base your decision?

NOTE: Writing assignments for "The Language of Radio, Television, and Newspapers" appear on p. 153.

6
Must a Great Newspaper Be Dull?

WALKER GIBSON

In this essay from Tough, Sweet and Stuffy, *Walker Gibson, professor of English at the University of Massachusetts, analyzes newspaper reporting and confrónts the question "Must a great newspaper be dull?" While he grants the impossibility of "straight" reporting, Gibson points to the inherent dangers in trying not to be dull. By looking at a single incident as reported by* The New York Times, *the* New York Herald Tribune, *and* Time *magazine, Gibson compares and contrasts the various stylistic alternatives available to the reporter.*

This essay considers some examples of how the news of the day is   1
expressed for us, and how, in some of its expressions, a bastard
form of the Tough Talker[1] can be detected.

We begin with a conventional sample of "straight" reporting,   2
though concerning events that lend themselves to excitable treatment. Here is a reporter for *The New York Times* (Claude Sitton)
beginning his lead article on the race riots in Birmingham, Alabama,
in the issue for May 8, 1963.

> The police and firemen drove hundreds of rioting Negroes off the streets
> today with high-pressure hoses and an armored car. The riot broke out

---

[1] *Ed. note:* Earlier in *Tough, Sweet and Stuffy* Gibson defines the Tough Talker:
"What I mean by Tough Talk is most easily discovered in works of fiction where a
narrator-hero identifies himself as a hard man who has been around. . . . His rhetoric
. . . shows its limitations openly: short sentences, 'crude' repetitions of words, simple
grammatical structures with little subordinating. (I have no use for elegant variation,
for the worn-out gentilities of traditional prose.) His tense intimacy with his assumed
reader, another man who has been around, is implied by colloquial patterns from oral
speech and by a high frequency of the definite article. He lets his reader make logical
and other connections between elements. (You know what I mean; I don't have to
spell it all out for *you*.) He prefers naming things to describing them, and avoids
modification, especially when suggestive of value. All these habits of behavior suggest that he is self-conscious about his language—even about language generally. He
is close-lipped, he watches his words." (pp. ix, 41).

143

after from 2,500 to 3,000 persons rampaged through the business district in two demonstrations and were driven back. The Negroes rained rocks, bottles and brickbats on the law-enforcement officials as they were slowly forced backward by the streams of water. The pressure was so high that the water skinned bark off trees in the parks and along sidewalks. Policemen from surrounding cities and members of the Alabama Highway Patrol rushed to a nine-block area near the business district to help quell the riot. An undetermined number of persons were injured in the demonstrations against segregation. They included the Rev. Fred L. Shuttlesworth, a prominent Negro leader, and two city policemen and a Jefferson County deputy sheriff.

(The National Association for the Advancement of Colored People called for peaceful picketing in 100 cities around the country to protest the actions of the Birmingham officials. In Greenfield Park, N.Y., a group of Conservative rabbis left for Birmingham in a "testimony on behalf of the human rights and dignity" of Negroes.)

I have called this an example of "straight" reporting, and my quotation marks are intended to suggest, of course, that straightness is as absolutely impossible in writing as it is in higher mathematics. Readers of a semantic turn of mind, looking for loaded language in that introduction, might easily challenge some of it. The Negroes "rampaged" through the business district, and "rained" missiles on the police. The sentence about the velocity of the fire hoses would not have been composed by a Southern reporter. But on the whole it is hard to see how the job could have been done much straighter than it has been done here. A little dull, considering the circumstances? Unfeeling? Perhaps a little Stuffy? Or is the horror the more vivid because of the writer's very restraint? At any rate, taking this account as a base of operations, let us look at some alternative ways of reporting that day's events in Birmingham.

At the time when these events took place, the *New York Herald Tribune* was conducting a publicity campaign directed a little desperately at an obvious front-running competitor. MUST A GREAT NEWSPAPER BE DULL?, the billboards were asking, and the answer, in the negative, was presumably to be found in the style of the *Tribune*'s own pages. On the same day when the *Times* piece appeared, the *Tribune*'s story, under the byline of Charles Portis, began as follows:

Three times during the day, waves of shouting, rock-throwing Negroes had poured into the downtown business district, to be scattered and driven back by battering streams of water from high-pressure hoses and swinging clubs of policemen and highway patrolmen. Now the deserted streets were littered with sodden debris. Here in the shabby streets of the Negro section one of the decisive clashes in the Negro battle against segregation was taking place. Last night a tense quiet settled over the riot-racked city after a day in which both sides altered their battle tactics. The Negro crowds, who for days have hurled themselves against police barriers, divided into small, shifting bands, darted around the police and poured hundreds of separate patrols into the downtown business districts. The police, who had crowded hundreds into the city's jails, abandoned efforts to arrest the demonstrators. They concentrated on herding the mobs toward the 16th Street Baptist Church, headquarters for these unprecedented demonstrations. By day's end, Gov. George Wallace had ordered some 250 state highway patrolmen in to aid beleaguered local police and had warned at an opening session of the Legislature that he would prosecute Negroes for murder if anyone died in the Birmingham riots.

As often, we may begin by asking just where in place and time the two assumed authors are situated. The *Times* man is not, as far as we can tell, anywhere in particular. He is sitting in his hotel room typing out an account of what he has seen or heard during the day just ended. Or he is at a telephone dictating this information to New York. Who knows? Little or no distinction has been made between speaker and assumed author. There is no pretense that the reporter is anywhere else but where, in realistic fact, we must assume he *is*, as a working journalist. But the *Tribune* man is far more complex in locating himself. He uses, first, two verb tenses in identifying the time of utterance. During the day waves of Negroes *had poured* (first sentence). When is now? Presumably at the end of the day, at the time of writing. Why, then, *were* littered; why not *are* littered? This particular posture, of using "now" for a time spoken of as already having happened, is common in fiction, where an *imagined* voice can use "now" in that curious and palpably made-up way. The assumed author pretends with one word (now) that he is really there at the moment, while with another word (were) he reminds us that he isn't. Third sentence: *Here* in the shabby streets of the Negro section. Where is here? Where is the speaker? Well, the speaker is apparently in the shabby streets, but the *writer* certainly isn't in the streets. Squatting on the sidewalk with typewriter or telephone? Scarcely. What the writer has done, then, is to invent an imagined speaker, *on the model of the novelist,* who, because he is imaginary, can speak of the situation more authoritatively than any mere hotel-bound reporter. And authoritative this speaker (or, better, narrator) certainly is. It follows, to take a minor example, that he can call the streams from the fire hoses "battering," almost as if he felt them himself. (Compare the *Times* man's sentence about the fire hoses and the bark of trees: evidence he presumably observed personally.)

Or, to take a more conspicuous example, it follows that this narrator can label the riot as "one of the decisive clashes in the Negro battle against segregation." How does he know that? He knows it because he is a made-up man, because he is like a teller of a tale, and it is his privilege and his business to know.

Further manifestations of this narrator's free-swinging position can be found in a number of his words and phrases. His willingness to use metaphor (however unoriginally) is characteristic. "Hundreds of rioting Negroes" (*Times*) are "waves" in the *Tribune*. The crowds "hurled themselves" while the police were "herding" the mobs toward the church. Throughout the passage the writer's liberal use of modification is significant. . . . [W]e find here a perceptible difference between the two pieces of prose in the number of words used as modifiers—that is, considerably more in the *Tribune* article. . . . [I]t is the omniscient assumed author who takes the liberty of modifying his nouns with adjectives. Why not? He knows, and can well afford to give us the qualities of things, not just their names. And the difference in genre is of course the whole point: [in contrast to] writing a clear piece of fiction, the *Tribune* purports to express actual events.

By such language the day's news is transformed into a tale told by a fictitious teller. It may not be dull, but as anyone can see, it can be dangerous. What the *Tribune* writer has done is to impose on a real life situation an omniscient narrator of the sort familiar to traditional fiction. Must a great newspaper be dull? In this case, at least, the avoidance of "dullness" has been accomplished at the cost of making Birmingham a fictitious place, the kind of place where someone "in charge" (the narrator) can truly know the score. I do not disguise my own moral indignation at this literary make-believe. For Birmingham and its troubles are not fiction; they are serious and complicated matters to be cautiously expressed. Furthermore, insofar as naive readers may not recognize the *Tribune*'s fictitiousness, and may assume that this is a Real Birmingham being described, the damage done in the long run to people's minds may be serious.

There is a problem of *genre* here that has attracted some attention just recently. With the publication of Truman Capote's enormously popular *In Cold Blood* (1965), the issue was explicitly raised. Was this factual journalism, or was it fiction? Mr. Capote has made much of his "invention" of new style, combining the two. The fictional omniscience of his narrating voice is supposed to be justified by years of research, note-taking, tape-recording, and all the industry of the cautious reporter. Nevertheless he feels free to enter the minds of his protagonists and give us their "thoughts." Where are we? This muddle has upset some of his critics, notably Mr. F.

W. Dupee, who has complained that Capote is "exploiting the factual authority of journalism and the atmospheric license of fiction."

But the device of the omniscient narrator in newswriting, as an   9
attempt to avoid dullness, has been with us for quite a while. It has been most conspicuous in *Time,* "the weekly news-magazine." The style of *Time* has irked a great many people, and has inspired parodies of considerable venom. *Time*'s style has also, obviously, impressed many readers favorably, as the magazine's success over the years must demonstrate. It has not generally been understood that both the outrage and the admiration originate in one pervasive device of style: the intrusion into the news of an omniscient narrator, on the model of works of fiction.

Any random sampling of *Time*'s pages will show this omniscient   10
speaker at work. Such a speaker can, for example, know what is going on inside the minds of other people—a privilege open to the fictitious narrator alone.

> The cold war, the President felt, was a stalemate. He sensed a deepening international discouragement . . .

He can *know* the true significance of the events he describes:

> To eye and ear, the desultory discussion in the Senate seemed like anything but what it actually was: one of the most . . .

He can be in possession of the most vivid details concerning events no human could possibly know:

> Leaping from his bed one night last January, Dahomey's President Hubert Maga excitedly telephoned military headquarters to report that his residence was being shelled. He soon went back to sleep. As it turned out . . .

He can temptingly throw out details about a character he is introducing, *as if* the reader already knew whom he was talking about—the suspense-building technique of the story-teller:

> They called him "Tawl Tawm." His flamboyant Senate oratory could drown an opponent in sweet molasses or hogtie him in barbed wire. He smoked ten 15¢ cigars a day and wore his white hair so long that it crested in curls at the nape of his neck. He dressed . . .

This piece is not headlined at all—such as "Senator Connolly Dies." Instead it is *titled*—"Tawl Tawm"—in the slightly mysterious way that stories are conventionally titled.

In fact *Time*'s dependence on models of fiction shows up clearly   11
in its headings, where puns and echoes based on actual titles of fiction are common. "Revolution in the Afternoon," "Sounds in the

Night," "The Monkey's Pa," are examples from a single issue. These instances of semi-literary semi-sophistication have their bearing on the tone of the magazine, in which the reader is flattered by being in the know with respect to such little jokes. But tricks of title are only a minor weapon in *Time*'s arsenal for putting the reader (fictitiously) in the know. It is the consistent omniscience of the narrating voice that primarily does the job.

How did *Time* describe the events of May 7, 1963, in Birmingham, Alabama? As follows: 12

> The blaze of bombs, the flash of blades, the eerie glow of fire, the keening cries of hatred, the wild dance of terror at night—all this was Birmingham, Alabama.
>
> Birmingham's Negroes had always seemed a docile lot. Downtown at night, they slouched in gloomy huddles beneath street lamps talking softly or not at all. They knew their place: they were "niggers" in a Jim Crow town, and they bore their degradation in silence.
>
> But last week they smashed that image forever. The scenes in Birmingham were unforgettable. There was the Negro youth, sprawled on his back and spinning across the pavement while firemen battered him with streams of water so powerful that they could strip the bark off trees. There was the Negro woman, pinned to the ground by cops, one of them with his knee dug into her throat. There was the white man who watched hymn-singing Negroes burst from a sweltering church and growled: "We ought to shoot every damned one of them." And there was the little Negro girl, splendid in a newly starched dress, who marched out of a church, looked toward a massed line of pistol-packing cops, and called to a laggard friend: "Hurry up, Lucile. If you stay behind you won't get arrested with our group."

The postures of Knowing taken here are obvious enough and   13
hardly need stressing. "All this was Birmingham." The narrator knows the past, for the Negroes "had always seemed" docile. He has seen them "in gloomy huddles" over a long period of time; this concrete description implies close personal knowledge. They knew their place, he says, echoing ironically the white man's cliché, of which again he seems to have an intimate knowledge. "But last week they smashed that image *forever*": now he knows the future too. Is that the news? Or is it the kind of statement an all-knowing story-teller can make about a place he has invented? (Of course we have to say, for this writer, that subsequent events have justified some of his fictitious wisdom!)

The suspicion is tempting that the *real* author of this piece never   14
left his air-conditioned office in Manhattan's Time-Life Building. What he may have done was to read a lot of other people's accounts

of Birmingham, including the *Times* man's observation about fire hoses and tree bark, which he then paraphrased in the manner of the novelist. More accurately, I suppose, this prose is the work of several hands, one or two of whom may actually have been on the scene in Birmingham.

But omniscience is not the only thing to notice about this narrator's use of words. The reader who reacts to that barrage of definite articles in *Time*'s first sentence may be reminded of an old friend.   15

> The blaze of bombs, the flash of blades, the eerie glow of fire, the keening cries of hatred, the wild dance of terror . . .

Part of the speaker's relation with the reader is that of a shared knowledgeable awareness of just the sort of "blaze" and "flash" and "eerie glow" the speaker is talking about. *You* know what I mean. It is the familiar intimacy of the Tough Talker, who implies that he already knows his reader before the story opens.

Actually, once the first sentence is over with, the writer for *Time*   16 uses somewhat fewer definite articles than the writers of our other two Birmingham passages. But he has additional rhetorical characteristics that, statistically at least, carry him much closer to Frederic Henry[2] than is the case with the other two. Most important is the sheer size of his words. A count of monosyllables in all three passages shows that whereas in the *Times* and *Tribune* a little over half of the words are of one syllable, over three-quarters of *Time*'s diction is monosyllabic. In a count of longer words, those of three syllables or more, the *Times* piece shows 15 percent, the *Tribune* 12 percent, and *Time* only 5 percent. And even these are simple and repetitious; "Birmingham" appears three times. We recall that the Tough Talker is chary with modification. If we list the words in each passage being used to modify nouns (omitting articles and demonstrative and personal pronouns), we discover that the *Time* writer, for all his eerie glows and keening cries, has the least modification of the three, while the *Tribune* piece has the most.

A chart of such information may be useful: 17

	Times	Tribune	Time
Total words in passage	193	201	214
Average sentence length	22	25	19
Monosyllables (% of total words)	55%	57%	78%
Longer words (3 syllables & over)	15%	12%	5%
Modifiers of nouns	15%	19%	11%

Do such figures prove anything? Probably not by themselves,   18

[2] *Ed. note:* The hero of Ernest Hemingway's *A Farewell to Arms*.

unless we can feel, in the tone of the *Time* passage, that particular intensity and intimacy we noted in the introduction to *A Farewell to Arms.* Can we? For all the embarrassing bad writing in the *Time* passage, I hope it is clear that we can. The speaker, surely "a hard man who has been around in a violent world," expects of us intimacy of a special closeness. If we are to become the sympathetic assumed reader of these words (which I personally find most difficult), we share a world defined in tight-lipped simplicity of language. It is a world where policemen are always cops and violence is taken for granted, and where crude pathos (the little Negro girl at the end) is expected to move us deeply right through the toughness. Beneath that harsh voice (as often, even in Hemingway) there beats all too visibly a heart of sugar. In fact the triteness of the piece is such as to give us momentary pause about our whole response so far. Can this very triteness be intended? Those piled-up alliterative clichés at the start—the blaze of bombs, the keening cries—suggest possibly an even further intimacy with the reader that may conceivably run something like this: You and I know this is mostly a verbal game. You recognize as I do the familiar theatrical phrases from who-done-it literature with which I adorn this account, and you recognize that I'm not trying to *tell you* anything about Birmingham. I'm just wittily entertaining you for a few moments after a busy day. After all, you've already read last week's newspapers. This is decorative.

If there is anything to the suspicions I have just uttered (and I am   19 truly doubtful), then Timestyle has to be seen as cynical in the extreme. For if, as seems remotely possible, the sophisticated reader is to see this writer's pose as after all not tough and intense, but mock-tough, then the two of them, reader and writer, are engaged in a most irresponsible game. These are not events to play games with. The real trouble is that I, as a reader, can't tell whether this is a game or not.

And if it is not, then we return to locate again one huge distinc-   20 tion between the Tough Talker we saw in Hemingway and the one we see here. It is true that some of the Tough Talker's rhetoric is here visible: short sentences, simplified diction, relatively low modification. But omniscience has been added! We have an intense, human-sounding, tough-talking narrator *without* any human limitations. He knows. When, in other words, you invent a voice that asserts deep and violent feeling, and close intimacy with the reader, and omniscience, you have a public address system of formidable power. And when you apply that voice to the "reporting" of the *news,* you have committed an act of intellectual dishonesty.

In this comparison of three expressions of the news, the restraint   21
of *The New York Times* has seemed to come off with highest marks.
But let not the *Times* relax its vigil. The fact is that the charms of
fiction-writing have beguiled the *Times* writers too, though usually
without the rhetoric of the Tough Talker. We can see fictitious
omniscience especially in the Sunday supplement called "The News
of the Week in Review," where, in summarizing the week's news, it
is apparently tempting to talk as if one knew what happened.

THE COUP
The time was just before 3 A.M. in Washington on Friday. In the "situation room" in the White House basement, a command center which
receives diplomatic and intelligence reports from around the world, a
message from the U.S. Embassy in Saigon clattered off one of the
teletype machines. A watch officer phoned.

Without belaboring the point one can certainly make out in these
lines the suspenseful devices of the novelist, from the mysterious
title and *in-medias-res* beginning to the teletype machine that clattered off a message. Who heard it clatter? This is a case of the *Times*
man having read his *Time* too well and too often rather than the
other way around.

One appreciates any effort by journalists to make the reading of   22
the news less of a chore and a bore. Nobody wants to be dull. But if
the alternative to dullness is dishonesty, it may be better to be dull.
On the other hand there are surely other alternatives. Without trying
to tell the newswriter his business, I should suppose that a concrete
and sober account of what a reporter *did* during his day's work
would be, in many cases, neither dull nor dishonest. Such an account would not, to be sure, leave us with the satisfied feeling of
knowing the Real Scoop on Birmingham, or the White House, or the
Wide World. But as I have already said too often, this is not a
feeling to be encouraged anyway.

QUESTIONS ON CONTENT

1. What does Gibson mean by "straight" reporting? Do you agree
with Gibson's statement that "straightness is as absolutely impossible in writing as it is in higher mathematics"? Explain.

2. What comments does Gibson make regarding the use of metaphor
and modification in newswriting? Does he consider their use appropriate in all types of newswriting? Explain.

3. What "pervasive device of style" is responsible for much of both the outrage and admiration directed at *Time*? Describe other devices mentioned by Gibson characteristic of "Timestyle." Can you add to Gibson's list? What effects do you think each has?

4. After reading this article, how would you answer the question Gibson raises in his title: "Must a great newspaper be dull?"

QUESTIONS ON RHETORIC

1. What three things does Gibson compare in this essay? What is the basis of his comparison? Does Gibson point out differences between like things or similarities between different things? Explain. What are the differences or similarities?

2. How has Gibson organized his comparison of the three publications? In answering this question, you may find it helpful to outline the essay.

3. Discuss the importance of a writer's stance, the point Gibson makes by asking "just where in place and time" *The New York Times* and the *New York Herald Tribune* writers are located. How can a writer reveal location and, by implication, point of view?

4. What is the function of Gibson's chart in paragraph 17? How helpful do you find the chart in understanding his comparison? What does his analysis tell you about the intended audience for each publication? Explain.

VOCABULARY

velocity	indignation	docile
pretense	explicitly	intimacy
conspicuous	pervasive	triteness
perceptible	intrusion	formidable

CLASSROOM ACTIVITIES

1. Write three paragraphs in which you describe the same incident, person, scene, or thing. In the first paragraph, use language that will produce a neutral impression; in the second, language that will produce a favorable impression; and in the third, language that will produce an unfavorable impression. Keep the factual content of each of your paragraphs constant; vary only the language.

WRITING ASSIGNMENTS FOR "THE LANGUAGE OF RADIO, TELEVISION, AND NEWSPAPERS"

1. Write an essay in which you compare and contrast a national tabloid newspaper (e.g., the *National Enquirer*) with your local newspaper. You may wish to consider one or more of the following:
   a. types of stories covered
   b. placement of stories
   c. formality or informality of writing
   d. amount and type of advertising
   e. amount of visual material
   f. intended audience

2. Choose an editorial dealing with a controversial issue. Assume that you have been offered equal space in the newspaper in which to present the opposing viewpoint. Write an editorial in the form of a rebuttal. Hand in both your editorial and the original that stimulated it.

3. Imagine that you are away at school. Recently you were caught in a radar speed trap—you were doing 40 miles per hour in a 25-mile-per-hour zone—and have just lost your license; you will not be able to go home this coming weekend, as you had planned. Write two letters in which you explain why you will not be able to get home, one to your parents and the other to your best friend.

4. Attend a sports event on your campus and take notes on what happens during that event. Write an account of the sports event which relies on your notes and makes use of effective metaphors and strong action verbs.

NOTE: Suggested topics for research papers appear on p. 293.

NOTABLE QUOTATIONS

The following quotations are drawn from the articles in this section. They are presented as additional topics for classroom discussion or for writing assignments.

"Silence, like the white space between magazine articles, signalled conclusions and promised beginnings. Silence served as comma, period and paragraph, just as those marks served to signal silence." *Dye*

"After all, Archie is the arch-conservative and arch-debunker, and all his remarks are in one way or another 'suppository.' " *Rosa and Eschholz*

"Among animals, only men seem susceptible to narcissism." *Gilbert*

"Sportswriters have been comparing such and such an athlete to this or that animal since the dawn of sports." *Gilbert*

"American speech is conceded to be energetic and picturesque, possibly as an expression or reflection of national activity and variety." *Schultz*

"There is no more outstanding characteristic of news stories rushed into print during the football season than the use of action verbs in the headlines." *Schultz*

"Despite all its pretenses of representing the public, the average newspaper is simply a business enterprise that sells news and uses that lure to sell advertising space." *Friedrich*

"Like any other business, a newspaper obeys the law of supply and demand, and most newspapers have discovered that a sex murder attracts more readers than does a French cabinet crisis." *Friedrich*

"It is the omniscient assumed author who takes the liberty of modifying his nouns with adjectives." *Gibson*

"Nobody wants to be dull. But if the alternative to dullness is dishonesty, it may be better to be dull." *Gibson*

V

Jargon, Jargon, Jargon

1
CB Radio:
The Electronic "Toy"

THOMAS FENSCH

Some of the most colorful language to appear recently in the United States is that associated with CB radio. In the following selection, excerpted from Smokeys, Truckers, CB Radios & You, *Thomas Fensch discusses how the slang terms, the emergency 10-codes, and the "handles" add to the liveliness of this specialized language. Fensch also explains how this new language has evolved to meet the needs of its users.*

$\mathbf{A}$ long a busy interstate highway, a motorist witnesses a two-car   1
accident. Reaching under his dashboard, he grabs a hand micro-
phone, pushes the talk button and transmits in code:

> Breaker 9, Breaker 9, We have a 10–50 at I–81 and 490. Advise 10–51,
> 10-52. Repeat, 10–51, 10–52 at I–81 and 490. 10–4, Smokey. . . .

What he actually said was: 2

> Channel 9, Channel 9 (emergency frequency), We have an accident (10–
> 50) at the intersection of routes 81 and 490. We need a wrecker (10–51)
> and an ambulance (10–52). Acknowledge, please, police. . . .

The code is that of Citizens Band radio, the amazing electronic   3
communication system which is saving lives and property and is
ending "isolation on the road," as one major Citizens Band manufacturer phrases it, for countless thousands of motorists on the
nation's highways.

The most obvious form of Citizens Band activity is highway use   4
—reporting accidents, road conditions, locating traffic jams—and
police radar traps.

But more and more, CB radio, as it is commonly known, is used   5
to keep housing projects guarded during peak vandalism hours; CB
teams keep long-haul truckers advised of changing road conditions

and changing weather, and members of REACT, Inc. (which stands for *R*adio *E*mergency *A*ssociated *C*itizens *T*eams), a national "Good Samaritan" organization, aid in every conceivable situation when rapid, two-way local communications are imperative.

Now, CB is sweeping the country—because of its inherent con-   6 venience, the fact that CB equipment is now within the financial reach of every family budget, and because the safety factor alone makes CB sets invaluable. The final reason, of course, is the mystique of the long-haul trucker who uses it, and the just-plain-fun of talking as you drive down the thruway.

Citizens Band began in the late 1940s. Established by law in   7 1949, the citizen "band" is in the shortwave range and formerly was an amateur band known as "11 meters." The CB frequency usually is referred to as "27 mhz" (megahertz). In 1958, the federal government widened the citizen band by allowing "Class D" service; local, two-way communications, which were ideal for delivery trucks, service station wreckers and other business uses. The operations were simple: the CB user filled out a simple form and mailed it and an application fee (formerly $20), to the Federal Communications Commission. When he received his license, he bought a CB set for his car, truck, or wrecker, and bought a second or "base" set for his home, or service station, or store. The "mobile set," which can fit in any powered vehicle, can be installed by any electronics store or by most amateur radio operators and most home handymen. It is easier to tune than a color TV set. The user does not have to know Morse Code, which amateur radio operators must know. The CB user should know the federal laws and regulations which govern CB use, and the CB enthusiast should also be familiar with the "10-Codes," the emergency codes which are in common use among CB users and law enforcement units, such as police departments and fire and rescue squads.

CB grew rapidly in the early and mid '60s with a great amount of   8 illegal hamming on the band. Stricter FCC rules then slowed its growth until the boom began with the energy crisis of 1973–1974. When Congress passed a national law making 55 miles per hour the national speed limit, suddenly truckers who had CB sets in their trucks began to use them to alert each other to the location of "Smokey taking pictures" (police with radar). The term "Smokey" or "Smokey the Bear" for any police officer is perhaps the most popular CB term. It comes from the fact that certain highway patrol units, including the Ohio State Highway Patrol, use the flatbrimmed campaign hat seen on Smokey the fire-prevention bear. Paid by the trip, long-haul truckers could not make money driving under 55 mph. Alerted to the location of radar traps (or "bear traps") by other truckers, the drivers could bypass the "picture takers," and continue over 55 mph.

CB suddenly became big news. The truckers developed their [9] own slang. The "Smokey" slang became quite sophisticated. Here are a few CB slang terms.

Feed the bears	Pay a traffic fine
Bear in the air	Police using a helicopter or airplane for traffic surveillance
Flip-flop	Long-haul trucker's return trip
Seat covers	Pretty girls in autos
Picture taker [or] camera [or] X-rays	Police radar

Happily, however, for every trucker or citizen in an automobile [10] using CB code to spot and avoid radar, 10 or 15 or 100 CB users are standing ready to aid the police during emergencies. At first, local and state police units were angered and resentful of CB users who operated their sets to avoid the 55 mph speed limit.

But CB radio spread: lawbreakers became the minority; and [11] drivers used the radios to "end their isolation on the road." They bought CB sets, installed them in the autos, and talked with the truckers who drove on the nation's interstate highways and turnpikes. . . .

EMERGENCY CODES

Perhaps the most important part of the language of Citizens Band [12] are the "10-codes," the numerical codings which CB users and police, fire department and rescue units use. There are two distinctly different codes, the "CB 10 Code," and the "Police 10 Code," which, of necessity, is longer and more detailed. . . .

Citizens Band 10 Code

Term	Usage	Meaning
10–1	"I've got a 10–1 on your last transmission."	Receiving poorly

Term	Usage	Meaning
10–2	"We have a 10–2 now."	Receiving well
10–3	"Roger, 10–3."	Stop transmitting
10–4	"10–4, on that."	Acknowledged, understood
10–5	"10–5 to base."	Relay message
10–6	"We'll be 10–6 until 12 P.M."	Busy
10–7	"We're 10–7 now."	Out of service; leaving the air
10–8	"We're 10–8 and mobile."	In service, ready for call
10–9	"10–9 your last 10–20."	Repeat, transmission bad
10–10	"We're 10–10 here now."	Transmission ended, ready for call
10–11	"You're 10–11 on us."	Talking too rapidly
10–12	"We'll be 10–12 for two hours."	Officials or visitors present
10–13	"What's the 10–13 west to Rochester?"	Advise on weather and road conditions
10–18	"You were 10–1 during that 10–18."	Engineering test
10–20	"What's your 10–20?"	What's your location?
10–21	"Give your wife a 10–21."	Call by telephone
10–23	"10–23 for 5 minutes."	Standby
10–24	"Understand your 10–24 call."	Trouble at station
10–25	"Do you have 10–25 with the county mounties?"	Do you have contact with . . .
10–30	"His ratchet jawing is definitely 10–30 all the way."	Does not conform with rules and regulations
10–33	"We have a 10–33 because of ice."	Emergency traffic situation at this location
10–36	"Gimme a 10-36."	Correct time
10–65	"We're 10–65 now."	Clear for message

Term	Usage	Meaning
10–92	"You are getting out 10–92 now."	Your quality is poor or weak
10–99	"You are definitely 10–99."	Unable to receive your message

CB SLANG AND USAGE PATTERNS

Now that you've got your new CB unit in your car, and you've got 13
your license from the FCC (it doesn't hurt to keep a Xerox of your
license in the glove compartment of your car), you're ready for the
road. But you won't have any fun or communicate properly if you
don't understand CB slang, and how it is used. Below are most of
the common CB terms: on the left is the phrase; on the right the
explanation, and in the center is the phrase used correctly. Remember, however, that slang changes rapidly; one phrase in Iowa may
mean completely the opposite in Wyoming; or a phrase which may
mean the same in Wyoming and Los Angeles *now* may be meaningless and not used six months from now.

If in doubt: ASK. But remember too, that if you don't know the 14
term, good old everyday common English is OK—even if you're
talking to Uncle Charlie. 10–4?

Term	Usage	Meaning
Beaver	"That's some good looking beaver."	girl
Back	"Back to you, Charley."	your turn, now
Back door	"Looks like I got the back door, this trip."	behind your vehicle (or) end unit of chain
Back down	"We got to back down, we got a Smokey ahead."	slow down
Back out	"I'm going to back out now."	stop transmitting
Base station	"I'm at the base station now."	CB set at a fixed location, usually operator's home
Beam	"I'm throwing my beam toward you."	directional antenna
Bear	"We got a bear ahead on I-81."	police. See: Smokey
Bear cave (or) Bear den	"There's a bear den ahead 5 miles."	police headquarters

Term	Usage	Meaning
Bear in the air	"We got a bear in the air here."	police using an airplane or heli-copter for traffic check
Big switch	"We're going to pull the big switch now."	turn off CB set
Big 10–4	"That's a big 10–4."	acknowledged with feeling
Bleeding	"Someone's bleeding all over you."	interference from another channel
Break (or) Breaker	"Breaker, breaker."	I want to talk (or interrupt)
Breaker	"Go ahead, breaker."	one who interrupts
Brown bottles	"We got a whole lot of brown bottles."	beer
Camera	"We got a Smokey with a camera ahead."	police with radar
Catch	"We'll catch you later."	to talk to
Chicken coop	"The chicken coop is open tonight."	truck weigh station
Choke and puke	"Let's stop to choke and puke."	trucker's coffee shop
Clear (or) clean	"We're clear south to Cortland."	no police
Come again	"Come again your 10–20."	repeat your transmission
Comeback	"Thanks for the comeback."	return call
Come on	"What's your 10–20? Come on."	over to you
County mountie	"We got a county mountie at the intersec-tion of 42 and 250."	sheriff's deputies
Covered up	"Somebody covered you up that time. Come on."	signal interfered
Cut the coax	"I'm gonna cut the coax now."	turn off the set
Ears	"I got my ears on."	CB set
18-wheeler	"You in the 18-wheeler?"	semi-truck
88s	"Eighty-eights to you."	Goodbye
Eyeball	"I'll eyeball you later."	face-to-face meeting

Term	Usage	Meaning
Feed the bears	"I can't afford to feed the bears this week."	pay a traffic fine
Final	"This'll be my final."	last transmission
Five-five	"Better stay at 5-5 now."	55 mile-an-hour road
Flip-flop	"Catch you on the flip-flop."	long-haul trucker's return trip
4-wheeler	"You in that red 4-wheeler?"	car
Getting out	"How am I getting out?"	being heard
Good buddy	"How ya doin', good buddy?"	typical greeting
Gone	"We're gone."	final transmission
Green stamps	"I don't have any green stamps to feed the bears."	money
Green stamp road	"Guess I'll avoid the green stamp road."	toll road
Hammer	"I'm gonna put the hammer down, now."	accelerator (truck)
Handle	"The handle here is Skyrocket."	CB nickname
Hole-in-the-wall	"Catch you east of the Blue Mountain hole-in-the-wall."	tunnel
Holler	"Give me a holler soon, good buddy."	call
Home-20	"Catch me at my home-20."	at home
Landline	"I'll catch you on the landline tonight."	telephone
Lay an eye on	"Can you lay an eye on me yet?"	have in sight
Local yokel	"We got a local yokel on the interstate now."	local police
Mail	"I've been reading your mail."	listening to CB talk
Mercy	"Mercy, how you're getting out."	used for emphasis
Mile markers	"I was going so fast, the markers looked like a picket fence."	highway mile posts

Term	Usage	Meaning
Mobile	"We're on the mobile now."	CB set in a car or other vehicle
Move, moving	"We're behind a Smokey who's on the move."	changing location
Negative	"That's a negative."	no
Negative copy	"That's a negative copy."	did not receive transmission
Negatory	"That's a negatory."	no (used for emphasis)
Oil, 40-weight oil	"That sure was awful 40-weight oil."	trucker's coffee
On the side	"We'll be on the side now."	listening (or standing by)
Over the shoulder	"If you're in that 18-wheeler, I'm over your shoulder."	behind
Picture taker	"We got a picture taker in sight, moving south on the interstate."	radar cruiser
Pink slip (or) Piece of candy	"Old Jack got his first pink slip yesterday for using overpowered gear."	violation notice from the FCC for improper CB use
Plain wrapper	"We got a plain wrapper moving east on Route 690."	police in unmarked cruiser
Putting on	"What am I putting on you?"	signal strength
Ratchet jaw	"He's a real ratchet jaw."	incessant broadcaster
Radio check	"Give me a radio check please."	signal check
Read	"I read you good now."	hear
Rig	"Just got a new rig."	CB set
Rocking chair	"Looks like I got the rocking chair this trip."	in the middle of a string of vehicles
Roger	"Roger on that, Skyrocket."	understand, acknowledge
Salt shaker	"We got to back down behind that salt shaker."	salt- or sand-spreading truck
Say again	"Say again your 10–20."	repeat (aviation term)

Term	**Usage**	**Meaning**
73s	"73s to you, good buddy."	best regards, best wishes (amateur radio term)
Shout	"Thanks for the shout."	transmission
Smokey, Smokey bears	"We got two Smokeys ahead."	state highway patrolmen (known for the flat-brimmed campaign hat, also used in pictures of "Smokey" the fire-prevention bear)
Super slab	"We'll make better time on the super slab."	turnpike, super highway
Taking pictures	"We got a Smokey taking pictures on 490 east of 62."	using radar
Ten-four (10–4)	"That's a 10–4."	acknowledge
Tijuana Taxi	"We got a Tijuana taxi moving west."	police car
Thermos bottle	"We see a thermos bottle and a county mountie."	tank truck, liquid gas truck
Throwing	"What kind of signal am I throwing your way?"	transmitting
10–20	"What's your 10–20?"	location
Uncle Charley (or) The Man (or) Candyman	"I just got a pink slip from Uncle Charlie."	FCC inspectors, who issue violations for improper CB use
Walked all over	"Come on, good buddy, somebody walked all over you."	overpowered by a stronger signal
Wall-to-wall bears	"Looks like we got wall-to-wall bears here."	saturated with police
Wrapper	"There's a Smokey moving south in a plain green wrapper."	paint color
X-rays	"We see a Smokey takin' X-rays."	radar

QUESTIONS ON CONTENT

1. What is the origin of the term "CB"?

2. What are the different uses that Fensch describes for CB radio?

3. How does Fensch account for the CB boom that began in the early 1970s?

4. What do you think are the functions of the emergency codes (10-codes)? What are their advantages?

5. CB slang varies from state to state, and new terms are constantly being added. Add any terms you know of that are not mentioned in the article. Have you heard any of the terms in the list used with a different meaning?

QUESTIONS ON RHETORIC

1. This article begins with an anecdote. Is this an effective opening? Why or why not?

2. Look at the way the "CB 10 Code" and the list of CB slang are set up. Would these lists be as effective if the column headed "Usage" had been omitted? Why or why not?

VOCABULARY

inherent	invaluable	vandalism
imperative	mystique	conceivable

CLASSROOM ACTIVITIES

1. Fensch writes, "A very large part of the mystique and fascination of Citizens Band radio is the 'handle'—the on-the-air nickname adopted by almost everybody. With the exception of profanity, which is banned by the FCC, 'anything goes' as far as the individual nickname, or handle, is concerned." Study the following sample list of CB handles:

Annie Oakley	Brown-Eyed Devil	Brush Man
Batman	Blue Grass Boy	Cisco Kid
Blue Beard	Bouncer	Corn Silk
Beer Mug	Black Widow	California Blue Eyes
Bud Man	Bugs Bunny	Curly
Buffalo Bill	Booze Hound	Cupcake

China Doll	Kilroy	Red Baron
Crazy Ears	King Budweiser	Robin Hood
Daisy Mae	Lone Ranger	Red Eye
Dick Tracy	Little Orphan Annie	
Eagle Scout	Limey	Six Pack
Easy Rider	Little Teenager	Silver Bullet
	Lone Wolf	Silver Dog
Flower Girl		Short Snort
Flying Dutchman	Mountain Girl	Sneaky Pete
Foxy Lady	Music Man	Sundowner
Gypsy Rose	Motorcycle Mamma	Trapper John
Grandma	Mr. Breadbox	Tinker Bell
Goldilocks		Tarantula
Gumshoes Sr.	Navajo	
Green Hornet	Nomad	Uncle Charlie
	One-Eyed Jack	Virginia Hillbilly
Hot Toddy		Vulture
Happy Hooker	Pied Piper	
Hawaii 5–0	Papa Bear	Wounded Knee
High Voltage	Pill Popper	White Velvet
	Pie Crust	Wine Drinker
Ichabod	Pink Panther	Water Boy
Iron Man	Playmate	Yellow Submarine
Jaguar	Queen Bee	Yogi Bear
Jungle Jim	Road Runner	Yankee Peddler
Kojak	Radar Man	Zebra III

Choose five handles and discuss their connotations; try to explain why an individual might have chosen these handles.

NOTE: Writing assignments for "Jargon, Jargon, Jargon" appear on p. 191.

2

Is Your Team
Hungry Enough, Coach?

EDWIN NEWMAN

Edwin Newman, author of Strictly Speaking *and* A Civil Tongue, *was born in New York City in 1919. Writing for newspapers at summer camp, George Washington High School, and the University of Wisconsin prepared him for his career as a reporter and a writer. In 1952 he joined NBC and headed their news bureaus in London, Rome, and Paris before returning to New York in 1961. In this selection from* Strictly Speaking, *Newman, NBC's "house grammarian," takes a close look at the jargon of the sports world.*

M eaning no disrespect, I suppose there is, if not general rejoic-   1
ing, at least a sense of relief when the football season ends. It's a
long season.

I have an additional reason for watching football fade out with-   2
out much regret. That reason is a protective interest in the English
language. The phrase "pretty good," as in "He hit him pretty
good," and "We stopped them pretty good," and "He moves pretty
good for a big man," gets worked out pretty good from late September to mid-January. After which it should be given a pretty good
rest, or allowed to rest pretty good, or at any rate left to basketball,
where they hit the backboards pretty good.

Basketball, of course, cannot be played without referees, and   3
generally they do the officiating pretty good, but not always. Said K.
C. Jones, coach of the Capital Bullets of the NBA, explaining why
he would not comment on the officiating in a play-off game against
New York: "No sense in risking a $2,000 fine. To hell with it. They
read the papers pretty good for our remarks."

After basketball, baseball. Al Downing of the Los Angeles   4
Dodgers, who threw home run number 715 to Henry Aaron: "I was
trying to get it down to him, but I didn't and he hit it good—as he
would. When he first hit it, I didn't think it might be going. But like a

168

great hitter, when he picks his pitch, chances are he's going to hit it pretty good.''

Pretty good has its final flowering in football on the Sunday of the Superbowl, when opinion is likely to be general that one reason the winners beat the losers was that they stopped their running game pretty good. The losers might have been able to make up for this even though they were hurting pretty good, meaning that some of their players were injured, if they had got their passing game going pretty good, but they didn't, and that was that: the winners were the world champions.

When the majestic ocean liner the *QE 2* tossed gently in the balmy Atlantic, her engines dead, early in April, 1974, a number of American football players and coaches were aboard, showing films and giving chalk talks as part of the entertainment. One was Hank Stram, coach of the Kansas City Chiefs. Stram told a reporter that after emergency repairs the ship had ''moved along pretty good'' for thirty minutes. It is necessary to stay in shape during the off-season.

At the 1974 Superbowl, Pat Summerall, in search of a more analytical explanation, attributed the success of the Miami Dolphins' defense to their having ''so many different variations,'' leaving us to suppose that the Minnesota Vikings' defense failed because their variations were uniform. Ray Scott, working with Summerall, told us that Larry Csonka ''apparently is injured around his one eye.'' He may have had Csonka confused with the legendary fullback Cyclops, who helped the Giants defeat the Titans but, unlike Csonka, never played on a world championship team.

World champions—there's another point. Are they really? They are the champions of the National Football League, but they have not played any teams in other leagues. No doubt they could beat them—the others are minor leagues, after all—but that still would not make them world champions. American football is not played in other countries, and it is a little hard to be world champion in a game that is played in your country only. It is as though a Siamese claimed to be world champion in boxing Thai-style, or a Scotsman claimed to be world champion in tossing the caber. World championships require some international competition, and in American-style football there isn't any.

The same is true of the baseball World Series. It may be a series, but it is grandiose to speak of the world. Perhaps it is a harmless conceit, but the American and National leagues do not represent the world, even with two divisions each and a team in Montreal.

The teams aren't usually very good, either. In these days talent is spread so thin by expansion that some players doing regular duty swagger up to the plate with .189 batting averages and nobody thinks there is anything untoward about it. These players are often said to have a way of coming through with timely hits. When you're batting .189, any hit you get is likely to be timely.

Still, whether the World Series is played is determined not by the   11 quality of the teams but by the annual occurrence of October, and again, whatever the quality of the teams, the series must end in seven games or less, which is the sports-page version of seven games or fewer. Equally inescapable is the pre-series analysis, in which the experts, paid and unpaid, compare the opposing sides, weigh their strengths and weaknesses, evaluate their physical condition, take note of the weather, calculate which side has more of that magical substance, momentum, and point out that the breaks can nullify any advantage, that anything can happen in a short series, and that you still have to win them one at a time.*

In this arcane atmosphere you may find yourself reading an ex-   12 planation of why, although Team A's first baseman hits better with men on than Team B's does, Team B's first baseman has more rbis. The explanation is that the man with more rbis (runs batted in, or ribbies to the cognoscenti) had more chances to bat in runs because he came up fourth in the order whereas the other came up sixth. However, the man who batted sixth might have done better had he been allowed to bat in the cleanup position, and indeed he wanted to but allowed himself to be placed in the sixth position for the higher good of the team and an interest-free loan from the club owner.

Even for the most knowing, comparisons are difficult in a time   13 when a manager may platoon left field with four players of different sizes, depending on the height of the outfield grass, but once the experts' analyses are complete, they interview the managers. The answers are purely ritualistic, but nobody minds. It is part of the great fall classic. I will omit the questions and give only the answers.

"Getting runs home is the name of the game, and my boys have   14 shown all year that they can get the runs home."

"Pitching is the name of the game, and we have the pitching."   15

"I think our rookies will do pretty good."   16

"I think our veterans will do pretty good. Their records speak   17 for themselves."

"The double play is the name of the game, and our guys can   18 really turn it over."

"Hustle is the name of the game, and nobody is going to outhus-   19 tle us."

---

* In boxing there is a rough equivalent of this: They both only got two hands.

"Pride is the name of the game, and we didn't come this far to   20
lose."

"Kirilenko closed with a rush this season and got his average up   21
to .219, and I look for some real power hitting from him."

"Frelinghuysen has good speed and good power. But we think   22
we can handle him."

"Yes, I think so." (I'd better give the question here. It was "Do   23
you think you can put it all together?")

Putting it all together was identified as the key to success a few   24
years ago, and it has swept all other explanations before it. When
the series has ended, it accounts for one team's coming out with the
right to fly the championship flag while the other does not. Many
things go into putting it all together: pitchers reach back and give it
everything they've got; infielders go skyward after errant throws;
pivot men in twin killings elude sliding runners (nobody has come up
with a synonym for slide); outfielders swing potent bats and scamper
to the farthermost barrier to haul in arching blasts, while on the side
that did not put it all together outfielders also scamper to the farthermost barrier to haul in arching blasts but swing once-potent bats,
now shackled; bloopers barely escape desperate grasps; balls are
deposited in the distant seats; heady days of glory are relived; speed
on the base paths pays off; somebody trots out his assortment of
breaking pitches, to his opponents' almost total frustration; and it is
found once more that there is no substitute for the high hard one
when the high hard one is needed. And, when starters get into
trouble, relief pitchers warm up and the announcers tell us, "There
is activity in the bullpen." Ogden Nash once wrote a poem about a
relief pitcher named MacTivity so that he could say, "There is
MacTivity in the bullpen."

The interview before the World Series closely resembles the   25
spring training season interview. Again it is a two-character affair.
The sports writer is named Buck and the manager is named Al.
Buck's first question is, "Well, Al, how do you think you'll do this
year?" Al is not thrown by this. He says, "Well, I think we'll do
pretty good. I think we'll do all right."

Buck follows that up like a hawk. He says, a shade aggressively,   26
"Well, are you predicting the pennant, Al?" Al replies that well,
they won it last year, and the other teams are going to have to beat
them. He knows one thing: they are not going to beat themselves.

The interview has been under way for about a minute at this   27
point, and nobody has said anything about the name of the game.
This is now remedied. Buck asks Al where he thinks his main
strength lies, and Al replies that scoring runs is the name of the game

and his boys can get the runs home. Buck then says that some
people think pitching is the name of the game, and Al says it is, it is,
and he thinks his pitchers will do pretty good, but he still has one
outstanding need, a reliever who can go at top speed for a full inning
without tiring. He has such a man on the roster, a Cuban named
Felix Miguel Arbanzas Lopez y Puesto, a real flame thrower, but
there is some question about Castro's letting him out and the FBI's
letting him in.

Buck asks about right field, normally occupied by High Pockets   28
Kirilenko, a somewhat moody player who (as we know) closed with
a rush last season and got his average up to .219. Al says that
Kirilenko has good speed and good power, but because of that big
.219 average Kirilenko is holding out for a share of the concession
revenue, a commitment by the club owner to cover any losses he
may sustain on his investments in the stock market, and the services
of a hairdresser before each game.

If High Pockets doesn't get in line, Al will try the French Cana-   29
dian rookie, Willie LaBatt. LaBatt has been up before, but he really
shattered the fences in the Australian Instructional League over the
winter, and he may be ready. Al also has hopes for his new first
baseman, Cy (The Eel) Lamprey, who should be a ballplayer because he grew up in the shadow of Ebbets Field. In fact, Lamprey
was lost briefly under the debris when they tore it down, but they
dug him out and he looks pretty good.

The team will, however, miss second baseman Ron Larrabee,   30
who had so much range to his left that he crashed into the first-base
stands going after a grounder and broke his shoulder at a crucial
juncture of last year's pennant race. Larrabee is therefore hobbled
by injuries and not yet ready.

The interview is approaching its climax. Soon fielding is the   31
name of the game, and so is base running. Buck's last question is
whether pride isn't really the name of the game, and whether Al,
who has pride, can communicate it to his players. Al replies that if
he didn't think he could, he wouldn't be there, and while you never
know in baseball, his team has a real good shot. Buck says, "You
better believe it," and there, to the regret of all, the interview ends.

There is an alternative ending, more appropriate in some cases—   32
for example, in Al's, since his team made it into the series last year.
It is:

"Is your team hungry enough, Al?"   33
"I don't think a team can ever be hungry enough."   34

In the closing days of the 1973 baseball season, I watched on   35
television a game between the Pittsburgh Pirates and the Montreal

Expos that was delayed by rain several times and for a total of more than three hours. At one point the play-by-play announcer, Jim Simpson, remarked that it was "raining pretty good." He must have been embarrassed because he immediately added, "It's raining pretty hard."

There is no way to measure the destructive effect of sports broadcasting on ordinary American English, but it must be considerable. In the early days sports broadcasting was done, with occasional exceptions such as Clem McCarthy, by nonexperts, announcers. Their knowledge of the sports they described varied, but their English was generally of a high order. If they could not tell you much about the inside of the game they were covering, at any rate what they did tell you you could understand.

Then came the experts, which is to say the former athletes. They could tell you a great deal about the inside, but—again with some exceptions—not in a comprehensible way. They knew the terms the athletes themselves used, and for a while that added color to the broadcasts. But the inside terms were few, and the nonathlete announcers allowed themselves to be hemmed in by them—"He got good wood on that one," "He got the big jump," "He really challenged him on that one," "They're high on him," "They came to play," "He's really got the good hands," and "That has to be," as in "That has to be the best game Oakland ever played."

The effect is deadening on the enjoyment to be had from watching sports on television or reading about them and, since sports make up so large a part of American life and do so much to set its tone, on the language we see and hear around us.

There is one sports announcer who does not go where the former athletes lead him. That is Howard Cosell. Cosell is a phenomenon, or as some have it, phenomena. Nothing can shake him away from his own bromides, of which the supply is unquenchable. Cosell can range from a relative paucity ("Despite the relative paucity of scoring . . .") to a veritable plethora ("Let's continue on this point of this veritable plethora of field goals") without drawing a breath, and there is every reason to believe that when he says "relative paucity" and "veritable plethora" he is not kidding; he means it.

Only Cosell would have described the mood of the crowd at the Bobby Riggs–Billie Jean King match as "an admixture" or remarked that for Riggs "It has not been a comedic night." Only Cosell would speak of a football team "procuring a first down," or say that a fighter was "plagued by minutiae," or that the cards of the referee and judges, made public after each round in a fight in Quebec, "vivified" the problem facing the fighter who was behind. During a Monday night football game nobody else would say, "The Redskins have had two scoring opportunities and failed to avail themselves both times," or that "The mist is drifting over the stadium like a description in a Thomas Hardy novel." At any rate, we may hope that nobody else would say it.

I am far from arguing that the language of athletes and former   41
athletes never adds to the gaiety of the nation. Jake LaMotta, the old middleweight, interviewed long after his fighting days were over, told his questioner that he had no fear of the future because "I got too much growing for me." Another middleweight, Rocky Graziano, during his fighting days was pleased with his reception in the Middle West. He said, "They trutt me right in Chicago." An old ballplayer, Joe Hauser, had the same sort of genius. Near the end of his career, badly slowed down, he was retired on what should have been a single to right. He said with some bitterness, "They trun me out at first."

Joe Jacobs, manager of the German heavyweight Max Schmeling   42
in the 1930s, described his dreamlike condition when a decision unexpectedly went against his man: "I was in a transom." Before their first fight Joe Frazier said of Muhammad Ali, "He don't phrase me," and was right on both counts, and Ali spoke of not being "flustrated," which he rarely was. In one of the disputes over rules at the 1972 Olympics, a United States swimming coach spoke of signing "alphadavits." We would all be poorer without this. . . .

QUESTIONS ON CONTENT

1. Why does Newman object to the phrase "pretty good"? In each of his examples, does his objection seem justified to you? Explain.

2. Why does Newman criticize the statements made by Pat Summerall and Ray Scott (paragraph 7)? Who was Cyclops?

3. Although Newman admits that "there is no way to measure the destructive effect of sports broadcasting on ordinary American English," he claims that "it must be considerable." How well does Newman substantiate this claim?

4. After giving examples of the speech of Rocky Graziano, Joe Jacobs, and Muhammad Ali, Newman states, "We would all be poorer without this." What does Newman mean by this statement?

5. After giving many examples of sports jargon, Newman says, "The effect is deadening on the enjoyment to be had from watching sports on television or reading about them and, since sports make up so large a part of American life and do so much to set its tone, on the

language we see and hear around us." Would George Orwell agree with this statement? Why or why not?

QUESTIONS ON RHETORIC

1. Where does Newman state his thesis in this essay? How convincingly does he support his thesis?

2. Newman effectively links the paragraphs by repeating key words and by using transitional words or phrases. Examine the first sentence in each of Newman's paragraphs and identify the repeated key word or transitional expression.

3. Reread paragraph 24, in which Newman considers the phrase "putting it all together." How does he develop this paragraph? What is the function of the quotation from the Ogden Nash poem about MacTivity?

4. What is Newman's attitude toward Howard Cosell, and how is that attitude revealed?

VOCABULARY

disrespect	swagger	errant
protective	weigh	roster
analytical	nullify	juncture
grandiose		

CLASSROOM ACTIVITIES

1. In preparation for a class discussion on sports jargon, carefully read the sports section of your local newspaper. Identify examples of sports jargon. Would Edwin Newman find any of your examples objectionable? Why or why not? Do you feel that jargon has a place in sports writing? Explain.

NOTE: Writing assignments for "Jargon, Jargon, Jargon" appear on p. 191.

3

The Language of the Law

DAVID MELLINKOFF

Most of us find the language used by lawyers to be frequently unintelligible and therefore intimidating. Legalese, however, is extremely influential, and one might even argue that much of its power derives from its very obscurity. Not wishing to grant such an absurdity, David Mellinkoff, himself an attorney, claims in this excerpt from his book The Language of the Law *that there is no legitimate reason for our legal system to be a major dispenser of gobbledygook.*

Intelligible and unintelligible have an overpowering sound of abso-   1
luteness that limits their usefulness in discussion of the language of
the law. It is a very empty phrase that someone, somewhere, cannot
squeeze a drop of sense from, yet some glittering nonsense discour-
ages the effort. Take this specimen, spawned by a current vogue for
legislation about emergency calls on party lines:

> In every telephone directory . . . there shall be printed in type not
> smaller than any other type appearing on the same page, a notice
> preceded by the word "warning" printed in type at least as large as the
> largest type on the same page, . . .

This is no misprint. It had models in the laws of sister states, and   2
in turn has become a model for others. Take comfort that some
draftsmen have refused to buy this pre-wrapped shoddy, stopping
the word flow when they had had enough for law, for good English,
and for people—after the word *warning*. Take comfort too that
complete gibberish is not the typical instance of language mangling
by lawyers.

It is still aiming too low to be satisfied with language that is only   3
"capable of being understood," the standard definition of *intelligible*. The general antipathy to absolutes has for centuries split
intelligible into degrees, and as used in this book it means "easily

understood,'' what some mean by clear or plain. Its opposite—
unintelligible—covers the full muddy spectrum available to lawyers.
From the shortest nonsense—*ss*.[1] Through long rows of unnecessarily unclear words and constructions, variously distinguished as obscure, vague, ambiguous, and in other circles called doubletalk,
officialese, gobbledygook, federal prose, etc., etc. Down into the
scraps of language which at best are not easily understood, such as
and/or and *or/and*.

This breadth of range is a further reminder that intelligibility is   4
not synonymous with brevity, though verbosity does make it easier
for the writer to lose himself while losing his reader.

Likewise, intelligibility is not dependent upon precision, which   5
sometimes must be sacrificed for quick understanding, as in the
traffic signs which tell pedestrians to WAIT (without saying for how
long), and to WALK (without adding, ''if you want to.'') The sacrifice
of precision for intelligibility needs mention, not to encourage slop-
piness but appropriateness, and to offset the single-minded teaching
which reverses the rites—making intelligibility always the goat.
There are still times when magic words make a legal difference—
e.g., *consideration for the lease* (instead of *prepaid rent*), or the
weaker magic of *liquidated damages* (instead of *forfeiture* or *pen-
alty*). Even so, there is little legal prose of any sort which cannot be
made more intelligible than it usually is.

Once the draftsman starts with a clear understanding of what it is   6
he wants to say, making himself understood is more a matter of how
than of what. If the simplest truth goes in fuzzy, it will come out that
way. And if complexity goes in clear, it can come out that way—
gospel or not. Even ''. . . Holmes was sometimes clearly wrong; but
. . . when this was so he was always wrong clearly.''

Any legal prose can be made more intelligible if the draftsman is   7
striving for intelligibility, but even the careful draftsman sometimes
finds more pressing concerns—some legitimate. There is, for example, the deliberate use of language which everyone recognizes as
being easily misunderstood, accepted for the sake of quick agreement. This sort of *calculated ambiguity* is left for later. Also left for
later is the deliberate use of language which though not always
easily understood is quickly felt, the language of ceremony and
persuasion.

On the blacker side is the art of planned confusion, which has its   8
advocates, its gray and off-white shadings, and above all its patterns
for identification. The patterns are so strong that at times the
''planned'' aspect has dropped deep into the inner lawyer, to become merely habitual without taint of sinister purpose.

[1] Editors' note: ss abbreviates the Latin *scilicet* (namely).

Planned confusion takes two major forms: (1) saying-nothing   9
and making it look like something, and (2) saying-something and
making it look like nothing, or like something else. The law has no
monopoly on either form, but as wholesale dealers in words lawyers
have found the patterns too useful.

At its mildest, nonprofessional saying-nothing takes the form of   10
small talk, the polite lying that is the mark of civilized society. Thus,

we say	instead of
I find it stimulating	Absolute nonsense
Most interesting	What a bore
Very stately	Real ugly
We must get together soon	Thank God, you're leaving town

Related to this is the lawyer's   11

"progress" letter	instead of
Your matter is being given due consideration in the light of the pertinent statutes and case law, and you will be further advised in due course.	Right now it looks like you're stuck. But don't go shopping for another lawyer.

A more widespread malady of nothingness at the bar is the *one-*   12
legged subjunctive. Its most prevalent forms are *it would seem* and *it*
may well be, which make no more sense when joined together like
this:

> It would seem also that a further and more far reaching effect of the
> instant judgment may well be to encourage other persons to breach their
> obligations . . .

Variants are *one might wish* and the emphatically spurious *it may*
very well be.

Unlike the bald fraud of *yes and no,* these phrases equivocate   13
even on being equivocal. *It would seem* (that is the appearance of
things, says the writer)—and you wait in vain for the other shoe to
drop. Not *it would seem to be, but the fact is,* just way up in the air,
it would seem. So that the writer can never be called to account. Not
what I thought or believed or what the fact was, just what it seemed
to be. And then again, *it may well be* something completely different
or *it may well not be.* I'm not sure or won't say; at least I haven't
said.

The lawyer's addiction to *it would seem* is related to the old and 14
continuing law use of French *semble* (it seems). But that is a technical expression of uncertainty and lack of authority which still has a
place (in footnotes), and should be kept there. A more intelligible
statement of guess is *one of the possibilities is,* and a candid *I don't
know* would win the law some friends.

A more vicious way of saying-nothing is the lawyer's *agreement* 15
to agree, or—as it frequently appears by design or accident—*subject
to change by mutual consent.* Of course. It always is. Like the
whereas recital, this phrase gives the hurried bargainer the false
impression that something has been taken care of. It is eyewash or
worse.

One step deeper into bad morals is saying something calculated 16
to mislead. This is a species of unintelligibility related to the practice
of using fine print to make contracts illegible. The object of each is
the same—to force law on the victim without arousing suspicion that
it is there. Various paths lead to the same sinkhole.

One of them is using words so ordinary in appearance that the 17
reader thinks he understands. Here is a sample. Without counsel,
the citizen in the hurried sanctuary of the voting booth ponders
"Yes" or "No" on a—

ballot	meaning
ASSESSMENT OF GOLF COURSES. Assembly Constitutional Amendment No. 29. Establishes manner in which non-profit golf-courses should be assessed for purposes of taxation.	Private golf courses shall be taxed less than other private property.

These ballot words are carefully designed to produce a "yes" 18
vote (which they did). First, they speak of the "manner" of *doing
something*—"assessment," "establishes," "assessed," "tax-
ation." So that attention is diverted from the fact that the words are
consistent with a way of *not doing something*—not assessing, not
taxing. Second, they speak of *non-profit,* which (if it means anything
to the voter) has a vaguely charitable sound, unconnected with expensive memberships. Yet on the statute books, the words will
mean what they mean to lawyers—". . . not designed primarily to
pay dividends . . ." If the ballot measure had said what it meant, the
issue would have been clear and the vote in doubt.

Another form of saying-something is the disarmingly disingen-   19
uous letter agreement. Here boring repetition and amiable fairness
combine to mask the one sharp tooth:

> We agree to pay all bills in full promptly as they come in, including
> without limitation of the generality of the foregoing all bills for labor,
> services, and materials, supplies, utilities, taxes, permits, fees, royal-
> ties, and everything else directly or indirectly for or used in connection
> with the construction of your building, you of course to reimburse us for
> everything spent for labor, services, and materials, supplies, utilities,
> taxes, permits, fees, royalties, overhead, and everything else directly or
> indirectly for or used in connection with the construction of your
> building.

QUESTIONS ON CONTENT

1. Mellinkoff argues that legal prose should be "intelligible"—that
is, "easily understood"—but that it does not necessarily need to be
brief or precise. Explain this apparent paradox.

2. How does Mellinkoff defend "calculated ambiguity"? Give some
examples of it.

3. What does Mellinkoff mean by "planned confusion"? Do you
agree that it is sometimes justifiable?

4. What, according to Mellinkoff, is "the one-legged subjunctive"?
Why does he object to it?

5. Identify and discuss "the one sharp tooth" in the letter agreement quoted by Mellinkoff.

6. In their introductory note, the editors say, "Legalese, however,
is extremely influential and one might even argue that much of its
power derives from its very obscurity." How might this obscurity
intimidate us? How might this intimidation make us more easily
exploitable by our legal system?

QUESTIONS ON RHETORIC

1. What is the function of the quotation about telephone directories
that appears in paragraph 1? Why does Mellinkoff place it so near
the opening of the selection?

2. Paragraph 3 of this essay contains three complete sentences fol-

lowed by three sentence fragments. Is this an effective paragraph? Why or why not?

3. Does Mellinkoff sustain an objective tone in this selection or does he permit his personal feelings to become apparent to the reader? Would the essay be more or less effective if he had used a different tone? Why?

VOCABULARY

brevity	antipathy	monopoly
malady	equivocal	spurious
vogue	synonymous	

CLASSROOM ACTIVITIES

1. The following item appeared in the *San Francisco Chronicle.*

State Makes it Perfectly Clear

SACRAMENTO   For some time the public has wondered what to make of most bureaucratic twaddle—but a new State law has set the record straight at last.

From the revised State code of the Division of Consumer Services, Department of Consumer Affairs, Title 4: subsection 2102, comes the official word:

"Tenses, Gender and Number: For the purpose of the rules and regulations contained in this chapter, the present tense includes the past and future tenses, and the future, the present; the masculine gender includes the feminine, and feminine, the masculine; and the singular includes the plural, and the plural the singular."

Our Correspondent

Comment on this example of legalese.

NOTE: Writing assignments for "Jargon, Jargon, Jargon" appear on p. 191.

4

Occupational Euphemisms

H. L. MENCKEN

The editors of Time *reported not so long ago on an attempt in Germany to merchandise and make more respectable the "oldest profession in the world." Large, comfortable hotels used for prostitution are now called "Eros-centers," and the girls who work in them are called "Erostesses." This amusing use of euphemisms is only one more in a long history of attempts by people to elevate themselves by retitling their occupations. In this selection, H. L. Mencken, outspoken journalist, social critic, and commentator on American English during the 1920s and 1930s, has provided us with what has become a classic discussion of this topic.*

The American, probably more than any other man, is prone to be   1
apologetic about the trade he follows. He seldom believes that it is
quite worthy of his virtues and talents; almost always he thinks that
he would have adorned something far gaudier. Unfortunately, it is
not always possible for him to escape, or even for him to dream
plausibly of escaping, so he soothes himself by assuring himself that
he belongs to a superior section of his craft, and very often he
invents a sonorous name to set himself off from the herd. Here we
glimpse the origin of a multitude of characteristic American euphemisms, e.g., *mortician* for *undertaker, realtor* for *real-estate agent,
electragist* for *electrical contractor, aisle manager* for *floor-walker,
beautician* for *hairdresser, exterminating engineer* for *rat-catcher,*
and so on. *Realtor* was devised by a high-toned real-estate agent of
Minneapolis, Charles N. Chadbourn by name. He thus describes its
genesis:

> It was in November, 1915, on my way to a meeting of the Minneapolis
> Real Estate Board that I was annoyed by the strident peddling of a
> scandal sheet: "All About the Robbery of a Poor Widow by a Real
> Estate Man." The "real estate man" thus exposed turned out to be an

obscure hombre with desk-room in a back office in a rookery, but the incident set me to thinking. "Every member of our board," I thought, "is besmirched by this scandal article. Anyone, however unworthy or disreputable, may call himself a real estate man. Why do not the members of our board deserve a distinctive title? Each member is vouched for by the board, subscribes to its Code of Ethics, and must behave himself or get out." So the idea incubated for three or four weeks, and was then sprung on the local brethren.

As to the etymology of the term, Mr. Chadbourn says: 2

> Real estate originally meant a royal grant. It is so connected with land in the public mind that *realtor* is easily understood, even at a first hearing. The suffix -or means a doer, one who performs an act, as in *grantor, executor, sponsor, administrator.*

The Minneapolis brethren were so pleased with their new name   3
that Mr. Chadbourn was moved to dedicate it to the whole profession. In March, 1916, he went to the convention of the National Association of Real Estate Boards at New Orleans, and made a formal offer of it. It was accepted gratefully, and is now defined by the association as follows:

> A person engaged in the real estate business who is an active member of a member board of the National Association of Real Estate Boards, and as such, an affiliated member of the National Association, who is subject to its rules and regulations, who observes its standards of conduct, and is entitled to its benefits.

In 1920 the Minneapolis Real Estate Board and the National   4
Association of Real Estate Boards applied to Judge Joseph W. Molyneaux of Minneapolis for an injunction restraining the Northwestern Telephone Exchange Company from using *realtor* to designate some of its hirelings, and on September 10 the learned judge duly granted this relief. Since then the National Association has obtained similar injunctions in Virginia, Utah and other States. Its general counsel is heard from every time *realtor* is taken in vain, and when, in 1922, Sinclair Lewis applied it to George F. Babbitt, there was an uproar. But when Mr. Chadbourn was appealed to he decided that Babbitt was "fairly well described," for he was "a prominent member of the local board and of the State association," and one could scarcely look for anything better in "a book written in the ironic vein of the author of 'Main Street.'" Mr. Chadbourn believes that *realtor* should be capitalized, "like *Methodist* or *American*," but so far it has not been generally done. In June, 1925, at a meeting of the National Association of Real Estate Boards in Detroit, the past presidents of the body presented him with a gold watch as a

token of their gratitude for his contribution to the uplift of their profession. On May 30, 1934, the following letter from Nathan William MacChesney, general counsel of the National Association, appeared in the *New Republic*:

> [*Realtor*] is not a word, but a trade right, coined and protected by law by the National Association of Real Estate Boards, and the term is a part of the trade-mark as registered in some forty-four States and Canada. Something over $200,000 has been spent in its protection by the National Association of Real Estate Boards in attempting to confine its use to those real estate men who are members of the National Association of Real Estate Boards, subject to its code of ethics and to its discipline for violation. It has been a factor in making the standards of the business generally during the past twenty years, and the exclusive right of the National Association of Real Estate Boards has been sustained in a series of court decisions, a large number of injunctions having been issued, restraining its improper use.

In 1924 the *Realtor's Bulletin* of Baltimore reported that certain   5
enemies of realtric science were trying to show that *realtor* was derived from the English word *real* and the Spanish word *toro,* a bull, and to argue that it thus meant *real bull.* But this obscenity apparently did not go far; probably a hint from the alert general counsel was enough to stop it. During the same year I was informed by Herbert U. Nelson, executive secretary of the National Association, that "the real-estate men of London, through the Institute of Estate Agents and Auctioneers, after studying our experience in this respect, are planning to coin the word *estator* and to protect it by legal steps." This plan, I believe, came to fruition, but *estator* never caught on, and I can't find it in the Supplement to the Oxford Dictionary. *Realtor,* however, is there—and the first illustrative quotation is from *Babbitt!* In March, 1927, J. Foster Hagan, of Ballston, Va., reported to *American Speech* that he had encountered *realtress* on the window of a real-estate office there, but this charming derivative seems to have died a-bornin'. In 1925 or thereabout certain ambitious insurance solicitors, inflamed by *realtor,* began to call themselves *insurors,* but it, too, failed to make any progress.

Electragist, like realtor, seems to be the monopoly of the lofty   6
technicians who affect it: "it is copyrighted by the Association of Electragists International, whose members alone may use it." But *mortician* is in the public domain. It was proposed by a writer in the *Embalmers' Monthly* for February, 1895, but the undertakers, who were then *funeral-directors,* did not rise to it until some years later. On September 16, 1916, some of the more eminent of them met at Columbus O., to form a national association, on the lines of the

American College of Surgeons, the American Association of University Professors, and the Society of the Cincinnati, and a year later they decided upon National Selected *Morticians* as its designation. To this day the association remains so exclusive that, of the 24,000 undertakers in the United States, only 200 belong to it. But any one of the remaining 23,800 is free to call himself a *mortician,* and to use all the other lovely words that the advance of human taxidermy has brought in. *Mortician,* of course, was suggested by *physician,* for undertakers naturally admire and like to pal with the resurrection men, and there was a time when some of them called themselves *embalming surgeons.* A *mortician* never handles a *corpse;* he *prepares a body* or *patient.* This business is carried on in a *preparation-room* or *operating-room,* and when it is achieved the patient is put into a *casket* and stored in the *reposing-room* or *slumber-room* of a *funeral-home.* On the day of the funeral he is moved to the *chapel* therein for the last exorcism, and then hauled to the cemetery in a *funeral-car* or *casket-coach.* The old-time shroud is now a *négligé* or *slumber-shirt* or *slumber-robe,* the mortician's worktruck is an *ambulance,* and the cemetery is fast becoming a *memorial-park.* In the West cemeteries are being supplanted by public mausoleums, which sometimes go under the names of *cloisters, burial-abbeys,* etc. To be laid away in one runs into money. The vehicle that morticians use for their expectant hauling of the ill is no longer an *ambulance,* but an *invalid-coach. Mortician* has been a favorite butt of the national wits, but they seem to have made no impression on it. In January, 1932, it was barred from the columns of the Chicago *Tribune.* "This decree goes forth," announced the *Tribune,* "not for lack of sympathy with the ambition of undertakers to be well regarded, but because of it. If they haven't the sense to save themselves from their own lexicographers, we shall not be guilty of abetting them in their folly." But *mortician* not only continues to flourish; it also begets progeny, e.g., *beautician, cosmetician, radiotrician* and *bootician.* The barbers, so far, have not devised a name for themselves in *-ician,* but they may be trusted to do so anon. In my youth they were *tonsorial artists,* but in recent years some of them have been calling themselves *chirotonsors.* Practically all American press-agents are now *public relations counsels, contact-managers* or *publicists,* all tree-trimmers are *tree-surgeons,* all milk-wagon and bakery-wagon drivers have become *salesmen,* nearly all janitors are *superintendents,* many gardeners have become *landscape-architects* (in England even the whales of the profession are simple *landscape-gardeners),* cobblers are beginning to call themselves *shoe-rebuilders,* and the corn-doctors, after a generation

as *chiropodists,* have burst forth as *podiatrists.* The American fond-
ness for such sonorous appellations arrested the interest of W. L.
George, the English novelist, when he visited the United States in
1920. He said:

> Business titles are given in America more readily than in England. I
> know one *president* whose staff consists of two typists. Many firms have
> four *vice-presidents.* In the magazines you seldom find merely an *editor;*
> the others need their share of honor, so they are *associate* (not *assist-
> ant*) editors. A dentist is called a *doctor.* I wandered into a university,
> knowing nobody, and casually asked for the *dean.* I was asked, "Which
> *dean?*" In that building there were enough deans to stock all the English
> cathedrals. The master of a secret society is *royal supreme knight com-
> mander.* Perhaps I reached the extreme at a theatre in Boston, when I
> wanted something, I forgot what, and was told that I must apply to the
> *chief of the ushers.* He was a mild little man, who had something to do
> with people getting into their seats, rather a comedown from the pomp
> and circumstance of his title. Growing interested, I examined my pro-
> gramme, with the following result: It is not a large theatre, but it has a
> *press-representative,* a *treasurer* (box-office clerk), an *assistant treasurer*
> (box-office junior clerk), an *advertising-agent,* our old friend the *chief of
> the ushers,* a *stage-manager,* a *head electrician,* a *master of properties* (in
> England called *props*), a *leader of the orchestra* (pity this—why not
> *president*) and a *matron* (unknown).

George might have unearthed some even stranger magnificoes in   7
other playhouses. I once knew an ancient bill-sticker, attached to a
Baltimore theatre, who boasted the sonorous title of *chief lithogra-
pher.* Today, in all probability, he would be called a *lithographic-
engineer.* For a number of years the *Engineering News-Record,* the
organ of the legitimate engineers, used to devote a column every
week to just such uninvited invaders of the craft, and some of the
species it unearthed were so fantastic that it was constrained to
reproduce their business cards photographically in order to convince its readers that it was not spoofing. One of its favorite exhibits
was a bedding manufacturer who first became a *mattress-engineer*
and then promoted himself to the lofty dignity of *sleep-engineer.* No
doubt he would have called himself a *morphician* if he had thought
of it. Another exhilarating specimen was a tractor-driver who advertised for a job as a *caterpillar-engineer.* A third was a beautician who
burst out as an *appearance-engineer.* In an Atlanta department-store
the *News-Record* found an *engineer of good taste*—a young woman
employed to advise newly-married couples patronizing the furniture
department, and elsewhere it unearthed *display-engineers* who had
been lowly window-dressers until some visionary among them made

the great leap, *demolition-engineers* who were once content to be house-wreckers, and *sanitary-engineers* who had an earlier incarnation as garbage-men. The *wedding-engineer* is a technician employed by florists to dress churches for hymeneal orgies. The *commencement-e.* arranges college and high-school commencements; he has lists of clergymen who may be trusted to pray briefly, and some sort of fire-alarm connection, I suppose, with the office of Dr. John H. Finley, the champion commencement orator of this or any other age. The *packing-e.* is a scientist who crates clocks, radios and chinaware for shipment. The *correspondence-e.* writes selling-letters guaranteed to pull. The *income-e.* is an insurance solicitor in a new falseface. The *dwelling-e.* replaces lost keys, repairs leaky roofs, and plugs up rat-holes in the cellar. The *vision-e.* supplies spectacles at cut rates. The *dehorning-e.* attends to bulls who grow too frisky. The *Engineering News-Record* also discovered a *printing-e.*, a *furniture-e.*, a *photographic-e.*, a *financial-e.* (a stock-market tipster), a *paint-e.*, a *clothing-e.*, *a wrapping-e.* (a dealer in wrapping-paper), a *matrimonial-e.* (a psychoanalyst specializing in advice to the lovelorn), a *box-e.* (the *packing-e.* under another name), an *automotive-painting-e.*, a *blasting-e.*, a *dry-cleaning-e.*, a *container-e.*, a *furnishing-e.*, a *socioreligious-e.* (an uplifter), a *social-e.* (the same), a *feed-plant-e.*, a *milk-e.*, a *surface-protection-e.*, an *analyzation-e.*, a *fiction-e.*, a *psychological-e.* (another kind of psychoanalyst), a *casement-window-e.*, a *shingle-e.*, a *fumigating-e.*, a *laminated-wood-e.*, a *package-e.* (the *packing-e.* again), a *horse-e.*, a *podiatric-e.* (a corn-doctor), an *ice-e.*, a *recreation-e.*, a *tire-e.*, a *paint-maintenance-e.*, a *space-saving-e.*, a *film-e.*, (or *film-gineer*), a *criminal-e.* (a criminologist), a *diet-kitchen-e.*, a *patent-e.*, an *equipment-e.*, a *floor-covering-e.*, a *society-e.*, a *window-cleaning-e.*, a *dust-e.*, a *hospitalization-e.*, a *baking-e.*, a *directory-e.*, an *advertising-e.*, a *golf-e.* (a designer of golf courses), a *human-e.* (another variety of psychoanalyst), an *amusement-e.*, an *electric-sign-e.*, a *household-e.*, a *pageant-e.*, an *idea-e.*, a *ballistics-e.*, a *lace-e.* and a *sign-e.* Perhaps the prize should go to the *dansant-e.* (an agent supplying dancers and musicians to nightclubs), or to the *hot-dog-e.* The exterminating-engineers have a solemn national association and wear a distinguishing pin; whether or not they have tried to restrain non-member rat-catchers from calling themselves *engineers* I do not know. In 1923 the *Engineering News-Record* printed a final blast against all the pseudo-engineers then extant, and urged its engineer readers to boycott them. But this boycott apparently came to nothing, and soon thereafter it abated its indignation and resorted to laughter. Next to *engineer*, *expert* seems to be the favorite talisman of Americans eager to augment their estate and dignity in this world. Very often it is hitched to an explanatory prefix, e.g., *housing-, planning-, hog-, erosion-, marketing-, boll-weevil-,* or *sheep-dip-,* but sometimes the simple adjective *trained-* suffices. When the Brain Trust came into power in Washington, the town began to swarm with such quacks, most of them recent graduates of the far-flung colleges of the land. One day a humorous member of Congress printed an immense list of them in the *Congressional Record,* with their salaries and academic dignities. He found at least one whose expertness was acquired in a seminary for chiropractors. During the John Purroy Mitchel "reform" administration in New York City (1914–18) so many bogus *experts* were put upon the payroll that special designations for them ran out, and in prodding through the Mitchel records later on Bird S. Coler discovered that a number had been carried on the books as *general experts.*

QUESTIONS ON CONTENT

1. A euphemism is a supposedly pleasant or higher-status term that is used in place of a blunt or lower-status term. Do you think there is a substantial difference between "real estate man" and "realtor"? Why do you think that Chadbourn was offended by "real estate man"?

2. Why, according to Mencken, do Americans use so many occupational euphemisms?

3. Usually it is those who are in the occupations themselves who call for occupational euphemisms. Do you feel that Mencken or anyone else is justified in criticizing such desires or euphemistic usages? Explain.

4. In paragraph 1, Mencken draws attention to a basic contradiction of American life. What is this contradiction? Can it be resolved?

QUESTIONS ON RHETORIC

1. What is the relationship of paragraph 1 to the rest of Mencken's essay?

2. How does Mencken introduce his lengthy discussion of the use of the term *engineer?* Do you consider this method effective?

3. How does Mencken reveal his attitude toward occupational euphemisms? Consider carefully the language of the essay—for example, "for undertakers naturally admire and like to pal with the resurrection men"; "in England even the whales of the profession are

simple *landscape-gardeners*"; "sonorous appellations"; "hymeneal orgies."

4. Throughout this essay, Mencken writes of the person involved in an occupation as "he"; the essay begins:

> The American, probably more than any other *man,* is prone to be apologetic about the trade *he* follows. *He* seldom believes that it is quite worthy of *his* virtues and talents; almost always *he* thinks that *he* would have adorned something far gaudier. Unfortunately, it is not always possible for *him* to escape, or even for *him* to dream plausibly of escaping, so *he* soothes *himself* by assuring *himself* that *he* belongs to a superior section of *his* craft . . . [italics added].

Mencken wrote at a time when use of the male pronoun forms and the generic *man* was not considered sex-biased. Today many people object to the use of exclusively male references. How can the sentences be rewritten to eliminate the italicized references?

VOCABULARY

adorned	domain	plausibly
solicitors	progeny	derivative
injunction	abated	augment
fruition		

CLASSROOM ACTIVITIES

1. If you worked as a writer for a newspaper, would you prefer to be called a journalist, reporter, or newspaperman (newspaperwoman)? In a classroom discussion, explain your preference and give reasons for rejecting the other terms.

2. If euphemisms are a way of covering up something ugly, then occupational euphemisms indicate workers' attitudes toward their jobs. In his best-selling book *Working,* Studs Terkel collects workers' attitudes from virtually every job field. What insights does this excerpt from Terkel's introduction offer into the reasons why people feel a need for occupational euphemisms?

> This book, being about work, is, by its very nature, about violence—to the spirit as well as to the body. It is about ulcers as well as accidents, about shouting matches as well as fistfights, about nervous breakdowns as well as kicking the dog around. It is, above all (or beneath all), about daily humiliations. To survive the day is triumph enough for the walking wounded among the great many of us. . . .
> It is about a search, too, for daily meaning as well as daily bread, for recognition as well as cash, for astonishment rather than torpor; in short, for a sort of life rather than a Monday through Friday sort of

dying. Perhaps immortality, too, is part of the quest. To be remembered was the wish, spoken and unspoken, of the heroes and heroines of this book.

WRITING ASSIGNMENTS FOR "JARGON, JARGON, JARGON"

1. Elsewhere in his book *The Language of the Law,* David Mellinkoff states that "party line emergency statutes—bad enough in a lawyer's library—also invade the sanctity of the home. They require a notice in telephone books explaining the law to laymen." Mellinkoff quotes the following portions of the notices appearing in the California and New York directories, notices that were drafted from almost the same statutes:

California	New York
Penal Code section 384 makes it a misdemeanor	State law requires
for any person who shall willfully refuse to immediately relinquish a telephone party line	you to hang up the receiver of a party line telephone immediately
when informed that such line is needed for an emergency call . . .	when told the line is needed for an emergency call . . .
Also, any person who shall secure the use of a telephone party line	It is unlawful to take over a party line
by falsely stating that such line is needed for an emergency call shall be guilty of a misdemeanor.	by stating falsely that the line is needed for an emergency.

The California draftsman has taken the easy way—following the language of the statute, thus passing on to laymen technicality they don't need and words they don't understand. The New Yorker gives as much as the layman needs. He has avoided repetitions and chosen the ordinary, the direct, rather than the strange and roundabout. . . .

There is a small terroristic value in California's brandishing of the words *Penal Code, section 384, guilty, misdemeanor.* But for most citizens it is enough to learn from a telephone directory that certain conduct is against the law. Beyond the level of the parking ticket, when a layman needs to weigh the specific consequences of law-breaking, he is on his way to a lawyer or to prison. The New York draft is both shorter and more intelligible, with nothing essential lost.

Examine the party line emergency notice as it appears in your phone directory and write an essay in which you analyze the language used. Has the audience been taken into account by the writer of the notice? Has unnecessary legalese been eliminated? And has the law been made intelligible to the average person?

2. Select one of the following situations and write a dialogue that accurately uses the language of the people involved:

   a. A conference between a student and a teacher about the first paper of the semester
   b. A discussion between an executive and an auto mechanic about repairs to the former's Cadillac
   c. A conversation between a ten-year-old child and his/her mother about the condition of the child's room
   d. An interview by a newspaper reporter with the chief of police of a small town concerning a recent crime

3. Watch episodes from three different television shows featuring detectives, doctors, lawyers, or persons in some other occupation. Write an essay in which you analyze the professional language used in these shows, commenting on the general accuracy of the language and the similarities among the shows.

4. Interview an athlete or a coach about the prospects for the season, a recent game, an upcoming opponent, or any other aspect of the sport. Write an essay based on this interview, making sure that you accurately capture the statements made by the athlete or coach. Your essay should be focused and unified.

NOTE: Suggested topics for research papers appear on p. 293.

NOTABLE QUOTATIONS

The following quotations are drawn from the articles in this section. They are presented as additional topics for classroom discussion or for writing assignments.

"The most obvious form of Citizens Band activity is highway use— reporting accidents, road conditions, locating traffic jams—and police radar traps."   *Fensch*

"There is no way to measure the destructive effect of sports broadcasting on ordinary American English, but it must be considerable."   *Newman*

"It is still aiming too low to be satisfied with language that is only 'capable of being understood,' the standard definition of *intelligible.*"   *Mellinkoff*

"Planned confusion takes two major forms: (1) saying-nothing and making it look like something, and (2) saying-something and making it look like nothing, or like something else."   *Mellinkoff*

"The American, probably more than any other man, is prone to be apologetic about the trade he follows."   *Mencken*

"Next to *engineer, expert* seems to be the favorite talisman of Americans eager to augment their estate and dignity in this world."   *Mencken*

VI
Prejudice and Language

1

The Language
of Prejudice

GORDON ALLPORT

In this selection from The Nature of Prejudice, *Gordon Allport examines the connection between language and prejudice. Language plays a major role in the development and continuation of prejudice because human thinking is inextricably linked to language. Allport identifies and discusses some of the specific ways in which language, often very subtly, induces and shapes prejudice.*

Without words we should scarcely be able to form categories at all. A dog perhaps forms rudimentary generalizations, such as small-boys-are-to-be avoided—but this concept runs its course on the conditioned reflex level, and does not become the object of thought as such. In order to hold a generalization in mind for reflection and recall, for identification and for action, we need to fix it in words. Without words our world would be, as William James said, an "empirical sand-heap." 1

NOUNS THAT CUT SLICES

In the empirical world of human beings there are some two and a half billion grains of sand corresponding to our category "the human race." We cannot possibly deal with so many separate entities in our thought, nor can we individualize even among the hundreds whom we encounter in our daily round. We must group them, form clusters. We welcome, therefore, the names that help us to perform the clustering. 2

The most important property of a noun is that it brings many grains of sand into a single pail, disregarding the fact that the same grains might have fitted just as appropriately into another pail. To 3 state the matter technically, a noun *abstracts* from a concrete reality some one feature and assembles different concrete realities only with respect to this one feature. The very act of classifying forces us to overlook all other features, many of which might offer a sounder basis than the rubric we select. Irving Lee gives the following example:

> I knew a man who had lost the use of both eyes. He was called a "blind man." He could also be called an expert typist, a conscientious worker, a good student, a careful listener, a man who wanted a job. But he couldn't get a job in the department store order room where employees sat and typed orders which came over the telephone. The personnel man was impatient to get the interview over. "But you're a blind man," he kept saying, and one could almost feel his silent assumption that somehow the incapacity in one aspect made the man incapable in every other. So blinded by the label was the interviewer that he could not be persuaded to look beyond it.

Some labels, such as "blind man," are exceedingly salient and powerful. They tend to prevent alternative classification, or even cross-classification. Ethnic labels are often of this type, particularly if they refer to some highly visible feature, e.g., Negro, Oriental. They resemble the labels that point to some outstanding incapacity —*feeble-minded, cripple, blind man.* Let us call such symbols "labels of primary potency." These symbols act like shrieking sirens, deafening us to all finer discriminations that we might otherwise perceive. Even though the blindness of one man and the darkness of pigmentation of another may be defining attributes for some purposes, they are irrelevant and "noisy" for others.

Most people are unaware of this basic law of language—that every label applied to a given person refers properly only to one aspect of his nature. You may correctly say that a certain man is *human, a philanthropist, a Chinese, a physician, an athlete.* A given person may be all of these; but the chances are that *Chinese* stands out in your mind as the symbol of primary potency. Yet neither this nor any other classificatory label can refer to the whole of a man's nature. (Only his proper name can do so.)

Thus each label we use, especially those of primary potency, distracts our attention from concrete reality. The living, breathing, complex individual—the ultimate unit of human nature—is lost to sight. As in Fig. 1, the label magnifies one attribute out of all proportion to its true significance, and masks other important attributes of the individual. . . .

A category, once formed with the aid of a symbol of primary potency, tends to attract more attributes than it should. The cate-

LABELS OF PRIMARY POTENCY

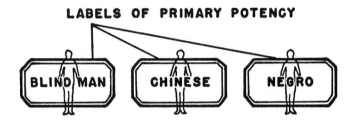

gory labeled *Chinese* comes to signify not only ethnic membership but also reticence, impassivity, poverty, treachery. To be sure, . . . there may be genuine ethnic-linked traits, making for a certain *probability* that the member of an ethnic stock may have these attributes. But our cognitive process is not cautious. The labeled category, as we have seen, includes indiscriminately the defining attribute, probable attributes, and wholly fanciful, nonexistent attributes.

Even proper names—which ought to invite us to look at the individual person—may act like symbols of primary potency, especially if they arouse ethnic associations. Mr. Greenberg is a person, but since his name is Jewish, it activates in the hearer his entire category of Jews-as-a-whole. An ingenious experiment performed by Razran shows this point clearly, and at the same time demonstrates how a proper name, acting like an ethnic symbol, may bring with it an avalanche of stereotypes. 8

> Thirty photographs of college girls were shown on a screen to 150 students. The subjects rated the girls on a scale from one to five for *beauty, intelligence, character, ambition, general likability.* Two months later the same subjects were asked to rate the same photographs (and fifteen additional ones introduced to complicate the memory factor). This time five of the original photographs were given Jewish surnames (Cohen, Kantor, etc.), five Italian (Valenti, etc.), and five Irish (O'Brien, etc.); and the remaining girls were given names chosen from the signers of the Declaration of Independence and from the Social Register (Davis, Adams, Clark, etc.).
>
> When Jewish names were attached to photographs there occurred the following changes in ratings:
>
> decrease in liking
> decrease in character
> decrease in beauty
> increase in intelligence
> increase in ambition
>
> For those photographs given Italian names there occurred:
>
> decrease in liking
> decrease in character

decrease in beauty
decrease in intelligence

Thus a mere proper name leads to prejudgments of personal attributes. The individual is fitted to the prejudice ethnic category, and not judged in his own right.

While the Irish names also brought about depreciated judgment, the depreciation was not as great as in the case of the Jews and Italians. The falling of likability of the "Jewish girls" was twice as great as for "Italians" and five times as great as for "Irish." We note, however, that the "Jewish" photographs caused higher ratings in *intelligence* and in *ambition*. Not all stereotypes of out-groups are unfavorable.

The anthropologist, Margaret Mead, has suggested that labels of 9 primary potency lose some of their force when they are changed from nouns into adjectives. To speak of a Negro soldier, a Catholic teacher, or a Jewish artist calls attention to the fact that some other group classifications are just as legitimate as the racial or religious. If George Johnson is spoken of not only as a Negro but also as a *soldier,* we have at least two attributes to know him by, and two are more accurate than one. To depict him truly as an individual, of course, we should have to name many more attributes. It is a useful suggestion that we designate ethnic and religious membership where possible with *adjectives* rather than with *nouns.*

EMOTIONALLY TONED LABELS

Many categories have two kinds of labels—one less emotional and 10 one more emotional. Ask yourself how you feel, and what thoughts you have, when you read the words *school teacher,* and then *school marm.* Certainly the second phrase calls up something more strict, more ridiculous, more disagreeable than the former. Here are four innocent letters: m-a-r-m. But they make us shudder a bit, laugh a bit, and scorn a bit. They call up an image of a spare, humorless, irritable old maid. They do not tell us that she is an individual human being with sorrows and troubles of her own. They force her instantly into a rejective category.

In the ethnic sphere even plain labels such as Negro, Italian, 11 Jew, Catholic, Irish-American, French-Canadian may have emotional tone for a reason that we shall soon explain. But they all have their higher key equivalents: nigger, wop, kike, papist, harp, canuck. When these labels are employed we can be almost certain that the speaker *intends* not only to characterize the person's membership, but also to disparage and reject him.

Quite apart from the insulting intent that lies behind the use of 12 certain labels, there is also an inherent ("physiognomic") handicap in many terms designating ethnic membership. For example, the proper names characteristic of certain ethnic memberships strike us as absurd. (We compare them, of course, with what is familiar and therefore "right.") Chinese names are short and silly; Polish names intrinsically difficult and outlandish. Unfamilar dialects strike us as ludicrous. Foreign dress (which, of course, is a visual ethnic symbol) seems unnecessarily queer.

But of all these "physiognomic" handicaps the reference to color, clearly implied in certain symbols, is the greatest. The word Negro comes from the Latin *niger* meaning black. In point of fact, no Negro has a black complexion, but by comparison with other blonder stocks, he has come to be known as a "black man." Unfortunately *black* in the English language is a word having a preponderance of sinister connotations: the outlook is black, blackball, blackguard, blackhearted, black death, blacklist, blackmail, Black Hand. In his novel *Moby Dick,* Herman Melville considers at length the remarkably morbid connotations of black and the remarkably virtuous connotations of white. 13

Nor is the ominous flavor of black confined to the English language. A cross-cultural study reveals that the semantic significance of black is more or less universally the same. Among certain Siberian tribes, members of a privileged clan call themselves "white bones," and refer to all others as "black bones." Even among Uganda Negroes there is some evidence for a white god at the apex of the theocratic hierarchy; certain it is that a white cloth, signifying purity, is used to ward off evil spirits and disease. 14

There is thus an implied value-judgment in the very concept of *white race* and *black race.* One might also study the numerous unpleasant connotations of *yellow,* and their possible bearing on our conception of the people of the Orient. 15

Such reasoning should not be carried too far, since there are undoubtedly, in various contexts, pleasant associations with both black and yellow. Black velvet is agreeable, so too are chocolate and coffee. Yellow tulips are well liked; the sun and moon are radiantly yellow. Yet it is true that "color" words are used with chauvinistic overtones more than most people realize. There is certainly condescension indicated in many familiar phrases: dark as a nigger's pocket, darktown strutters, white hope (a term originated when a white contender was sought against the Negro heavyweight champion, Jack Johnson), the white man's burden, the yellow peril, black boy. Scores of everyday phrases are stamped with the flavor of prejudice, whether the user knows it or not. 16

We spoke of the fact that even the most proper and sedate labels   17
for minority groups sometimes seem to exude a negative flavor. In
many contexts and situations the very terms *French-Canadian,
Mexican,* or *Jew,* correct and nonmalicious though they are, sound a
bit opprobrious. The reason is that they are labels of social deviants.
Especially in a culture where uniformity is prized, the name of *any*
deviant carries with it *ipso facto* a negative value-judgment. Words
like *insane, alcoholic, pervert* are presumably neutral designations
of a human condition, but they are more: they are finger-pointings at
deviance. Minority groups are deviants, and for this reason, from
the very outset, the most innocent labels in many situations imply a
shading of disrepute. When we wish to highlight the deviance and
denigrate it still further we use words of a higher emotional key:
crackpot, soak, pansy, greaser, Okie, nigger, harp, kike.

Members of minority groups are often understandably sensitive   18
to names given them. Not only do they object to deliberately insulting epithets, but sometimes see evil intent where none exists. Often
the word Negro is spelled with a small *n,* occasionally as a studied
insult, more often from ignorance. (The term is not cognate with
white, which is not capitalized, but rather with Caucasian, which is.)
Terms like "mulatto," or "octoroon" cause hard feeling because of
the condescension with which they have often been used in the past.
Sex differentiations are objectionable, since they seem doubly to
emphasize ethnic difference: why speak of Jewess and not of Prot-
estantess, or of Negress and not of whitess? Similar overemphasis is
implied in the terms like Chinamen or Scotchman; why not American man? Grounds for misunderstanding lie in the fact that minority
group members are sensitive to such shadings, while majority members may employ them unthinkingly.

THE COMMUNIST LABEL

Until we label an out-group it does not clearly exist in our minds.   19
Take the curiously vague situation that we often meet when a person
wishes to locate responsibility on the shoulders of some out-group
whose nature he cannot specify. In such a case he usually employs
the pronoun "they" without an antecedent. "Why don't they make
these sidewalks wider?" "I hear they are going to build a factory in
this town and hire a lot of foreigners." "I won't pay this tax bill;
they can just whistle for their money." If asked "who?" the
speaker is likely to grow confused and embarrassed. The common
use of the orphaned pronoun *they* teaches us that people often want

and need to designate out-groups (usually for the purpose of venting hostility) even when they have no clear conception of the out-group in question. And so long as the target of wrath remains vague and ill-defined specific prejudice cannot crystallize around it. To have enemies we need labels.

Until relatively recently—strange as it may seem—there was no   20
agreed-upon symbol for *communist*. The word, of course, existed but it had no special emotional connotation, and did not designate a public enemy. Even when, after World War I, there was a growing feeling of economic and social menace in this country, there was no agreement as to the actual source of the menace.

A content analysis of the *Boston Herald* for the year 1920 turned   21
up the following list of labels. Each was used in a context implying some threat. Hysteria had overspread the country, as it did after World War II. Someone must be responsible for the postwar malaise, rising prices, uncertainty. There must be a villain. But in 1920 the villain was impartially designated by reporters and editorial writers with the following symbols:

> alien, agitator, anarchist, apostle of bomb and torch, Bolshevik, communist, communist laborite, conspirator, emissary of false promise, extremist, foreigner, hyphenated-American, incendiary, IWW, parlor anarchist, parlor pink, parlor socialist, plotter, radical, red, revolutionary, Russian agitator, socialist, Soviet, syndicalist, traitor, undesirable.

From this excited array we note that the *need* for an enemy   22
(someone to serve as a focus for discontent and jitters) was considerably more apparent than the precise *identity* of the enemy. At any rate, there was no clearly agreed upon label. Perhaps partly for this reason the hysteria abated. Since no clear category of "communism" existed there was no true focus for the hostility.

But following World War II this collection of vaguely inter-   23
changeable labels became fewer in number and more commonly agreed upon. The out-group menace came to be designated almost always as *communist* or *red*. In 1920 the threat, lacking a clear label, was vague; after 1945 both symbol and thing became more definite. Not that people knew precisely what they meant when they said "communist," but with the aid of the term they were at least able to point consistently to *something* that inspired fear. The term developed the power of signifying menace and led to various repressive measures against anyone to whom the label was rightly or wrongly attached.

Logically, the label should apply to specifiable defining attrib-   24
utes, such as members of the Communist Party, or people whose

THE LANGUAGE OF PREJUDICE   203

allegiance is with the Russian system, or followers, historically, of Karl Marx. But the label came in for far more extensive use.

What seems to have happened is approximately as follows. Having suffered through a period of war and being acutely aware of devastating revolutions abroad, it is natural that most people should be upset, dreading to lose their possessions, annoyed by high taxes, seeing customary moral and religious values threatened, and dreading worse disasters to come. Seeking an explanation for this unrest, a single identifiable enemy is wanted. It is not enough to designate "Russia" or some other distant land. Nor is it satisfactory to fix blame on "changing social conditions." What is needed is a human agent near at hand: someone in Washington, someone in our schools, in our factories, in our neighborhood. If we *feel* an immediate threat, we reason, there must be a near-lying danger. It is, we conclude, communism, not only in Russia but also in America, at our doorstep, in our government, in our churches, in our colleges, in our neighborhood.

Are we saying that hostility toward communism is prejudice? Not necessarily. There are certainly phases of the dispute wherein realistic social conflict is involved. American values (e.g., respect for the person) and totalitarian values as represented in Soviet practice are intrinsically at odds. A realistic opposition in some form will occur. Prejudice enters only when the defining attributes of "communist" grow imprecise, when anyone who favors any form of social change is called a communist. People who fear social change are the ones most likely to affix the label to any persons or practices that seem to them threatening.

For them the category is undifferentiated. It includes books, movies, preachers, teachers who utter what for them are uncongenial thoughts. If evil befalls—perhaps forest fires or a factory explosion—it is due to communist saboteurs. The category becomes monopolistic, covering almost anything that is uncongenial. On the floor of the House of Representatives in 1946, Representative Rankin called James Roosevelt a communist. Congressman Outland replied with psychological acumen, "Apparently everyone who disagrees with Mr. Rankin is a communist."

When differentiated thinking is at a low ebb—as it is in times of social crises—there is a magnification of two-valued logic. Things are perceived as either inside or outside a moral order. What is outside is likely to be called "communist." Correspondingly—and here is where damage is done—whatever is called communist (however erroneously) is immediately cast outside the moral order.

This associative mechanism places enormous power in the hands of a demagogue. For several years Senator McCarthy managed to discredit many citizens who thought differently from himself by the simple device of calling them communist. Few people were able to see through this trick and many reputations were ruined. But the famous senator has no monopoly on the device. As reported in the *Boston Herald* on November 1, 1946, Representative Joseph Martin, Republican leader in the House, ended his election campaign against his Democratic opponent by saying, "The people will vote tomorrow between chaos, confusion, bankruptcy, state socialism or communism, and the preservation of our American life, with all its freedom and its opportunities." Such an array of emotional labels placed his opponent outside the accepted moral order. Martin was re-elected. . . .

Not everyone, of course, is taken in. Demagogy, when it goes   30
too far, meets with ridicule. Elizabeth Dilling's book, *The Red Network,* was so exaggerated in its two-valued logic that it was shrugged off by many people with a smile. One reader remarked, "Apparently if you step off the sidewalk with your left foot you're a communist." But it is not easy in times of social strain and hysteria to keep one's balance, and to resist the tendency of a verbal symbol to manufacture large and fanciful categories of prejudiced thinking.

VERBAL REALISM AND SYMBOL PHOBIA

Most individuals rebel at being labeled, especially if the label is   31
uncomplimentary. Very few are willing to be called *fascistic, socialistic,* or *anti-Semitic.* Unsavory labels may apply to others; but not to us.

An illustration of the craving that people have to attach favora-   32
ble symbols to themselves is seen in the community where white people banded together to force out a Negro family that had moved in. They called themselves "Neighborly Endeavor" and chose as their motto the Golden Rule. One of the first acts of this symbol-sanctified band was to sue the man who sold property to Negroes. They then flooded the house which another Negro couple planned to occupy. Such were the acts performed under the banner of the Golden Rule.

Studies made by Stagner and Hartmann show that a person's   33
political attitudes may in fact entitle him to be called a fascist or a socialist, and yet he will emphatically repudiate the unsavory label, and fail to endorse any movement or candidate that overtly accepts them. In short, there is a *symbol phobia* that corresponds to *symbol*

realism. We are more inclined to the former when we ourselves are concerned, though we are much less critical when epithets of "fascist," "communist," "blind man," "school marm" are applied to others.

When symbols provoke strong emotions they are sometimes re-   34
garded no longer as symbols, but as actual things. The expressions "son of a bitch" and "liar" are in our culture frequently regarded as "fighting words." Softer and more subtle expressions of contempt may be accepted. But in these particular cases, the epithet itself must be "taken back." We certainly do not change our opponent's attitude by making him take back a word, but it seems somehow important that the word itself be eradicated.

Such verbal realism may reach extreme length.   35

> The City Council of Cambridge, Massachusetts, unanimously passed a resolution (December, 1939) making it illegal "to possess, harbor, sequester, introduce or transport, within the city limits, any book, map, magazine, newspaper, pamphlet, handbill or circular containing the words Lenin or Leningrad."

Such naiveté in confusing language with reality is hard to comprehend unless we recall that word-magic plays an appreciable part in human thinking. The following examples, like the one preceding, are taken from Hayakawa.

> The Malagasy soldier must eschew kidneys, because in the Malagasy language the word for kidney is the same as that for "shot"; so shot he would certainly be if he ate a kidney.

> In May, 1937, a state senator of New York bitterly opposed a bill for the control of syphilis because "the innocence of children might be corrupted by a widespread use of the term. . . . This particular word creates a shudder in every decent woman and decent man."

This tendency to reify words underscores the close cohesion that   36
exists between category and symbol. Just the mention of "communist," "Negro," "Jew," "England," "Democrats," will send some people into a panic of fear or a frenzy of anger. Who can say whether it is the word or the thing that annoys them? The label is an intrinsic part of any monopolistic category. Hence to liberate a person from ethnic or political prejudice it is necessary at the same time to liberate him from *word fetishism.* This fact is well known to students of general semantics who tell us that prejudice is due in large part to verbal realism and to symbol phobia. Therefore any program for the reduction of prejudice must include a large measure of semantic therapy.

QUESTIONS ON CONTENT

1. Allport quotes William James's statement that without words our lives would be an "empirical sand-heap." What did James mean by the phrase? What are the implications of a world in which we could not determine categories?

2. Nouns or names provide an essential service in making categorization possible. Yet, according to Allport, nouns are also words that "cut slices." What is inherently unfair about nouns?

3. What does Allport mean by the "orphaned pronoun *they*"? Why is it used so often?

4. Allport seems to use the terms *noun, label,* and *symbol* interchangeably. What distinctions do you make among these terms?

5. What are "labels of primary potency"? Why are they so important? Can and should we avoid the use of such labels?

6. Why may "labels of primary potency lose some of their force when they are changed from nouns into adjectives"? Do you agree that "it is a useful suggestion that we designate ethnic and religious membership where possible with *adjectives* rather than with *nouns*"? Why or why not?

7. What do the terms *reify, verbal realism, symbol phobia, word fetishism,* and *symbol realism* mean? How could you apply these terms to the whole range of "four-letter" or "taboo" words to make linguistic sense of the concept of pornography?

QUESTIONS ON RHETORIC

1. The first three paragraphs of Allport's essay become progressively less abstract. Explain how these paragraphs logically narrow our focus to the noun and how it functions.

2. Allport includes six fairly lengthy quotations in his essay. What is their function? Do you think they are effective? Why or why not?

3. In paragraph 17, identify the topic sentence. What method is used to develop the paragraph?

VOCABULARY

rudimentary	intrinsic	sinister
ethnic	inherent	morbid

array   ludicrous   sedate
cohesion

CLASSROOM ACTIVITIES

1. Individuals who are in show business often change their names.
Listed below are the professional names and the original names of a
number of celebrities. Discuss the significance of the changes.

Professional Name	Original Name
Tony Curtis	Bernard Schwartz
Mick Jagger	Michael Phillip
Simone Signoret	Simone Kaminker
Roy Rogers	Leonard Slye
Raquel Welch	Raquel Tejada
James Garner	James Bumgarner
Bob Dylan	Robert Zimmerman
Doris Day	Doris von Kappelhoff
John Wayne	Marion Michael Morrison
Cyd Charisse	Tula Finklea
Anne Bancroft	Annemarie Italiano
Michael Caine	Maurice J. Micklewhite
Jack Benny	Benjamin Kubelsky
Connie Francis	Concetta Franconero
Ringo Starr	Richard Starkey
Hugh O'Brian	Hugh J. Krampe

NOTE: Writing assignments for "Prejudice and Language" appear on p. 226.

2
Words with Built-in Judgments

S. I. HAYAKAWA

In Language in Thought and Action, *from which the following selection is taken, general semanticist S. I. Hayakawa explores the complex relationships that exist between reality and the language we use to describe it. He discusses the power that some words have to evoke both informative connotations and affective connotations and how an awareness of this power can help us avoid both stirring up traditional prejudices and unintentionally giving offense.*

The fact that some words arouse both informative and affective connotations simultaneously gives a special complexity to discussions involving religious, racial, national, and political groups. To many people the word "communist" means simultaneously "one who believes in communism" (informative connotations) and "one whose ideals and purposes are altogether repellent" (affective connotations). Words applying to occupations of which one disapproves ("pickpocket," "racketeer," "prostitute"), like those applying to believers in philosophies of which one may disapprove ("atheist," "heretic," "materialist," "Holy Roller," "radical," "liberal"), likewise often communicate *simultaneously* a fact and a judgment on the fact.

In some parts of the southwestern United States there is strong prejudice against Mexicans, both immigrant and American-born. The strength of this prejudice is indirectly revealed by the fact that newspapers and polite people have stopped using the word "Mexican" altogether, using the expression "Spanish-speaking person" instead. "Mexican" has been used with contemptuous connotations for so long that it has become, in the opinion of many people in the region, unsuitable for polite conversation. In some circles, the word is reserved for lower-class Mexicans, while the "politer" term is used for the upper class. There are also terms, such as "chicano" and "Latino," that Mexican-American and Spanish-speaking groups have chosen to describe themselves.

In dealing with subjects about which strong feelings exist, we are   3
compelled to talk in roundabout terms if we wish to avoid arousing traditional prejudices, which hinder clear thinking. Hence we have not only such terms as "Spanish-speaking persons" but also, in other contexts, "problem drinkers" instead of "drunkards," and "Hansen's disease" instead of "leprosy."

These verbal stratagems are necessitated by the strong affective   4
connotations as well as by the often misleading implications of their blunter alternatives; they are not merely a matter of giving things fancy names in order to fool people, as the simple-minded often believe. Because the old names are "loaded," they dictate traditional patterns of behavior toward those to whom they are applied. When everybody "knew" what to do about "little hoodlums," they threw them in jail and "treated 'em rough." Once in jail, little hoodlums showed a marked tendency to grow up into big hoodlums. When thoughtful people began to observe such facts, they started rethinking the problem, using different terminologies. What is the best way of describing these troubled and troublesome youths? Shall they be described as "defectives" or "psychopathic personalities"? Or as "maladjusted" or "neurotic"? Shall we say they are "deprived," "disadvantaged," "frustrated," or "socially displaced"? Shall we say they are "troubled by problems of identity"? Are they in need of "confinement," "punishment," "treatment," "education," or "rehabilitation"? It is through trying out many, many possible terms such as these that new ways of dealing with the problem are discovered and devised.

The meaning of words, as we have observed, changes from   5
speaker to speaker and from context to context. The words "Japs" and "niggers," for instance, although often used both as a designation and an insult, are sometimes used with no intent to offend. In some classes of society and in some geographical areas, there are people who know no other words for Japanese, and in other areas there are people who know no other words for Negroes. Ignorance of regional and class differences of dialect often results in feelings being needlessly hurt. Those who believe that the meaning of a word is *in the word* often fail to understand this simple point of differences in usage. For example, an elderly Japanese woman of my acquaintance used to squirm at the mention of the word "Jap," even when used in an innocuous or complimentary context. "Whenever I hear that word," she used to say, "I feel dirty all over."

The word "nigger" has a similar effect on most Negroes. A distinguished Negro sociologist tells of an incident in his adolescence when he was hitchhiking far from home in regions where Negroes are hardly ever seen. He was befriended by an extremely kindly white couple who fed him and gave him a place to sleep in their home. However, they kept calling him "little nigger"—a fact which upset him profoundly, even while he was grateful for their kindness. He finally got up courage to ask the man not to call him by that "insulting term." 6

> "Who's insultin' you, son?" said the man.
> "You are, sir—that name you're always calling me."
> "What name?"
> "Uh . . . you know."
> "I ain't callin' you no names, son."
> "I mean your calling me 'nigger.' "
> "Well, what's insultin' about that? You are a nigger, ain't you?"

As the sociologist says now in telling the story, "I couldn't think of an answer then, and I'm not sure I can now." 7

In case the sociologist reads this book, we are happy to provide him with an answer, although it may be twenty-five years late. He might have said to his benefactor, "Sir, in the part of the country I come from, white people who treat colored people with respect call them Negroes, while those who wish to show their contempt for colored people call them niggers. I hope the latter is not your intention." And the man might have replied, had he been kindly in thought as he was in deed. "Well, you don't say! Sorry I hurt your feelings, son, but I didn't know." And that would have been that. Many black people have rejected the term "Negro" as itself an insulting term and prefer to be called blacks or Afro-Americans. Some "hip" terms that Negroes use for themselves are "moulenjam," "splib," "member," "blood," and "boots." 8

Negroes, having for a long time been victims of unfair persecution because of race, are often even more sensitive about racial appellations than the Japanese woman previously mentioned. It need hardly be said that Negroes suffer from the confusion of informative and affective connotations just as often as white people—or Japanese. Such Negroes, and those white sympathizers with the Negro cause who are equally naive in linguistic matters, tend to feel that the entire colored "race" is vilified whenever and wherever the word "nigger" occurs. They bristle even when it occurs in such expressions as "niggertoe" (the name of an herb; also a dialect term for Brazil nut), "niggerhead" (a type of chewing tobacco), "nig- 9

gerfish" (a kind of fish found in West Indian and Floridan waters)—
and even the word "niggardly" (of Scandinavian origin, unrelated,
of course, to "Negro") has to be avoided before some audiences.

Such easily offended people sometimes send delegations to visit   10
dictionary offices to demand that the word "nigger" be excluded
from future editions, being unaware that dictionaries . . . perform a
historical, rather than legislative, function. To try to reduce racial
discrimination by getting dictionaries to stop including the word
"nigger" is like trying to cut down the birth rate by shutting down
the office of the county register of births. When racial discrimination
against Negroes is done away with, the word will either disappear or
else lose its present connotations. By losing its present connotations, we mean, first, that people who need to insult their fellow men
will have found more interesting grounds on which to base their
insults and, second, that people who are called "niggers" will no
longer fly off the handle any more than a person from New England
does at being called a "Yankee."

One other curious fact needs to be recorded about words applied   11
to such hotly debated issues as race, religion, political heresy, and
economic dissent. Every reader is acquainted with certain people
who, according to their own flattering descriptions of themselves,
"believe in being frank" and like to "tell it like [sic] it is." By
"telling it like it is," they usually mean calling anything or anyone
by the term which has the strongest and most disagreeable affective
connotations. Why people should pin medals on themselves for
"candor" for performing this nasty feat has often puzzled me.
Sometimes it is necessary to violate verbal taboos as an aid to
clearer thinking, but more often "calling a spade a spade" is to
provide our minds with a greased runway down which we may slide
back into old and discredited patterns of evaluation and behavior.

QUESTIONS ON CONTENT

1. Explain the distinction Hayakawa draws between "informative
connotations" and "affective connotations."

2. Why, according to Hayakawa, have many people in the American Southwest stopped using the term "Mexican"?

3. How can names, as Hayakawa asserts, "dictate traditional patterns of behavior toward those to whom they are applied"?

4. On what basis does Hayakawa argue that "verbal stratagems"
are often a necessity?

5. Why is it important to realize that the meanings of words may change "from speaker to speaker and from context to context"?

6. In what ways are Hayakawa's "words with built-in judgments" similar to Allport's "labels of primary potency" (Allport, paragraph 4)?

QUESTIONS ON RHETORIC

1. Most of the paragraphs in Hayakawa's essay are organized in the same way. Explain how they are organized, paying particular attention to the topic sentences.

2. With only a few exceptions, the paragraphs of this essay are similar in length. Describe any relationship you see between this fact and the similarity in structure of the paragraphs.

3. How effective is the metaphor of the "greased runway" in the final paragraph? Explain.

VOCABULARY

simultaneously	psychopathic	dissent
repellent	innocuous	candor
contemptuous	benefactor	rehabilitation

CLASSROOM ACTIVITIES

1. Hayakawa lists a number of terms (*pickpocket, racketeer, prostitute, atheist, heretic, materialist, Holy Roller, radical, liberal, Mexican, drunkard, leprosy, hoodlums, Japs, niggers*) that evoke simultaneously both affective connotations and informative connotations. Think of three other terms that also do this. Explain the affective and informative connotations of each term.

NOTE: Writing assignments for "Prejudice and Language" appear on p. 226.

3

How "White" Is
Your Dictionary?

WILLIAM WALTER DUNCAN

William Walter Duncan is concerned about the ways in which our dictionaries actually reinforce our prejudices. Comparing dictionary entries for the terms "black" and "white," he argues that they are not complete and that they should be improved.

During a recent discussion on semantics in one of my classes, I   1
asked some twenty students to tell me what they think of when the
word *white* is mentioned. I got such responses as: "purity," "the
color," "snow," "something clean," but not one negative connotation for the word.

I then asked about the word *black* and got: "something very   2
dark," "dirty," "black lies," "death," but not one positive connotation. When I pointed this out to the class, one "white" student
immediately exclaimed, "But there are no positive connotations for
black."

At this point one of the "black" students—all of whom had   3
previously remained silent—responded angrily, and understandably
so, pointing out that in his mind there are many negative connotations for *white* and many positive ones for *black*.

After a few moments of tension among some of the students, I   4
turned the discussion into an examination of the word *black,* using
the unabridged edition of *The Random House Dictionary of the
English Language.* All of the definitions of the word in this dictionary are either negative or neutral in nature. Not until the phrases,
specifically item no. 22, *in the black,* does one find a positive connotation for the word, the sole entry in more than fifty lines of fine
print that can be said to be of a positive nature. Even when *black
clothing* is mentioned, one finds: "esp. as a sign of mourning: *He
wore black at the funeral.*"

In contrast with *black, white* has a preponderance of positive meanings, but none with negative connotations—not one word about *white* associated with death, as in *white as a ghost,* or with evil, as in *a white mask of deception.*

Now a dictionary is merely a report of the ways words are used. (The precedent set by Samuel Johnson for the expression of personal biases in the definition of some words has long since been rejected by lexicographers.) And the Random House dictionary, in its treatment of the words *white* and *black,* is not essentially different from other dictionaries. For example, here is the way *Funk & Wagnalls Standard College Dictionary* (Harcourt, Brace & World, 1963) treats the word:

> black adj. 1. Having no brightness or color; Reflecting no light; opposed to *white.* 2. Destitute of light; in total darkness. 3. Gloomy; dismal; forbidding: a *black* future. 4. Having a very dark skin, as a Negro. 5. Soiled; stained. 6. Indicating disgrace or censure: a *black* mark. 7. Angry; threatening: *black* looks. 8. Evil; wicked; malignant: a *black* heart.

While all of the dictionaries which I have examined treat the word *black* in a similar manner, the statement that lexicographers merely report the way a word is used, a defense which one editor of a well-known dictionary recently made to me, needs to be examined carefully.

A dictionary is supposedly merely a record of what a language *was* at some point in the past. Even at the moment of publication, a dictionary is dated. No one, therefore, can reasonably expect the dictionaries now in use to have statements about the way the word *black* is currently being used by many people, as in the slogan *black is beautiful,* and only time will tell if *black* is going to become the standard term for *Negro.*

But even if the above arguments are accepted, American dictionaries have not made complete reports of the word *black.* Why, for instance, in listing the phrase *black clothing* were not references made to the formal attire which men sometimes wear to look their best, or to the black robes worn by judges or by academicians? Why weren't references made to the *black opal* or *pearl* or to other contexts in which the word carries a positive connotation?

While a dictionary cannot perhaps explain why a *black lie* is a repugnant case of mendacity and a *white* one an excusable falsehood, a dictionary can suggest that a reader compare one phrase with the other. This might lead many to realize the logical inconsistency of the two phrases and possibly the evil we perpetuate when we use them.

While a dictionary cannot be expected to explain why we call   11
some people "white" and others "black" when in reality there are
no black or white people—we are all colored—a dictionary can say
"a member of the so-called black race," as *Standard College* does,
and "a member of the so-called white race," as *Standard College*
does not.

While a correction and an improvement of the treatment of the   12
words *black* and *white* in our dictionaries may not eliminate prejudice associated with skin color, it could be a contribution to this
cause.

QUESTIONS ON CONTENT

1. How does Duncan define the term *dictionary*? What are his objec-
tions to this definition?

2. What, according to Duncan, is the philosophy of contemporary
dictionary makers regarding current usage?

3. What kinds of changes does Duncan want made in the entries for
black and *white*? Why does he suggest these changes? Do you agree
with him?

QUESTIONS ON RHETORIC

1. Duncan begins his article with an anecdote. Is this an effective
opening? Why or why not?

2. What is the tone of this essay: angry, strident, reasonable, emotional, logical? How does the tone affect your response to the essay?

VOCABULARY

connotation	destitute	perpetuate
unabridged	malignant	lexicographers
precedent	repugnant	

CLASSROOM ACTIVITIES

1. Read the following newspaper article. Be prepared, in classroom
discussion, to attack or defend the UN recommendations.

UN Group Urges Dropping of Words with Racist Tinge

In an effort to combat racial prejudice, a group of United Nations experts is urging sweeping revision of the terminology used by teachers, mass media and others dealing with race.

Words such as *Negro, primitive, savage, backward, colored, bushman* and *uncivilized* would be banned as either "contemptuous, unjust or inadequate." They were described as aftereffects of colonialism.

The report said that the terms were "so charged with emotive potential that their use, with or without conscious pejorative intent, to describe or characterize certain ethnic, social or religious groups, generally provoked an adverse reaction on the part of these groups."

The report said further that even the term *race* should be used with particular care since its scientific validity was debatable and that it "often served to perpetuate prejudice." The experts suggested that the word *tribe* should be used as sparingly as possible, since most of the "population groups" referred to by this term have long since ceased to be tribes or are losing their tribal character. A *native* should be called *inhabitant*, the group advised, and instead of *paganism* the words *animists, Moslems, Brahmans* and other precise words should be used. The word *savanna* is preferable to *jungle*, and the new countries should be described as *developing* rather than *underdeveloped*, the experts said.

NOTE: Writing assignments for "Prejudice and Language" appear on p. 226.

4

Sexism in English: A Feminist View

ALLEEN PACE NILSEN

Since culture influences language and language influences culture, we cannot reasonably study one subject without also studying the other. In an effort to see what role the dictionary plays in reflecting and influencing attitudes toward women in America, Alleen Pace Nilsen studied all the words relating to males and females in a recently published desk dictionary. She found that dictionary entries reflect deep-seated biases against women in several unexpected ways. Her findings raise some important questions about the possibility of establishing equal rights for women in this country.

Does culture shape language? Or does language shape culture? 1 This is as difficult a question as the old puzzler of which came first, the chicken or the egg, because there's no clear separation between language and culture.

A well-accepted linguistic principle is that as culture changes so 2 will the language. The reverse of this—as a language changes so will the culture—is not so readily accepted. This is why some linguists smile (or even scoff) at feminist attempts to replace *Mrs.* and *Miss* with *Ms.* and to find replacements for those all-inclusive words which specify masculinity, e.g., *chairman, mankind, brotherhood, freshman*, etc.

Perhaps they are amused for the same reason that it is the doctor 3 at a cocktail party who laughs the loudest at the joke about the man who couldn't afford an operation so he offered the doctor a little something to touch up the X-ray. A person working constantly with language is likely to be more aware of how really deep-seated sexism is in our communication system.

Last winter I took a standard desk dictionary and gave it a place 4 of honor on my night table. Every night that I didn't have anything more interesting to do, I read myself to sleep making a card for each entry that seemed to tell something about male and female. By spring I had a rather dog-eared dictionary, but I also had a collection of note cards filling two shoe boxes. The cards tell some rather interesting things about American English.

First, in our culture it is a woman's body which is considered important while it is a man's mind or his activities which are valued. A woman is sexy. A man is successful.

I made a card for all the words which came into modern English from somebody's name. I have a two-and-one-half inch stack of cards which are men's names now used as everyday words. The women's stack is less than a half inch high and most of them came from Greek mythology. Words coming from the names of famous American men include *lynch, sousaphone, sideburns, Pullman, rickettsia, Schick test, Winchester rifle, Franklin stove, Bartlett pear, teddy bear,* and *boysenberry.* The only really common words coming from the names of American women are *bloomers* (after Amelia Jenks Bloomer) and *Mae West jacket.* Both of these words are related in some way to a woman's physical anatomy, while the male words (except for *sideburns* after General Burnsides) have nothing to do with the namesake's body.

This reminded me of an earlier observation that my husband and I made about geographical names. A few years ago we became interested in what we called "Topless Topography" when we learned that the Grand Tetons used to be simply called *The Tetons* by French explorers and *The Teats* by American frontiersmen. We wrote letters to several map makers and found the following listings: *Nippletop* and *Little Nipple Top* near Mt. Marcy in the Adirondacks, *Nipple Mountain* in Archuleta County, Colorado, *Nipple Peak* in Coke County, Texas, *Nipple Butte* in Pennington, South Dakota, *Squaw Peak* in Placer County, California (and many other places), *Maiden's Peak* and *Squaw Tit* (they're the same mountain) in the Cascade Range in Oregon, *Jane Russell Peaks* near Stark, New Hampshire, and *Mary's Nipple* near Salt Lake City, Utah.

We might compare these names to Jackson Hole, Wyoming, or Pikes Peak, Colorado. I'm sure we would get all kinds of protests from the Jackson and Pike descendants if we tried to say that these topographical features were named because they in some way resembled the bodies of Jackson and Pike, respectively.

This preoccupation with women's breasts is neither new nor strictly American. I was amused to read the derivation of the word *Amazon.* According to Greek folk etymology, the *a* means "without" as in *atypical* or *amoral* while *mazon* comes from *mazōs* meaning "breast." According to the legend, these women cut off one breast so that they could better shoot their bows. Perhaps the feeling was that the women had to trade in part of their femininity in exchange for their active or masculine role.

There are certain pairs of words which illustrate the way in   10 which sexual connotations are given to feminine words while the masculine words retain a serious, businesslike aura. For example, being a *callboy* is perfectly respectable. It simply refers to a person who calls actors when it is time for them to go on stage, but being a *call girl* is being a prostitute.

Also we might compare *sir* and *madam*. *Sir* is a term of respect   11 while *madam* has acquired the meaning of a brothel manager. The same thing has happened to the formerly cognate terms, *master* and *mistress*. Because of its acquired sexual connotations, *mistress* is now carefully avoided in certain contexts. For example, the Boy Scouts have *scoutmasters* but certainly not *scoutmistresses*. And in a dog show the female owner of a dog is never referred to as the *dog's mistress,* but rather as the *dog's master.*

Master appears in such terms as *master plan, concert master,*   12 *schoolmaster, mixmaster, master charge, master craftsman,* etc. But *mistress* appears in very few compounds. This is the way it is with dozens of words which have male and female counterparts. I found two hundred such terms, e.g., *usher–usherette, heir–heiress, hero-heroine,* etc. In nearly all cases it is the masculine word which is the base with a feminine suffix being added for the alternate version. The masculine word also travels into compounds while the feminine word is a dead end; e.g., from *king–queen* comes *kingdom* but not *queendom,* from *sportsman–sportslady* comes *sportsman- ship* but not *sportsladyship,* etc. There is one—and only one—se- mantic area in which the masculine word is not the base or more powerful word. This is in the area dealing with sex and marriage. Here it is the feminine word which is dominant. *Prostitute* is the base word with *male prostitute* being the derived term. *Bride* ap- pears in *bridal shower, bridal gown, bridal attendant, bridesmaid,* and even in *bridegroom,* while *groom* in the sense of *bridegroom* does not appear in any compounds, not even to name the groom's attendants or his prenuptial party.

At the end of a marriage, this same emphasis is on the female. If   13 it ends in divorce, the woman gets the title of *divorcée* while the man is usually described with a statement, such as, "He's divorced." When the marriage ends in death, the woman is a *widow* and the *-er* suffix which seems to connote masculine (probably because it is an agentive or actor type suffix) is added to make *widower. Widower* doesn't appear in any compounds (except for *grass widower,* which is another companion term), but *widow* appears in several compounds and in addition has some acquired meanings, such as the extra hand dealt to the table in certain card games and an undesirable leftover line of type in printing.

If I were an anthropological linguist making observations about a   14
strange and primitive tribe, I would duly note on my tape recorder that I had found linguistic evidence to show that in the area of sex and marriage the female appears to be more important than the male, but in all other areas of the culture, it seems that the reverse is true.

But since I am not an anthropological linguist, I will simply go on   15
to my second observation, which is that women are expected to play a passive role while men play an active one.

One indication of women's passive role is the fact that they are   16
often identified as something to eat. What's more passive than a plate of food? Last spring I saw an announcement advertising the Indiana University English Department picnic. It read "Good Food! Delicious Women!" The publicity committee was probably jumped on by local feminists, but it's nothing new to look on women as "delectable morsels." Even women compliment each other with "You look good enough to eat," or "You have a peaches and cream complexion." Modern slang constantly comes up with new terms, but some of the old standbys for women are: *cute tomato, dish, peach, sharp cookie, cheese cake, honey, sugar,* and *sweetie-pie.* A man may occasionally be addressed as *honey* or described as a *hunk of meat,* but certainly men are not laid out on a buffet and labeled as women are.

Women's passivity is also shown in the comparisons made to   17
plants. For example, to *deflower* a woman is to take away her virginity. A girl can be described as a *clinging vine,* a *shrinking violet,* or a *wallflower.* On the other hand, men are too active to be thought of as plants. The only time we make the comparison is when insulting a man we say he is like a woman by calling him a *pansy.*

We also see the active-passive contrast in the animal terms used   18
with males and females. Men are referred to as *studs, bucks,* and *wolves,* and they go *tomcatting around.* These are all aggressive roles, but women have such pet names as *kitten, bunny, beaver, bird, chick, lamb,* and *fox.* The idea of being a pet seems much more closely related to females than to males. For instance, little girls grow up wearing *pigtails* and *ponytails* and they dress in *halters* and *dog collars.*

The active-passive contrast is also seen in the proper names   19
given to boy babies and girl babies. Girls are much more likely to be

given names like *Ivy, Rose, Ruby, Jewel, Pearl, Flora, Joy,* etc., while boys are given names describing active roles such as *Martin* (warlike), *Leo* (lion), *William* (protector), *Ernest* (resolute fighter), and so on.

Another way that women play a passive role is that they are 20 defined in relationship to someone else. This is what feminists are protesting when they ask to be identified as *Ms.* rather than as *Mrs.* or *Miss.* It is a constant source of irritation to women's organizations that when they turn in items to newspapers under their own names, that is, Susan Glascoe, Jeanette Jones, and so forth, the editors consistently rewrite the item so that the names read Mrs. John Glascoe, Mrs. Robert E. Jones.

In the dictionary I found what appears to be an attitude on the 21 part of editors that it is almost indecent to let a respectable woman's name march unaccompanied across the pages of a dictionary. A woman's name must somehow be escorted by a male's name regardless of whether or not the male contributed to the woman's reason for being in the dictionary, or in his own right, was as famous as the woman. For example, Charlotte Brontë is identified as Mrs. Arthur B. Nicholls, Amelia Earhart is identified as Mrs. George Palmer Putnam, Helen Hayes is identified as Mrs. Charles MacArthur, Zona Gale is identified as Mrs. William Llwelyn Breese, and Jenny Lind is identified as Mme. Otto Goldschmidt.

Although most of the women are identified as Mrs.——— or as 22 the wife of ———, other women are listed with brothers, fathers, or lovers. Cornelia Otis Skinner is identified as the daughter of Otis, Harriet Beecher Stowe is identified as the sister of Henry Ward Beecher, Edith Sitwell is identified as the sister of Osbert and Sacheverell, Nell Gwyn is identified as the mistress of Charles II, and Madame Pompadour is identified as the mistress of Louis XV.

The women who did get into the dictionary without the benefit of 23 a masculine escort are a group sort of on the fringes of respectability. They are the rebels and the crusaders: temperance leaders Frances Elizabeth Caroline Willard and Carry Nation, women's rights leaders Carrie Chapman Catt and Elizabeth Cady Stanton, birth control educator Margaret Sanger, religious leader Mary Baker Eddy, and slaves Harriet Tubman and Phillis Wheatley.

I would estimate that far more than fifty percent of the women 24 listed in the dictionary were identified as someone's wife. But of all the men—and there are probably ten times as many men as women —only one was identified as "the husband of . . ." This was the unusual case of Frederic Joliot who took the last name of Joliot-Curie and was identified as "husband of Irene." Apparently Irene, the daughter of Pierre and Marie Curie, did not want to give up her maiden name when she married and so the couple took the hyphenated last name.

There are several pairs of words which also illustrate the more powerful role of the male and the relational role of the female. For example a *count* is a high political officer with a *countess* being simply the wife of a count. The same is true for a *duke* and a *duchess* and a *king* and a *queen*. The fact that a king is usually more powerful than a queen might be the reason that Queen Elizabeth's husband is given the title of *prince* rather than *king*. Since *king* is a stronger word than *queen*, it is reserved for a true heir to the throne because if it were given to someone coming into the royal family by marriage, then the subjects might forget where the true power lies. With the weaker word of *queen*, this would not be a problem; so a woman marrying a ruling monarch is given the title without question. 25

My third observation is that there are many positive connotations connected with the concept of masculine, while there are either trivial or negative connotations connected with the corresponding feminine concept. 26

Conditioning toward the superiority of the masculine role starts very early in life. Child psychologists point out that the only area in which a girl has more freedom than a boy is in experimenting with an appropriate sex role. She is much freer to be a *tomboy* than is her brother to be a *sissy*. The proper names given to children reflect this same attitude. It's perfectly all right for a girl to have a boy's name, but not the other way around. As girls are given more and more of the boys' names parents shy away from using boy names that might be mistaken for girl names, so the number of available masculine names is constantly shrinking. Fifty years ago *Hazel, Beverly, Marion, Francis,* and *Shirley* were all perfectly acceptable boys' names. Today few parents give these names to baby boys and adult men who are stuck with them self-consciously go by their initials or by abbreviated forms such as *Haze* or *Shirl*. But parents of little girls keep crowding the masculine set and currently popular girls' names include *Jo, Kelly, Teri, Cris, Pat, Shawn, Toni,* and *Sam*. 27

When the mother of one of these little girls tells her to *be a lady*, she means for her to sit with her knees together. But when the father of a little boy tells him to *be a man*, he means for him to be noble, strong, and virtuous. The whole concept of manliness has such positive connotations that it is a compliment to call a male a *he-man*, a *manly man*, or a *virile man* (*virile* comes from the Indo-European *vir*, meaning "man"). In each of these three terms, we are implying that someone is doubly good because he is doubly a man. 28

Compare *chef* with *cook, tailor* and *seamstress*, and *poet* with   29
poetess. In each case, the masculine form carries with it an added
degree of excellence. In comparing the masculine *governor* with the
feminine *governess* and the masculine *major* with the feminine *ma-
jorette*, the added feature is power.

The difference between positive male and negative female con-   30
notations can be seen in several pairs of words which differ denota-
tively only in the matter of sex. For instance compare *bachelor* with
the terms *spinster* and *old maid*. *Bachelor* has such positive connotations that modern girls have tried to borrow the feeling in the term
bachelor-girl. *Bachelor* appears in glamorous terms such as *bachelor
pad, bachelor party*, and *bachelor button*. But *old maid* has such
strong negative feelings that it has been adopted into other areas,
taking with it the feeling of undesirability. It has the metaphorical
meaning of shriveled and unwanted kernels of popcorn, and it's the
name of the last unwanted card in a popular game for children.

Patron and *matron* (Middle English for *father* and *mother*) are   31
another set where women have tried to borrow the positive masculine connotations, this time through the word *patroness*, which literally means "female father." Such a peculiar term came about because of the high prestige attached to the word *patron* in such
phrases as *"a patron of the arts"* or *"a patron saint."* *Matron* is
more apt to be used in talking about a woman who is in charge of a
jail or a public restroom.

Even *lord* and *lady* have different levels of connotation. *Our*   32
Lord is used as a title for deity, while the corresponding *Our Lady* is
a relational title for Mary, the mortal mother of Jesus. *Landlord* has
more dignity than *landlady* probably because the landlord is more
likely to be thought of as the owner while the landlady is the person
who collects the rent and enforces the rules. *Lady* is used in many
insignificant places where the corresponding *lord* would never be
used, for example, *ladies room, ladies sizes, ladies aid society, lady-
bug*, etc.

This overuse of *lady* might be compared to the overuse of *queen*   33
which is rapidly losing its prestige as compared to *king*. Hundreds of
beauty queens are crowned each year and nearly every community
in the United States has its *Dairy Queen* or its *Freezer Queen*, etc.
Male homosexuals have adopted the term to identify the "feminine" partner. And advertisers who are constantly on the lookout
for euphemisms to make unpleasant sounding products salable have
recently dealt what might be a death blow to the prestige of the word
queen. They have begun to use it as an indication of size. For example, *queen-size* panty hose are panty hose for fat women. The mean-

ing comes through a comparison with *king-size,* meaning big. However, there's a subtle difference in that our culture considers it desirable for males to be big because size is an indication of power, but we prefer that females be small and petite. So using *king-size* as a term to indicate bigness partially enhances the prestige of *king,* but using *queen-size* to indicate bigness brings unpleasant associations to the word *queen.*

Another set that might be compared are *brave* and *squaw.* The   34
word *brave* carries with it the connotations of youth, vigor, and courage, while *squaw* implies almost opposite characteristics. With the set *wizard* and *witch,* the main difference is that *wizard* implies skill and wisdom combined with magic, while *witch* implies evil intentions combined with magic. Part of the unattractiveness of both *squaw* and *witch* is that they suggest old age, which in women is particularly undesirable. When I lived in Afghanistan (1967–1969), I was horrified to hear a proverb stating that where you see an old man you should sit down and take a lesson, but when you see an old woman you should throw a stone. I was equally startled when I went to compare the connotations of our two phrases *grandfatherly advice* and *old wives' tales.* Certainly it isn't expressed with the same force as in the Afghan proverb, but the implication is similar.

In some of the animal terms used for women the extreme unde-   35
sirability of female old age is also seen. For instance consider the unattractiveness of *old nag* as compared to *filly,* of *old crow* or *old bat* as compared to *bird,* and of being *catty* as compared to being *kittenish.* The chicken metaphor tells the whole story of a girl's life. In her youth she is a *chick,* then she marries and begins feeling *cooped up,* so she goes to *hen parties* where she *cackles* with her friends. Then she has her *brood* and begins to *henpeck* her husband. Finally she turns into *an old biddy.*

QUESTIONS ON CONTENT

1. What are the three main conclusions about sexism in the English language that Nilsen draws based on her study of the entries in a desk dictionary?

2. What point does Nilsen make about each of the following:
   a. English words derived from the name of a person
   b. geographical names
   c. pairs of words, one masculine and the other feminine
   d. the use of words referring to foods, plants, and animals in connection with women

e. the first names given to male and female infants
f. the use of *Ms.*
g. dictionary entries concerning famous women
h. positive and negative connotations connected with the concepts "masculine" and "feminine"

3. Like any attempt to change the status quo, women's attempts to change language have aroused a great deal of opposition. To what is this opposition reacting? Does the opposition seem justified? What techniques does the opposition employ?

QUESTIONS ON RHETORIC

1. What techniques does Nilsen use to support her conclusions? Is her evidence convincing? Why or why not?

2. What is the tone of this essay? How does Nilsen maintain this tone?

3. In essays of substantial length such as this one, short transitional paragraphs are often used to link the main sections of the essay. Identify two such paragraphs in Nilsen's article. Are they effective? When should they be used? When should they be avoided?

VOCABULARY

scoff	counterparts	shriveled
amoral	delectable	atypical
cognate	temperance	

CLASSROOM ACTIVITIES

1. In the sentences that follow, each of the italicized words is a generic term—that is, a term that supposedly refers to all people, male and female, that it designates. Explain why each of these uses is or is not sexist:
   a. My favorite anthropology course is "The Cultures of *Man.*"
   b. Over three hundred *bachelor's* degrees were awarded at the last commencement.
   c. "Madam *Chairman*," he said; "I protest the ruling of the chair."
   d. All *men* are created equal.
   e. Usually women executives are just *yesmen.*
   f. "Don't try to make me your *whipping boy*," Caroline protested.

NOTE: Writing assignments for "Prejudice and Language" appear on p. 226.

WRITING ASSIGNMENTS FOR "PREJUDICE AND LANGUAGE"

1. Members of a group often have different perceptions of the characteristics of that group from those held by outsiders. What is your own image of the racial, national, religious, and social groups to which you belong? How do nonmembers view these groups? Write an essay in which you compare the two images and attempt to account for the differences.

2. Write an essay in which you compare and/or contrast the discussions of prejudice and language by Allport and Hayakawa.

3. William Walter Duncan in his essay "How 'White' Is Your Dictionary?" has investigated the unabridged *Random House Dictionary of the English Language* and the *Funk & Wagnalls Standard College Dictionary*, but he says that what he has found holds true for other dictionaries as well. Examine two other dictionaries, see how they define *black* and *white*, and write a paper describing the results of your research. Is Duncan correct?

NOTE: Suggested topics for research papers appear on p. 293.

NOTABLE QUOTATIONS

The following quotations are drawn from the articles in this section. They are presented as additional topics for classroom discussion or for writing assignments.

"Most people are unaware of this basic law of language—that every label applied to a given person refers properly only to one aspect of his nature." *Allport*

"Especially in a culture where uniformity is prized, the name of *any* deviant carries with it *ipso facto* a negative value-judgment." *Allport*

"Until we label an out-group it does not clearly exist in our minds." *Allport*

"When symbols provoke strong emotions they are sometimes regarded no longer as symbols, but as actual things." *Allport*

"In dealing with subjects about which strong feelings exist, we are compelled to talk in roundabout terms if we wish to avoid arousing traditional prejudices, which hinder clear thinking." *Hayakawa*

"Sometimes it is necessary to violate verbal taboos as an aid to clearer thinking, but more often 'calling a spade a spade' is to provide our minds with a greased runway down which we may slide back into old and discredited patterns of evaluation and behavior." *Hayakawa*

"A dictionary is supposedly merely a record of what a language *was* at some point in the past." *Duncan*

"A well-accepted linguistic principle is that as culture changes so will the language." *Nilsen*

"If I were an anthropological linguist making observations about a strange and primitive tribe, I would duly note on my tape recorder that I had found linguistic evidence to show that in the area of sex and marriage the female appears to be more important than the male, but in all other areas of the culture, it seems that the reverse is true." *Nilsen*

VII
Censorship
and Taboos

1
Verbal Taboo

S. I. HAYAKAWA

S. I. Hayakawa, former president of San Francisco State University and currently a United States Senator from California, is one of the leading semanticists in this country. In this excerpt from Language in Thought and Action, *Hayakawa examines the world of verbal taboos, the phenomenon that occurs in almost all languages when the distinction between language and reality becomes confused.*

In every language there seem to be certain "unmentionables"— 1
words of such strong . . . connotations that they cannot be used in polite discourse. In English, the first of these to come to mind are, of course, words dealing with excretion and sex. We ask movie ushers and filling-station attendants where the "lounge" or "rest room" is, although we usually have no intention of lounging or resting. "Powder room" is another euphemism for the same facility, also known as "toilet," which itself is an earlier euphemism. Indeed, it is impossible in polite society to state, without having to resort to baby talk or a medical vocabulary, what a "rest room" is for. (It is "where you wash your hands.") Another term is "John." There is now a book on the best "Johns" in New York.

Money is another subject about which communication is in some 2
ways inhibited. It is all right to mention *sums* of money, such as $10,000 or $2.50. But it is considered in bad taste to inquire directly into other people's financial affairs, unless such an inquiry is really necessary in the course of business. When creditors send bills, they almost never mention money, although that is what they are writing about. There are many circumlocutions: "We beg to call your attention to what might be an oversight on your part." "We would appreciate your early attention to this matter." "May we look forward to an early remittance?"

The fear of death carries over, quite understandably in view of 3
the widespread confusion of symbols with things symbolized, into

fear of the *words* having to do with death. Many people, therefore, instead of saying "died," substitute such expressions as "passed away," "went to his reward," "departed," and "went west." In Japanese, the word for death, *shi,* happens to have the same pronunciation as the word for the number four. This coincidence results in many linguistically awkward situations, since people avoid "*shi*" in the discussion of numbers and prices, and use "*yon,*" a word of different origin, instead.

Words having to do with anatomy and sex—and words even   4 vaguely suggesting anatomical or sexual matters—have, especially in American culture, remarkable . . . connotations. Ladies of the nineteenth century could not bring themselves to say "breast" or "leg"—not even of chicken—so that the terms "white meat" and "dark meat" were substituted. It was thought inelegant to speak of "going to bed," and "to retire" was used instead. In rural America there are many euphemisms for the word "bull"; among them are "he-cow," "cow-critter," "male cow," "gentleman cow." But Americans are not alone in their delicacy about such matters. When D. H. Lawrence's first novel, *The White Peacock* (1911), was published, the author was widely and vigorously criticized for having used (in innocuous context) the word "stallion." "Our hearts are warm, our bellies are full" was changed to "Our hearts are warm, and we are full" in a 1962 presentation of the Rodgers and Hammerstein musical *Carousel* before the British Royal Family.

These verbal taboos, although sometimes amusing, also produce   5 serious problems, since they prevent frank discussion of sexual matters. Social workers, with whom I have discussed this question, report that young people of junior high school and high school age who contract venereal disease, become pregnant out of wedlock, and get into other serious trouble of this kind are almost always profoundly ignorant of the most elementary facts about sex and procreation. Their ignorance is apparently due to the fact that neither they nor their parents have a vocabulary with which to discuss such matters: the nontechnical vocabulary of sex is to them too coarse and shocking to be used, while the technical, medical vocabulary is unknown to them. The social workers find, therefore, that the first step in helping these young people is usually a linguistic one: the students have to be taught a vocabulary in which they can talk about their problems before they can be helped further.

The stronger verbal taboos have, however, a genuine social   6 value. When we are extremely angry and we feel the need of expressing our anger in violence, uttering these forbidden words provides us with a relatively harmless verbal substitute for going berserk and smashing furniture; that is, the words act as a kind of safety valve in our moments of crisis.

It is difficult to explain why some words should have such power-   7
ful . . . connotations. . . . Some of our verbal reticences, especially the religious ones, have the authority of the Bible: "Thou shalt not take the name of the Lord thy God in vain; for the Lord will not hold him guiltless that taketh his name in vain" (Exodus 21:7). "Gee," "gosh almighty," and "gosh darn" are ways to avoid saying "Jesus," "God Almighty," and "God damn"; and carrying the biblical injunction one step further, we also avoid taking the name of the Devil in vain by means of such expressions as "the deuce," "the dickens," and "Old Nick." It appears that among all the people of the world, among the civilized as well as the primitive, there is a feeling that the names of the gods are too holy, and the names of evil spirits too terrifying, to be spoken lightly.

The primitive confusion of word with thing, of symbol with thing   8
symbolized, manifests itself in some parts of the world in a belief that the name of a person is *part of* that person. To know someone's name, therefore, is to have power over him. Because of this belief, it is customary among some peoples for children to be given at birth a "real name" known only to the parents and never used, as well as a nickname or public name to be called by in society. In this way the child is protected from being put in anyone's power. The story of Rumpelstiltskin is a European illustration of this belief in the power of names. . . .

QUESTIONS ON CONTENT

1. Into what categories does Hayakawa classify taboo words? Give an example of each subject area.

2. According to Hayakawa, what problems result from the exist-ence of verbal taboos? Explain.

3. Hayakawa says that the "stronger taboos have . . . a genuine social value." What is it?

4. Discuss Hayakawa's statement that there is "widespread confu-sion of symbols with things symbolized."

QUESTIONS ON RHETORIC

1. Which sentence in paragraph 4 presents the controlling idea? How does Hayakawa support this idea?

2. How does Hayakawa make the transition between paragraphs 5 and 6? What other transitional devices does he use in this essay?

3. Hayakawa assumes that his readers are familiar with the story of Rumpelstiltskin, a children's classic, and therefore does not retell the story to make his point. Is Hayakawa's assumption correct? Do you know the story?

VOCABULARY

connotations	symbols	ignorant
euphemism	coincidence	
inhibited	anatomical	

CLASSROOM ACTIVITIES

1. In recent years "concerned citizens" across the country have attempted to remove the *Dictionary of American Slang* as well as certain recent desk dictionaries from schools and libraries. They have done so to keep their children from being exposed to taboo language. What underlying assumption about the relationship between words and things do such efforts reflect? If these citizens were successful in removing these books, would their children be protected? Why or why not?

NOTE: Writing assignments for "Censorship and Taboos" appear on p. 259.

2
Four-Letter Words Can Hurt You

BARBARA LAWRENCE

Barbara Lawrence, associate professor of humanities at the State University of New York at Old Westbury, defines "obscenity" and explains why she finds the obscene language some students use to be "implicitly sadistic or denigrating to women."

Why should any words be called obscene? Don't they all describe natural human functions? Am I trying to tell them, my students demand, that the "strong, earthy, gut-honest"—or, if they are fans of Norman Mailer, the "rich, liberating, existential"—language they use to describe sexual activity isn't preferable to "phony-sounding, middle-class words like 'intercourse' and 'copulate'?" "Cop You Late!" they say with fancy inflections and gagging grimaces. "Now, what is *that* supposed to mean?"

Well, what is it supposed to mean? And why indeed should one group of words describing human functions and human organs be acceptable in ordinary conversation and another, describing presumably the same organs and functions, be tabooed—so much so, in fact, that some of these words still cannot appear in print in many parts of the English-speaking world?

The argument that these taboos exist only because of "sexual hangups" (middle-class, middle-age, feminist), or even that they are a result of class oppression (the contempt of the Norman conquerors for the language of their Anglo-Saxon serfs), ignores a much more likely explanation, it seems to me, and that is the sources and functions of the words themselves.

The best known of the tabooed sexual verbs, for example, comes from the German *ficken,* meaning "to strike"; combined, according to Partridge's etymological dictionary *Origins,* with the Latin sexual verb *futuere*; associated in turn with the Latin *fustis,* "a staff or cudgel"; the Celtic *buc*, "a point, hence to pierce"; the Irish *bot*, "the male member"; the Latin *battuere*, "to beat"; the Gaelic *batair*, "a cudgeller"; the Early Irish *bualaim*, "I strike"; and so forth. It is one of what etymologists sometimes call "the sadistic group of words for the man's part in copulation."

The brutality of this word, then, and its equivalents ("screw," "bang," etc.), is not an illusion of the middle class or a crotchet of Women's Liberation. In their origins and imagery these words carry undeniably painful, if not sadistic, implications, the object of which is almost always female. Consider, for example, what a "screw" actually does to the wood it penetrates; what a painful, even mutilating, activity this kind of analogy suggests. "Screw" is particularly interesting in this context, since the noun, according to Partridge, comes from words meaning "groove," "nut," "ditch," "breeding sow," "scrofula" and "swelling," while the verb, besides its explicit imagery, has antecedent associations to "write on," "scratch," "scarify," and so forth—a revealing fusion of a mechanical or painful action with an obviously denigrated object.

Not all obscene words, of course, are as implicitly sadistic or denigrating to women as these, but all that I know seem to serve a similar purpose: to reduce the human organism (especially the female organism) and human functions (especially sexual and procreative) to their least organic, most mechanical dimension; to substitute a trivializing or deforming resemblance for the complex human reality of what is being described.

Tabooed male descriptives, when they are not openly denigrating to women, often serve to divorce a male organ or function from any significant interaction with the female. Take the word "testes," for example, suggesting "witnesses" (from the Latin *testis*) to the sexual and procreative strengths of the male organ; and the obscene counterpart of this word, which suggests little more than a mechanical shape. Or compare almost any of the "rich," "liberating" sexual verbs, so fashionable today among male writers, with that much-derided Latin word "copulate" ("to bind or join together") or even that Anglo-Saxon phrase (which seems to have had no trouble surviving the Norman Conquest) "make love."

How arrogantly self-involved the tabooed words seem in comparison to either of the other terms, and how contemptuous of the female partner. Understandably so, of course, if she is only a "skirt," a "broad," a "chick," a "pussycat" or a "piece." If she is, in other words, no more than her skirt, or what her skirt conceals; no more than a breeder, or the broadest part of her; no more than a piece of a human being or a "piece of tail."

The most severely tabooed of all the female descriptives, inci- 9
dentally, are those like a "piece of tail," which suggest (either explicitly or through antecedents) that there is no significant difference
between the female channel through which we are all conceived and
born and the anal outlet common to both sexes—a distinction that
pornographers have always enjoyed obscuring.

This effort to deny women their biological identity, their individ- 10
uality, their humanness, is such an important aspect of obscene
language that one can only marvel at how seldom, in an era preoccu-
pied with definitions of obscenity, this fact is brought to our attention. One problem, of course, is that many of the people in the best
position to do this (critics, teachers, writers) are so reluctant today
to admit that they are angered or shocked by obscenity. Bored,
maybe, unimpressed, aesthetically displeased, but—no matter how
brutal or denigrating the material—never angered, never shocked.

And yet how eloquently angered, how piously shocked many of 11
these same people become if denigrating language is used about any
minority group other than women; if the obscenities are racial or
ethnic, that is, rather than sexual. Words like "coon," "kike,"
"spic," "wop," after all, deform identity, deny individuality and
humanness in almost exactly the same way that sexual vulgarisms
and obscenities do.

No one that I know, least of all my students, would fail to ques- 12
tion the values of a society whose literature and entertainment
rested heavily on racial or ethnic pejoratives. Are the values of a
society whose literature and entertainment rest as heavily as ours on
sexual pejoratives any less questionable?

QUESTIONS ON CONTENT

1. How does Lawrence explain the existence of taboos?

2. According to Lawrence, what harmful purpose do all obscene
words serve? Explain.

3. Why does Lawrence, as a woman, object to obscene language?
Could men object to obscene language on the same grounds?

QUESTIONS ON RHETORIC

1. Lawrence begins her essay with a series of questions. What functions do these questions serve?

2. Lawrence consciously avoids using any "obscene" words.

What, in your opinion, is gained or lost as a result of this strategy? Explain.

3. Comment on Lawrence's use of the words which have been italicized in the following sentence:

> And yet how *eloquently* angered, how *piously* shocked many of these same people become if denigrating language is used about any minority group other than women.

4. Should paragraphs 11 and 12 be combined? Why do you feel Lawrence has made them separate paragraphs? Explain.

5. What is the effect of Lawrence's final question?

VOCABULARY

preferable	analogy	contemptuous
grimaces	antecedent	pejoratives
oppression	implicitly	

CLASSROOM ACTIVITIES

1. Discuss in class the pros and cons of the proposition that women's use of "liberated" language is self-defeating. Why, in your opinion, do some women make a point of using such language?

NOTE: Writing assignments for "Censorship and Taboos" appear on p. 259.

3
The Corporate Censor

NICHOLAS JOHNSON

Nicholas Johnson, a former FCC commissioner, directs our attention to censorship in America—to the deliberate withholding of information from the public. While the government has been responsible for much censorship in the past, Johnson exposes another area of censorship—that by large, politically influential corporations. Since certain information is "inconsistent with corporate profits," it is often suppressed. Moreover, too often the public's airwaves are so clogged with "intellectual pabulum" that no time remains for first-rate entertainment, social commentary, or coverage of public affairs. Although several of the issues that Johnson addresses in this essay have been resolved, corporate censorship is still a problem that demands our attention. Johnson calls for television programing that will satisfy the full range of needs, tastes, and interests of Americans.

Julian Goodman, president of NBC, believes that television "is now under threat of restriction and control." Frank Stanton, president of CBS, says that "attempts are being made to block us." Elmer Lower, president of ABC News, thinks we may "face the prospect of some form of censorship."

I agree. Censorship *is* a serious problem in our country. My only dispute with these network officials involves just *who* is doing the censoring. They apparently believe it's the government. I disagree.

NBC recently cut Robert Montgomery's statements off the air when, during the Johnny Carson show, he mentioned a CBS station being investigated by the Federal Communications Commission. Folk singer Joan Baez was silenced by CBS when she wished to express her views about the Selective Service System on the Smothers Brothers show. Now, of course, the entire show has been canceled—notwithstanding the high ratings and its writers' recent Emmy. Sure there's censorship. But let's not be fooled into mistaking its source.

For at the same time that network officials are keeping off your television screens anything they find inconsistent with their corporate profits or personal philosophies, the FCC has been repeatedly defending their First Amendment rights against government censorship. Just recently, for example, the FCC ruled—over strong protests—that the networks' coverage of the Chicago Democratic Convention was protected by the Constitution's "freedom of the press" clause. In other decisions, the Commission refused to penalize radio station WBAI in New York for broadcasting an allegedly anti-Semitic poem, or a CBS-owned station for televising a "pot party."

Many broadcasters are fighting, not for *free* speech, but for *profitable* speech. In the WBAI case, for example, one of the industry's leading spokesmen, *Broadcasting* magazine, actually urged that WBAI be *punished* by the FCC—and on the same editorial page professed outrage that stations might not have an unlimited right to broadcast profitable commercials for cigarettes which may result in illness or death.

This country is a great experiment. For close to 200 years we have been testing whether it is possible for an educated and informed people to govern themselves. All considered, the experiment has worked pretty well. We've had our frustrations and disappointments as a nation, but no one has been able to come up with a better system, and most of the newer nations still look to us as a model.

Central to our system, however, is the concept of an educated and an informed people. As Thomas Jefferson said: "The way to prevent error is to give the people full information of their affairs." Our founding fathers were familiar with censorship by the King of England. They were going to replace a king with a representative Congress. But they were concerned lest any American institution become powerful enough to impede the flow of information to the people. So they provided in the First Amendment that "*Congress* shall make no law . . . abridging the freedom of speech. . . ." Why "Congress"? I believe they assumed Congress would be the only body powerful enough to abridge free speech. They were wrong.

A lot has happened to the creation and control of information in this country since 1789. That was an age of town meetings and handbills. Today most information comes from the three broadcasting networks, ABC, CBS, and NBC, and the two wire services, Associated Press and United Press International. As Professor John Kenneth Galbraith has reminded us in *The New Industrial State,* 70 years ago the large corporation confined itself to mass production in heavy industry. "Now," he writes, "it also sells groceries, mills grain, publishes newspapers, and provides public entertainment, all activities that were once the province of the individual proprietor or the insignificant firm.''

It is easy for us to forget how large, profitable, and politically   9
powerful some corporations have become. In 1948 about half of all manufacturing assets in the United States were controlled by 200 corporations; today a mere 100 corporations hold that power. A single corporation such as American Telephone and Telegraph (one of the FCC's many regulated companies) controls the wages and working conditions of 870,000 employees, purchases each year some $3.5 billion in goods and services, has assets of $37 billion, and has annual gross revenues in excess of $14 billion. This gross revenue is several times larger than the combined budgets of all the federal regulatory commissions, the federal court system, and the U.S. Congress; larger than the budget of each of the 50 states; a larger operation, indeed, than all but very few foreign governments.

I am not suggesting that large corporations are inherently evil.   10
Not at all. They have created much of our wealth. I am merely urging that we be aware of the fact that large corporations have the incentive and the power to control the information reaching the citizenry of our free society.

Sometimes corporate pressures to control what you see on tele-   11
vision are just plain silly. For example, in his book *TV—The Big Picture,* Stan Opotowsky reports that "Ford deleted a shot of the New York skyline because it showed the Chrysler building. . . . A breakfast-food sponsor deleted the line 'She eats too much' from a play because, as far as the breakfast-food company was concerned, nobody could ever eat too much." Often, however, corporate tampering with the product of honest and capable journalists and creative writers and performers can be quite serious. Sometimes there is a deliberate alteration of content; sometimes needed information is squeezed out by more profitable "entertainment" programming.

On February 10, 1966, the Senate was conducting hearings on   12
the Vietnam war. Fred Friendly, who was president of CBS News at the time, wanted you to be able to watch those hearings. His network management did not permit you to watch. If you were watching CBS that day you saw, instead of George Kennan's views opposing the Vietnam war, the fifth rerun of *I Love Lucy.* Fred Friendly quit CBS because of this decision, and subsequently wrote *Due to Circumstances Beyond Our Control* to tell the story. He began his book with the quotation, "What the American people don't know can kill them." Indeed it can. In Vietnam, about 35,000 so far. We have been shown miles of film from Vietnam, it's true.

But how much has television told you about the multibillion-dollar corporate profits from that war?

There are many other situations in which censorship exists side-by-side with large profits—and disease or death. The tobacco industry spends about $250 million a year on radio and television commercials designed to associate cigarette smoking, especially by the young, with fishing, football, the fresh air of the great outdoors, sexual prowess, and all other desirable attributes of a fun-packed adult world. In exchange for this investment, the industry sells on the order of $9 billion worth of cigarettes a year. Would it really surprise you to learn that the broadcasting industry has been less than eager to tell you about the health hazards of cigarette smoking? It shouldn't. Just recently, for example, a United States congressman alleged that the president of the National Association of Broadcasters had suppressed from Congress and the American public revealing information about the "substantial appeal to youth" of radio and television cigarette commercials. The relation of this forgetfulness to profits is clear: cigarette advertising provides the largest single source of television's revenue, about 8 percent. 13

The FCC has ruled that broadcasters can't present one point of view on a controversial issue and censor all others just to serve their own beliefs and profits. The "Fairness Doctrine" requires that all viewpoints be presented. The FCC applied this doctrine to cigarette commercials. And what was the response of the broadcasting industry? It fought the decision with all the economic and political strength at its command. It has finally gone all the way to the Supreme Court to argue that a doctrine which limits its power to keep *all* information about the health hazards of cigarette smoking from the American people is a violation of broadcasters' First Amendment rights! 14

Or how about the 50,000 people who die each year on our highways? Their deaths are due to many causes, of course, including their own intoxication and carelessness. But how many television stations told you—either before or after Ralph Nader came along—that most auto-safety engineers agree virtually *all* those lives could be saved if our cars were designed properly? Nader, in *Unsafe at Any Speed*, speculates about the "impact which the massive sums spent ($361,060,000 in 1964 on auto advertising alone) have on the communications media's attention to vehicle safety design." 15

Television certainly didn't take the lead in telling us about the unfit meat, fish, and poultry. (Chet Huntley was found to have been editorializing *against* the Wholesome Meat Act at a time when he 16 and his business partners were heavy investors in the cattle and meat business!) Bryce Rucker, in *The First Freedom,* notes that:

> Networks generally have underplayed or ignored events and statements unfavorable to food processors and soap manufacturers. Recent examples are the short shrift given Senate subcommittee hearings on, and comments favorable to, the 1966 "truth in packaging" bill and the high cost of food processing. Could it be that such behavior reflects concern for the best interests of, say, the top-50 grocery-products advertisers, who spent $1,314,893,000 in TV in 1965, 52.3 percent of TV's total advertising income?

What could be more essential than information about potentially harmful food and drugs?

All Americans are concerned about "the crime problem." Have you ever stopped to wonder why the only crimes most of us hear about are, in the words of the Presidential Commission on Law Enforcement and Administration of Justice, "the crimes that are the easiest for the poor and the disadvantaged to commit . . ."? What we haven't been told is that much of the crime in the United States is "white collar" crime; that the rich steal as much as or more than the poor. As the crime commission report defined it:

> The "white collar" criminal is the broker who distributes fraudulent securities, the builder who deliberately uses defective material, the corporation executive who conspires to fix prices, the legislator who peddles his influence and vote for private gain, or the banker who misappropriates funds. . . .

Did you ever find out from television, for example, that a *single* recent price-fixing case involved a "robbery" from the American people of more money than was taken in *all* the country's robberies, burglaries, and larcenies during the years of that criminal price fixing? The crime commission declared that "it is essential that the public become aware of the seriousness of business crime." Why is it the news media do not tell you about *these* threats to "law and order"?

One could go on and on. The inherent dangers in cyclamates (the artificial sweeteners in soft drinks) have been so widely discussed in Sweden that the government is considering prohibiting their use. The danger is scarcely known to the average American. Most of the nation's 160,000 coal miners have "black lung" disease (the disintegration of the lung from coal dust) in one form or another. Mine operators may refuse to pay for fresh-air masks—or support workmen's compensation legislation. Some television stations in coal-mining areas have, until recently, refused to televise programs offered them by doctors about this serious health hazard. Reports differ, and no one knows for sure, but one current sampling showed that 20 percent of the color-TV sets studied were emitting excess X-ray radiation. Natural-gas pipelines are exploding as predicted. And did you know that the life expectancy of the average American adult male has been *declining* in recent years? The list goes on almost without end.

Note what each of these items has in common: (1) human death, disease, dismemberment or degradation, (2) great profit for manufacturers, advertisers, and broadcasters, and (3) the deliberate withholding of needed information from the public. [19]

Many pressures produce such censorship. Some are deliberate, some come about through default. But all have come, not from government, but from private corporations with something to sell. Charles Tower, chairman of the National Association of Broadcasters Television Board, recently wrote a letter to *The New York Times* criticizing its attack on CBS for "censoring" the social commentary on the Smothers Brothers show. He said, [20]

> There is a world of difference between the deletion of program material by Government command and the deletion by a private party [such as a broadcaster]. . . . Deletion by Government command is censorship. . . . Deletion of material by private parties . . . is not censorship.

Another *Times* reader wrote in answer to Mr. Tower: "Mr. Tower's distinction . . . is spurious. The essence of censorship is the suppression of a particular point of view . . . over the channels of the mass media, and the question of who does the censoring is one of form only. . . ."

He's right. The results *are* the same. You and I are equally kept in ignorance, ill-prepared to "prevent error," and to engage in the process of self-governing which Thomas Jefferson envisioned—regardless of who does the censoring. [21]

A number of talented people *within* the broadcasting industry recognize its failings. One of the nation's leading black announcers told me of his first job as a disc jockey. He was handed a stack of records, but forbidden to read any news over the air. Said his boss: "You're not going to educate the Negroes of this community at my expense." A high ABC network executive was recently quoted in the pages of *TV Guide* as saying, "There are many vital issues that we won't go near. We censor ourselves." Eric Sevareid has said of the pressures involved in putting together a network news show: "The ultimate sensation is that of being bitten to death by ducks." And the executive editor of the San Francisco *Chronicle* has warned: "The press is in danger. Not the exciting kind of Holly- [22]

wood danger, but of dissolving into a gray mass of nonideas." For it is also a form of censorship to so completely clog the public's airwaves with tasteless gruel that there is no time left for quality entertainment and social commentary, no time "to give the people full information of their affairs." Mason Williams, the multitalented one-time writer for the Smothers Brothers, has left television in disgust and written a poem about his experiences with "The Censor," who, he says in conclusion,

> Snips out
> The rough talk
> The unpopular opinion
> Or anything with teeth
> And renders
> A pattern of ideas
> Full of holes
> A doily
> For your mind

Your mind. My mind. The mind of America.
The Rolling Stones said it long ago: 23

> When I'm drivin' in my car,
> When the man comes on the radio,
> He's tellin' me more and more
> About some useless information . . .
> Supposed to fire my imagination? . . .
> I can't get no satisfaction!*

Many Americans are trying to say something to each other. But the media haven't been listening. And you haven't been told. So some have turned to violence as a means of being heard. All you've been shown are the dramatic pictures; you know there's "something happening." But, like the Everyman of Bob Dylan's song, "You don't know what it is, do you, Mr. Jones?" The "silent screen" of television has left you in ignorance as to what it's all about.

The time may soon come when the media will have to listen.   24
From many directions come suggestions for change. Law professor Jerome Barron says the courts should recognize a "public right of access to the mass media." Free speech in this age of television, he believes, requires that citizens with something to say be permitted to say it over radio and television. Suppose you approach a television station with a "commercial" you have prepared either supporting or protesting the President's conduct of the Vietnamese war. It may no

*Copyright © Immediate Music Inc. 1965. Written by Mick Jagger & Keith Richards. Used by permission. All rights reserved. International copyright secured.

longer be sufficient for the station to say to you, "Sorry, we don't like your views, so we won't broadcast your announcement"—as a San Francisco station did last year to those trying to express their point of view regarding a *ballot proposition!* As the U.S. Supreme Court said a few days ago in the Red Lion case, upholding the constitutionality of the FCC's Fairness Doctrine:

> There is no sanctuary in the First Amendment for unlimited private censorship operating in a medium not open to all. Freedom of the press from governmental interference under the First Amendment does not sanction repression of that freedom by private interests.

It is too early to know the full, ultimate impact of this decision.

In Holland, any group that can get 15,000 persons to support its   25
list of proposed programs is awarded free time on the Dutch Television Network for a monthly program. There is even an organization for tiny and often eccentric splinter groups without 15,000 supporters. If a similar experiment were conducted in this country, groups interested in electronic music, drag racing, handicrafts, camping, as well as the League of Women Voters, the National Association for the Advancement of Colored People, local school boards, theater and drama associations, the Young Republicans (and, who knows, even the Smothers Brothers), could obtain television time to broadcast programs prepared under their supervision.

Or each network might devote a full one-third of its prime time   26
(6 P.M. to 11 P.M.) programing to something other than entertainment or sports. It could be nonsponsored cultural, educational, and public-affairs programing; if the networks were required to stagger such fare, then at any given time during the 6 P.M. to 11 P.M. period of greatest audiences the American viewer would have an alternative, a *choice.* There would still be at all times *two* networks with the commercial-laden, lowest-common-denominator mass entertainment of situation comedies, Westerns, quiz shows and old movies. The third, however, would have something else.

It would be wholly inappropriate for me as an FCC Commis-   27
sioner to insist that broadcasters present only the information, ideas, and entertainment that I personally find compatible. The FCC does not have, and would not want, the responsibility of selecting your television programs. But it would be equally irresponsible for me to sit idly by and watch the corporate censors keep from your TV screen the full range of needs, tastes, and interests of the American people.

The television-station owner, not the network, has ultimate re- 28
sponsibility for his programing. But somebody has to select his
programs, you say; nobody's perfect. You're right. And all I'm
urging is that, when in doubt, all of us—audience, networks, and
government—ought to listen a little more carefully to the talented
voices of those who are crying out to be heard. In short, I would far
rather leave the heady responsibility for the inventory in America's
"marketplace of ideas" to talented and uncensored *individuals*—
creative writers, performers, and journalists from *all* sections of this
great country—than to the *committees* of frightened financiers in
New York City. Wouldn't you? I think so.

QUESTIONS ON CONTENT

1. Since television cannot possibly report on everything that happens in the world, just as no individual can experience everything,
what, then, constitutes censorship? How does it differ from selectiv-
ity? Why is it undesirable?

2. By Johnson's definition, does not the FCC itself act as a
"censor"? Are there important differences between the censorship
practiced by the FCC and that practiced by large corporations? If
so, what are these differences?

3. Why, according to Johnson, do network officials keep certain
statements or portions of shows from the public? Explain.

4. Writing in 1969, Johnson claimed that the media did little to
publicize "white collar" crime. Has the situation changed since
then? Explain.

5. Are there contemporary issues other than those Johnson discusses that you feel are not adequately explored by the media?
Explain.

QUESTIONS ON RHETORIC

1. How does Johnson define censorship? Why is it not necessary for
him to give his readers a formal definition of the concept?

2. What types of information does Johnson use to substantiate his
argument?

3. Johnson makes frequent use of the short sentence in his essay.
Locate six examples of short sentences and explain the function of
each within the context of the paragraph in which it appears.

VOCABULARY

dispute	revenue	degradation
impede	sponsor	eccentric
proprietor	doctrine	

CLASSROOM ACTIVITIES

1. Public school teachers experience a great deal of pressure from various groups to exclude books from classroom use. Some of the most frequently assailed books are *The Catcher in the Rye, The Inner City Mother Goose, Soul on Ice, Huckleberry Finn, 1984, The Grapes of Wrath, Gulliver's Travels,* and, more recently, *Jonathan Livingston Seagull, The Bell Jar,* and *Go Ask Alice.* Probably some of these books have been read by members of your class. Discuss some possible reasons why these books might have been and continue to be attacked. How justified are the attacks?

2. The following news item appeared in the *Burlington Free Press* on June 4, 1977:

'Nigger' Can Be Erased in Maine

AUGUSTA, Maine (AP)—Names such as Nigger Hill and Nigger Island could be erased from the Maine map under a new law approved Friday by Gov. James B. Longley.

Longley signed a measure into law which allows people to complain to the Maine Human Rights Commission when they feel that the use of the term "nigger" in the name of a geographic site is offensive.

About 10 geographic features in Maine—hills, brooks and islands—include the term.

Rep. Gerald Talbot, D-Portland, the state's only black lawmaker, introduced the bill after he said he tried in vain to have the names changed by other means.

His measure originally called for banning the use of any name which is offensive to a nationality or racial group, but lawmakers amended the bill when they said it was too broad.

They said the original plan could have been extended to include terms such as "squaw."

The law will take effect in the fall.

Discuss in class whether this is an example of censorship or a sincere attempt to eradicate prejudice. In your opinion, was the law as originally proposed "too broad"? Why or why not?

NOTE: Writing assignments for "Censorship and Taboos" appear on p. 259.

4

Obscenity—
Forget It

CHARLES REMBAR

In the following essay, Charles Rembar, "an attorney who helped win land-mark decisions against censorship in the 1960s," presents his thoughts on what constitutes obscenity. Throughout the essay the author reiterates the idea that recent questions about obscenity are more properly questions that should be dealt with by laws other than those involving the First Amendment to the Constitution. Charles Rembar practices law in New York and is the author of two books: The End of Obscenity *and* Perspective.

There is, rather suddenly, a resurgence of interest in the legal field that goes by the name "obscenity." Not that it ever lacked for interest. The conjunction of sex and politics is irresistible. But now there is more than interest; there is consternation—on the part of those who fear for our morality, on the part of those who fear the First Amendment will founder on the convictions of Harry Reems and Larry Flynt.

I suggest we abandon the word obscenity. I do not mean that the law should ignore all the many and varied things that legislatures and courts have tried to deal with under this rubric. My suggestion rather is that we drop the word and turn our attention to the social interests actually involved. Then, perhaps, some sensible law-making and law enforcement will follow.

The law is verbal art. It depends for its effectiveness on compact, muscular words; overgrown, flabby words are useless in the law, worse than useless—confusing, damaging. "Obscene" as a description of the morally outrageous or the intellectually monstrous continues to be useful (and generally has little to do with sex). "Obscene" for legal purposes should be discarded altogether. It carries an impossible burden of passionate conviction from both sides of the question. And it diverts attention from real issues. The present litigation over what is called obscenity involves serious public concerns which the word obscures and distorts.

Draw back a bit. Exactly eleven years ago a battle against literary censorship came to a close. What had been censored, for three hundred years, was called, in law, obscenity. Obscenity in its traditional sense—impermissible writing about sex, impermissible either because of what it described or because of the words that were used —was at an end. Writers would be able to write as they pleased on the subject of sex, and use whatever language they thought best. They would no longer have to keep a mind's eye on the censor: they could pay full attention to their art and ideas. The field of legal struggle would move to other forms of expression—films, the stage, television, photography.

So much has changed in the last eleven years that one who had not lived through earlier times would find the freedom that writers now enjoy unremarkable. Yet in the few decades just then ended, such works as Dreiser's *An American Tragedy*, Lillian Smith's *Strange Fruit*, and Edmund Wilson's *Memoirs of Hecate County* had been the subjects of successful criminal prosecution. Recently, in contrast, there has been no suppression of books at all. Obscenity prosecutions are now directed at motion pictures and stage performances and magazines (the last not for their words but for their pictures).

The contest concluded in 1966 was essentially between accepted sexual morality (which sought to govern what was expressed as well as what was done) and the guaranties of the First Amendment. The books declared obscene had been attacked and suppressed for a double reason: because, in the view of the ruling group, they induced immoral behavior, and because their open publication was immoral in itself. The very first brief in the very first case of the series that changed the law—the trial of *Lady Chatterley*—put the question this way: "Should the courts chain creative minds to the dead center of convention at a given moment in time?" Conventional sexual morality was what was meant and understood.

Whether or not you agree with the view of those who sought to preserve morality by limiting speech and writing, obscenity as a legal concept was a fair description of what they objected to. It had been attacked as indefinable, but it was no harder to define, no vaguer, perhaps less vague, than other concepts the law engages every day—"the reasonable person," for example, or "good faith," not to mention "fair trial." Its scope had varied over the years, but that is true of all legal concepts. The important point for present purposes is that however uncertain its boundaries, the legal term "obscenity" served a specific social goal.

The real difficulty—which had not been suggested as a difficulty 8 until the twentieth century was well under way—was that the pursuit of the goal might run afoul of the First Amendment. Among the things settled in the series of cases that culminated in the *Fanny Hill* decision was that the attempt to enforce these moral standards through anti-obscenity laws must yield to the Amendment.

The First Amendment protects speech and press. Not all speech 9 and press; there are some exceptions—information helpful to an enemy in wartime, for example, or fraudulent statements to induce the purchase of stocks and bonds. (And even speech and press protected by the First Amendment remain subject to some regulation. You may not, without municipal permission, choose to hold a meeting in the middle of a busy street and proclaim your thoughts while traffic waits.) But obscenity is no longer an exception to freedom of speech and press in the traditional meaning of those terms. And it ought not be an exception for speech and press more broadly defined—communication in general.

"Suppress," however, means throttle altogether. Even the lib- 10 eral justices of the present Supreme Court, the dissenters from the Burger view, have allowed that expression can be in certain ways restricted. That is, the citizen who has something he wishes to communicate may not be silenced completely—he can be as obscene about it as he likes—but the flow of his expression can be channeled. These liberal justices have said that the First Amendment is not infringed by anti-obscenity laws that seek to safeguard children or to prevent the infliction of unwanted displays on a captive audience.

Another limitation on expression occurs when expression is 11 mixed with action. Consider the poor soul arrested for indecent exposure. No doubt he has something to communicate, if it is only "look at me," but what he does is also an act, and there is no possibility the Supreme Court would preclude the prosecution of the flasher on the theory that he is only invoking First Amendment rights.

The most libertarian of our justices, Hugo Black and William 12 Douglas, carved out and set aside "action brigaded with expression." Even while they were advancing their thesis that the First Amendment must be given an "absolute" construction—that speech and the press must be subject to no restraint whatever—they said that when behavior was involved, a different question was presented. The situation must be analyzed to determine which element, action or expression, can be said to dominate. The control of conduct has never been restricted by the First Amendment. Indeed, the control of conduct is the primary business of government. The prosecution of Harry Reems, actor in *Deep Throat,* poses an interesting problem. The film was made in Florida, where the actors performed their acts: Reems was prosecuted in Tennessee, a place where the film was shown. Behavior more than expression? In Florida maybe, it seems to me; in Tennessee, no.

It is in these three fields that legitimate problems remain—the protection of children, the unwilling audience, and action mixed with expression. In each instance, however, we would do better to use legal concepts other than obscenity. 13

When we are dealing with behavior rather than expression, the only question is what kind of behavior we ought to regulate— whether, for instance, any kind of private sex between (or among) consenting adults should be prohibited. The answer does not involve the First Amendment. Laws controlling conduct rather than communication, as we have seen, do not infringe freedom of speech or press. 14

The most prominent current topic on which this distinction may help arises from municipal efforts to deal with the ugly sore of commercial sex—Boston's delimitation of its "Combat Zone," Detroit's recently upheld dispersal ordinance, New York's attempt to restore the center of Manhattan to something like what it used to be. Prostitution, with its corollary crimes, is present. So are pornographic book stores. So are hard-core films. We tend to treat them as though they all present a single legal problem. They do not. Prostitution is behavior, not expression. Whether it should be licensed, or simply decriminalized, or continue to be prosecuted, is a troubling question, but it has nothing to do with the First Amendment. Prostitution is clearly on the conduct side of the conduct-expression divide. 15

But films and books and magazines are on the other side, and here the other concepts enter, and another distinction. We must distinguish between the willing audience and the captive audience. You can say or write or show what you please, but only to those who are willing to listen, or read, or view. *Tropic of Cancer* printed in volume form is one thing; *Tropic of Cancer* blared out by bullhorn in a public square is quite another. The right to express oneself is not the right to intrude expression on those who do not want it. 16

Privacy has been recognized as a constitutional right. It is ac- 17 tually a cluster of rights, one of which is the right to be let alone. Exhibition inside theaters is in this sense private; no one is compelled to enter. The same for books and magazines; no one is forced to read them. But once the stuff spills onto the streets—on theater marquees or posters, in storefront windows or newsstand displays—the privacy of those outside is assaulted. The liberty of those who like pornography is not inconsistent with the liberty of those who don't. Neither should be constrained by law—the one denied the means to gratify his voyeurism, the other forced to share it. If the people wish to forbid public exhibition of certain kinds—exhibition which dismays some of those who are trying to enjoy their clear right to use the streets and sidewalks free of assault—there is no First Amendment reason that ought to stand in the way. It need not be labeled obscenity. What is thrust upon the passerby can be regulated because the citizens feel it is disagreeable or offensive or unhealthy—that is, if there are enough such citizens so that under our democratic processes they constitute a majority.

Privacy is the modern idea that inheres in this situation. An ancient legal idea reinforces it. It is the traditional and useful and sensible idea of nuisance. In New York, 42nd Street constitutes a public nuisance. No need to cogitate and strain over whether the displays are obscene. Let the movies be shown in the theaters, but restrict, if the voters wish, what appears on their marquees. Let the magazines be sold—let the pimps to masturbators think of themselves as publishers—but keep their product off the front of newsstands.[1]

---

[1] These paragraphs may raise two questions in the reader's mind. I have stressed, in other writings, that the safeguards of the First Amendment are designed for minority views: there would be no need for the amendment if all we wanted to protect was what the majority deemed acceptable. Hence the references above to "a majority" and to "what the people wish" may seem, if one reads too quickly, rather odd. The answer is that these paragraphs deal with situations to which, if the prescription is followed, the First Amendment does not extend. And I am referring to the kind of thing at which anti-obscenity laws are aimed, not to political speech.

The second question is, How do you do it? How do you provide for the permission to publish and the prohibition of display—the permission to exhibit in closed theaters and the control of what is out on the street? Fifty difficult hypotheticals can be rattled off in fifty minutes. But this is true of almost any statutory regulation. Laws are hard to apply and enforce; this does not mean we should not have them. When, for instance, does merger become monopoly? When does an efficient business arrangement become restraint of trade? The fact that these are large, perplexing questions, which spawn thousands of more perplexing little questions, does not mean we ought not have our antitrust laws. To deal with all the legal questions my proposals might bring in their train would require a legal treatise. This short piece is necessarily elliptical, and I am not trying to draft the statutes. But I believe such statutes can be drawn, and enforced with fair success.

Finally, child abuse. Although there is disagreement about *how*   19
their cultural environment affects the emotional development of
children, there is consensus that the environment is a powerful factor. (If the reader of this piece has a liberal bent, it may help his
thinking on the subject to concentrate not on sex but on violence.) A
legislative effort to shield the child from certain representations of
sex (or violence) does not, in the view of the justices most concerned with freedom, infringe the First Amendment. Nor does the
legislature have to prove that ill effects inevitably flow from what it
prohibits. Since the First Amendment is not involved, the only constitutional inhibition is the due process clause, and there the test is
not whether the legislature is absolutely right, or even sure of the
efficacy of its statute. The test is whether there is a rational basis for
its concern, and whether what it tries to do about it is not altogether
foolish. The established constitutional formula for testing legislation
against the due process clause is that it not be "arbitrary and
unreasonable."

It is not arbitrary or unreasonable for the legislature to conclude   20
that inducing children to engage in sexual activity can harm them.
Nor is it arbitrary or unreasonable to prohibit the photographing of
children who have been induced to do so, or to interdict the publication and sale of magazines in which the photographs appear. The
publisher and the seller are principals in the abuse. Without them, it
would not occur.

There is also abuse of children in another situation—where the   21
child is audience rather than subject. Here television is the prime
subject of concern; children are overexposed to what comes
through the tube. It will not do to say the family should exercise
control. Pious introductions warning of "mature theme" and advice
to exercise "parental guidance" are stupid, unless they are cleverly
meant to be self-defeating, and in either event they are revolting. If
the children are not watching, the caveat has no purpose; if the
children are watching, the caveat is a lure. This is obscenity in its
larger, nonlegal sense.

Our habits have come to the point where the family in the home   22
is the captive audience par excellence. Neither the child's own judgment nor, as a practical matter, the authority of parents can make
effective choices. A legislative attempt to control the content of
television programs that had a reasonable basis in the aim to safeguard children would not violate the Constitution.

Our most liberal justices have pointed out that the world of the   23
child is not the world of the adult, and efforts to limit expression
have a special place where children are concerned. (Broadcasters

who resist control are making a claim to be free in the sense the right wing often uses—freedom to exploit monopolies.) Here again the standard is not obscenity.

Apart from these three fields, the First Amendment demands [24] that we must put up with a lot of what is disagreeable or even damaging. The point made by feminists—that porno films and magazines demean and exploit women—is a strong one. (It is even stronger than they think: the things they object to demean and exploit all people.) But the First Amendment, I believe, requires that we let the material be produced and published. So long as expression is involved and intrusion is not, and there is no question of child abuse, our arguments should be addressed not to the courts but to the producers and sellers of entertainment. That is not an entirely futile effort. The public can be affected by these arguments, and it is the public after all that makes the selling of entertainment a profitable venture. To the extent that these arguments do not prevail, we must accept the fact that the freedoms guaranteed by the First Amendment are costly freedoms. Very costly. Worth the cost, I would say.

The First Amendment has lately had to contend with more than [25] its old enemies. The effectiveness of any law—including our fundamental law, the Constitution—depends on the people's perception of it. The prime example of a law destroyed because too many saw it as fatuous was Prohibition. Freedom of the press has trouble enough as an operating concept—as distinguished from an incantation—without having to defend itself from those who like to call themselves its friends.

The voguish furor about anti-obscenity laws diminishes the public perception of the First Amendment in two ways. One is the [26] silliness—calculated or naive—of so many who rush to grab and wave the First Amendment banner. Lawyers defend topless bars with phrases out of *Areopagitica.* Blind to the fact that all constitutional law is a matter of degree, an actor solemnly proclaims: "Today Harry Reems, tomorrow Helen Hayes." Fatheadedness rarely helps a cause.

The other source of debilitation is a sort of constitutional imperialism. Freedom of expression is not our only liberty. It is, to my [27] mind, our most important liberty, the basis of all others. But it is part of an entire structure. It is entitled to no imperium; it must democratically live with other guaranties and rights.

The First Amendment has serious work to do. Invoked too often [28] and too broadly, it can grow thin and feeble. The restrictions I suggest are minimal, and specific, and—with the anachronistic concept of obscenity discarded—they allow more freedom than the courts have granted up to now. And, I think, they may help to avoid a dangerous dilution of First Amendment guaranties.

POSTSCRIPT

People to whom I have broached the idea submitted in this essay   29
have asked about its evolution. What goes on in the mind of a lawyer who once attacked obscenity laws so hard and now suggests legal restrictions on some of the things that are commonly called "obscene"?

A novelist, speaking from the feminist side, reads me an essay   30
she is doing. It mentions "Charles Rembar, the attorney who escorted Lady Chatterley and Fanny Hill to their triumphant American debuts, thereby unwittingly spreading his cloak—and ours—in the muddy path for a pack of porno hustlers." Not *unwittingly*, I say, and then I quote from *The End of Obscenity:*

> The current uses of the new freedom are not all to the good. There is an acne on our culture. Books enter the best-seller lists distinguished only by the fact that once they would have put their publishers in jail. Advertising plays upon concupiscence in ways that range from foolish to fraudulent. Theatre marquees promise surrogate thrills, and the movies themselves, even some of the good ones, include "daring" scenes— "dare" is a child's word—that have no meaning except at the box office. Television commercials peddle sex with an idiot slyness.

Among the lesser detriments of the new freedom is the deteriora-   31
tion of the television situation comedy, an art form that has not been altogether bad and has had, indeed, high moments. It suffers now from a blue-brown flood of double-meaning jokes, stupidities accompanied by high cackles from the studio audience. (How do they gather those people? Or is it only a Moog synthesizer?) On the other hand, among the more important benefits are the intelligent discussions, on television, of subjects that could not be publicly discussed before; it is difficult to remember, but a documentary on birth control could not have been aired some years ago. Also, just possibly, a new and wonderful trend in journalism: It may no longer be feasible to sustain a bad newspaper by loading it with leers; since sex stories are much less shocking today, the old circulation formula may be hard to work.

Do the suggestions I make jeopardize the freedom won eleven   32
years ago? I think not. In fact, in terms of what may be suppressed,

they expand it. The freedom was won for the printed word; for other forms of expression, the decisions carried implications of greater liberty than had theretofore been enjoyed, though not as complete as writers would enjoy. In arguing the cases, I said that not all media were the same, and called attention to the points that underlie the approach outlined above—the protection of children, the problem of action mixed with expression, and one's right not to be compelled to constitute an audience. (Don't pluck my sleeve as I am passing by, stop poking your finger on my chest; freedom includes freedom from your assailing my senses—these are fair demands that books don't interfere with.)

All that is new in my position is the proposal that we come to the   33
end of obscenity in another sense and turn our attention to the things society may rightfully care about.

The proposal is made with the thought that it can make the First   34
Amendment stronger.

QUESTIONS ON CONTENT

1. What does Rembar mean when he says "The law is verbal art"?

2. On what basis does Rembar argue that " 'obscene' for legal purposes should be discarded altogether"?

3. What changes have taken place in obscenity prosecutions in the past eleven years?

4. What exceptions are there to the rights we enjoy under the First Amendment? Give some examples.

5. In what three fields do "legitimate problems" regarding obscenity remain?

6. What does Rembar feel is "stupid" about warnings such as "mature theme" and "parental guidance"?

QUESTIONS ON RHETORIC

1. What is Rembar's thesis? Where is it stated?

2. Why is it essential that Rembar clearly define terms such as *obscenity, privacy,* and *suppress* in the essay? Explain.

3. What is the function of paragraph 13?

4. What is the meaning of Rembar's title, and where does he reveal its significance?

VOCABULARY

consternation	infliction	exploit
distorts	gratify	intrusion
fraudulent	consensus	jeopardize
	inevitably	

CLASSROOM ACTIVITIES

1. The following note, first published in *Time* (December 11, 1972), is another example of censorship, this time from an unexpected quarter:

Bowdler in Oregon

Some American place names have a unique resonance about them—places like Maggie's Nipples, Wyo., or Greasy Creek, Ark., Lickskillet, Ky., or Scroungeout, Ala. Collectors of Americana also savor Braggadocio, Mo., the Humptulips River in Washington, Hen Scratch, Fla., Dead Irishman Gulch, S. Dak., Cut 'N Shoot, Texas, Helpmejack Creek, Ark., Bastard Peak, Wyo., Goon Dip Mountain, Ark., Tenstrike, Minn., Laughing Pig, Wyo., Two Teats, Calif., or Aswaguscawadic, Me.

Not the least flavorsome was a sylvan place called Whorehouse Meadows, outside of Ontario, Ore. The meadow was named, with admirable directness, for some local women who once profitably entertained sheepherders there. But last week, the Oregon Geographic Names Board filed an official objection to a bit of bowdlerization by the Federal Bureau of Land Management. It discovered that the bureau, in drawing up a map of the area, had changed the name from Whorehouse Meadows to Naughty Girl Meadows. The bureau also cleaned up a nearby spot, deftly retitling it Bullshirt Springs, a change so small that the natives see no reason to contest it.

How are places and landmarks named? Why are some names more colorful than others? What is lost in the name changes mentioned in the *Time* article?

WRITING ASSIGNMENTS FOR "CENSORSHIP AND TABOOS"

1. Write an essay in which you compare and contrast the analysis of taboo words by Hayakawa and Lawrence.

2. Write an essay in which you attempt to persuade your reader either that censorship is never justifiable or that it is sometimes justifiable.

3. The names of cities. towns, rivers, and mountains, in addition to providing clues to settlement and migration patterns, reflect local history. After examining a map of your state or region, select six colorful place names and write an essay in which you discuss the origin of each name and what it tells of local history.

NOTE: Suggested topics for research papers appear on p. 293.

NOTABLE QUOTATIONS

The following quotations are drawn from the articles in this section. They are presented as additional topics for classroom discussion or for writing assignments.

"Money is another subject about which communication is in some ways inhibited." *Hayakawa*

"The stronger verbal taboos have . . . a genuine social value." *Hayakawa*

"Why should any words be called obscene? Don't they all describe natural human functions?" *Lawrence*

"Many broadcasters are fighting, not for *free* speech, but for *profitable* speech." *Johnson*

"I believe [our founding fathers] assumed Congress would be the only body powerful enough to abridge free speech. They were wrong." *Johnson*

"For it is also a form of censorship to so completely clog the public's air waves with tasteless gruel that there is no time left for quality entertainment and social commentary, no time to 'give the people full information of their affairs.'"   *Johnson*

"I suggest we abandon the word obscenity."   *Rembar*

"The law is verbal art."   *Rembar*

"Pious introductions warning of 'mature theme' and advice to exercise 'parental guidance' are stupid, unless they are cleverly meant to be self-defeating, and in either event they are revolting."   *Rembar*

VIII
Poems on Language

1 | Some Frenchmen

JOHN UPDIKE (1932-   )

Monsieur Etienne de Silhouette*
  Was slim and uniformly black;
His profile was superb, and yet
  He vanished when he turned his back.

Humane and gaunt, precise and tall
  Was Docteur J. I. Guillotin; †
He had one tooth, diagonal
  And loose, which, when it fell, spelled *fin*.

André Marie Ampère, ‡ a spark,
  Would visit other people's homes
And gobble volts until the dark
  Was lit by his resisting ohms.

Another type, Daguerre (Louis), §
  In silver salts would soak his head,
Expose himself to light, and be
  Developed just in time for bed.

* 1709–1767
† 1738–1814
‡ 1775–1836
§ 1789–1851

FOR DISCUSSION

1. In each stanza of this poem, Updike concerns himself with a Frenchman. What is the importance of each man? What do they all have in common?

2. Explain why Updike's wording is more appropriate than the following substitutions:

thin for *slim*
all for *uniformly*
crooked for *diagonal*
end for *fin*
show for *expose*

2 | The Naked and the Nude

ROBERT GRAVES (1895-   )

For me, the naked and the nude
(By lexicographers construed
As synonyms that should express
The same deficiency of dress
Or shelter) stand as wide apart
As love from lies, or truth from art.

Lovers without reproach will gaze
On bodies naked and ablaze;
The hippocratic eye will see
In nakedness, anatomy;
And naked shines the Goddess when
She mounts her lion among men.

The nude are bold, the nude are sly
To hold each treasonable eye.
While draping by a showman's trick
Their dishabille in rhetoric,
They grin a mock-religious grin
Of scorn at those of naked skin.

The naked, therefore, who compete
Against the nude may know defeat;
Yet when they both together tread
The briary pastures of the dead,
By Gorgons with long whips pursued,
How naked go the sometime nude!

FOR DISCUSSION

1. What, for Graves, is the difference between *naked* and *nude*? Do you agree with the distinction he makes? Why or why not?

2. What does Graves mean by *rhetoric* in the fourth line of the third stanza?

3. Explain the meaning of the last stanza, paying particular attention to the last line.

3 | Jabberwocky

LEWIS CARROLL [CHARLES LUTWIDGE DODGSON] (1832-1898)

'Twas brillig, and the slithy toves
  Did gyre and gimble in the wabe:
All mimsy were the borogoves,
  And the mome raths outgrabe.

"Beware the Jabberwock, my son!
  The jaws that bite, the claws that catch!
Beware the Jubjub bird, and shun
  The frumious Bandersnatch!"

He took his vorpal sword in hand:
  Long time the manxome foe he sought—
So rested he by the Tumtum tree,
  And stood awhile in thought.

And, as in uffish thought he stood.
  The Jabberwock, with eyes of flame,
Came whiffling through the tulgey wood.
  And burbled as it came!

One, two! One, two! And through and through
  The vorpal blade went snicker-snack!
He left it dead, and with its head
  He went galumphing back.

"And hast thou slain the Jabberwock?
  Come to my arms, my beamish boy!
O frabjous day! Callooh, Callay!"
  He chortled in his joy.

'Twas brillig, and the slithy toves
  Did gyre and gimble in the wabe:
All mimsy were the borogoves,
  And the mome raths outgrabe.

FOR DISCUSSION

1. Is "Jabberwocky" a nonsense poem? Explain.

2. Lewis Carroll blended *chuckle* and *snort* to make *chortle*. Identify another word in the poem that has been made by this blending process. What words were blended to produce the new word?

ADELE ALDRIDGE (1934-   )

DATE

MATE

intiM̆ATE

intiM̄ATE

intimiDATE

in time HATE

FOR DISCUSSION

1. What story does this poem tell?

2. What is the difference between the words in lines 3 and 4?

3. Why has Aldridge capitalized the words and parts of words that she has?

5 | *from* Knots

R. D. LAING (1927-   )

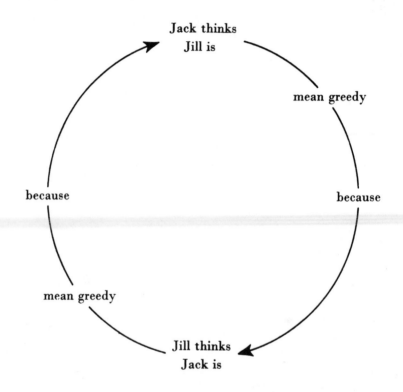

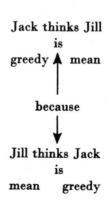

FOR DISCUSSION

1. This poem comes from Laing's book *Knots,* in which the individual poems are untitled. Does "Knots" seem to you an appropriate title for this poem? Why or why not?

2. How does the physical format of Laing's poem contribute to its effect on the reader?

6 | O Cheese

DONALD HALL (1928-   )

In the pantry the dear dense cheeses, Cheddars and harsh
Lancashires; Gorgonzola with its magnanimous manner;
the clipped speech of Roquefort; and a head of Stilton
that speaks in a sensuous riddling tongue like Druids.

O cheeses of gravity, cheeses of wistfulness, cheeses
that weep continually because they know they will die,
cheeses as blunt as gray rock,
cheeses of victory, cheeses wise in defeat.

Esrom as fundamental as a village family;
Pont l'Eveque intellectual, and quite well-informed; Ementhaler
decent and loyal, a little deaf in the right ear;
and Brie the revealing experience, instantaneous and profound.

O cheeses that dance in the moonlight, cheeses
that mingle with sausages, cheeses of Stonehenge,
cheeses of the Pacific Ocean, cheeses of new grass,
cheeses with gold threads like the threads in tapestries.

Reblochon openly sexual; Bresse Bleu like music in October;
Caerphilly like pine trees, small at the timberline;
Port du Salut in love; and Caprice des Dieux
eloquent, tactful, like a thousand-year-old hostess.

O cheeses that are shy, that linger in the doorway,
eyes looking down, cheeses spectacular as fireworks,
cheeses of Lascaux, of bison carved in stone, cheeses
fat as a cushion, lolling in bed until noon.

Camembert distant and formal, then suddenly laughing;
Gruyère an old neighbor returned for a visit; Liederkranz
fresh and ebullient, jumping like a small dog, noisy;
and Dolcelatte, always generous to a fault.

O village of cheeses, I make you this poem of cheeses,
O family of cheeses, living together in pantries,
O cheeses that keep to your own nature, like a lucky couple,
this solitude, this energy, these bodies slowly dying.

FOR DISCUSSION

1. What, in your opinion, is the purpose of this poem?

2. Discuss how Hall uses similes and personification to capture the essences of the many cheeses he mentions in this poem.

IX

Our Changing Language

1
The Acceleration of Language Change

ALVIN TOFFLER

Alvin Toffler's Future Shock *documents the acceleration of change in all aspects of contemporary life, an acceleration that disorients and frightens many people. In this passage from his book, Toffler turns his attention to the remarkable increase in our vocabulary, the transiency of many of our words, and other changes that are "convulsing" our language. Toffler feels that these changes raise serious questions about the future of our language and about our ability to communicate.*

If our images of reality are changing more rapidly, and the machinery of image-transmission is being speeded up, a parallel change is altering the very codes we use. For language, too, is convulsing. According to lexicographer Stuart Berg Flexner, senior editor of *The Random House Dictionary of the English Language*, "The words we use are changing faster today—and not merely on the slang level, but on every level. The rapidity with which words come and go is vastly accelerated. This seems to be true not only of English, but of French, Russian and Japanese as well." 1

Flexner illustrated this with the arresting suggestion that, of the estimated 450,000 "usable" words in the English language today, only perhaps 250,000 would be comprehensible to William Shakespeare. Were Shakespeare suddenly to materialize in London or New York today, he would be able to understand, on the average, only five out of every nine words in our vocabulary. The Bard would be a semi-literate. 2

This implies that if the language had the same number of words in Shakespeare's time as it does today, at least 200,000 words— perhaps several times that many—have dropped out and been replaced in the intervening four centuries. Moreover, Flexner conjec- 3 tures that a full third of this turnover has occurred within the last fifty years alone. This, if correct, would mean that words are now dropping out of the language and being replaced at a rate at least three times faster than during the base period 1564 to 1914.

This high turnover rate reflects changes in things, processes, and qualities in the environment. Some new words come directly from the world of consumer products and technology. Thus, for example, words like "fast-back," "wash-and-wear" or "flashcube" were all propelled into the language by advertising in recent years. Other words come from the headlines. "Sit-in" and "swim-in" are recent products of the civil rights movement; "teach-in" a product of the campaign against the Vietnam war; "be-in" and "love-in" products of the hippie subculture. The LSD cult has brought with it a profusion of new words—"acidhead," "psychedelic," etc.

At the level of slang, the turnover rate is so rapid that it has forced dictionary makers to change their criteria for word inclusion. "In 1954," says Flexner, "when I started work on the *Dictionary of American Slang,* I would not consider a word for inclusion unless I could find three uses of the word over a five-year period. Today such a criterion would be impossible. Language, like art, is increasingly becoming a fad proposition. The slang terms 'fab' and 'gear,' for example, didn't last a single year. They entered the teen-age vocabulary in about 1966; by 1967 they were out. You cannot use a time criterion for slang any more."

One fact contributing to the rapid introduction and obsolescence of words is the incredible speed with which a new word can be injected into wide usage. In the late 1950s and early sixties one could actually trace the way in which certain scholarly jargon words such as "rubric" or "subsumed" were picked up from academic journals, used in small-circulation periodicals like the *New York Review of Books* or *Commentary,* then adopted by *Esquire* with its then circulation of 800,000 to 1,000,000, and finally diffused through the larger society by *Time, Newsweek* and the larger mass magazines. Today the process has been telescoped. The editors of mass magazines no longer pick up vocabulary from the intermediate intellectual publications alone; they, too, lift directly from the scholarly press in their hurry to be "on top of things. . . ."

A more significant example of language turnover can be seen in the sudden shift of meaning associated with the ethnic term "black." For years, dark-skinned Americans regarded the term as racist. Liberal whites dutifully taught their children to use the term "Negro" and to capitalize the "N." Shortly after Stokely Carmichael proclaimed the doctrine of Black Power in Greenwood, Mississippi in June, 1966, however, "black" became a term of pride among both blacks and whites in the movement for racial justice. Caught off guard, liberal whites went through a period of confusion, uncertain as to whether to use Negro or black. Black was quickly legitimated when the mass media adopted the new meaning. Within a few months, black was "in," Negro "out."

Even faster cases of diffusion are on record. "The Beatles," says lexicographer Flexner, "at the height of their fame could make up any word they like, slip it into a record, and within a month it would be part of the language. At one time perhaps no more than fifty people in NASA used the word 'A-OK.' But when an astronaut used it during a televised flight, the word became part of the language in a single day. The same has been true of other space terms, too—like 'sputnik' or 'all systems go.'"

As new words sweep in, old words vanish. A picture of a nude girl nowadays is no longer a "pin-up" or a "cheesecake shot," but a "playmate." "Hep" has given way to "hip"; "hipster" to "hippie." "Go-go" rushed eagerly into the language at breakneck speed, but it is already gone-gone among those who are truly "with it."

The turnover of language would even appear to involve non-verbal forms of communication as well. We have slang gestures, just as we have slang words—thumbs up or down, thumb to nose, the "shame on you" gesture used by children, the hand moving across the neck to suggest a throat-slitting. Professionals who watch the development of the gestural language suggest that it, too, may be changing more rapidly.

Some gestures that were regarded as semi-obscene have become somewhat more acceptable as sexual values have changed in the society. Others that were used only by a few have achieved wider usage. An example of diffusion, Flexner observes, is the wider use today of that gesture of contempt and defiance—the fist raised and screwed about. The invasion of Italian movies that hit the United States in the fifties and sixties probably contributed to this. Similarly, the upraised finger—the "up yours" gesture—appears to be gaining greater respectability and currency than it once had. At the same time, other gestures have virtually vanished or been endowed with radically changed meaning. The circle formed by the thumb and forefinger to suggest that all goes well appears to be fading out; Churchill's "V for Victory" sign is now used by protesters to signify something emphatically different: "peace" not "victory."

There was a time when a man learned the language of his society and made use of it, with little change, throughout his lifetime. His "relationship" with each learned word or gesture was durable. Today, to an astonishing degree, it is not.

QUESTIONS ON CONTENT

1. How does Toffler explain the rapidity with which a word can gain popularity and then become obsolete? In what areas of our vocabulary is this process particularly rapid?

2. *Relevant, groovy,* and *rip-off* are examples of once popular words that are now much less frequently used. Give some other examples from your own experience. How do you account for this change in popular usage?

3. Toffler suggests that gestural language is also changing. Give several examples of gestures that have changed in meaning.

4. What kinds of words have changed more extensively than others? In answering this question, consider nouns, verbs, prepositions, and articles. What are the implications of your answer in terms of Toffler's assertion that if Shakespeare were to materialize today, he "would be a semi-literate"?

QUESTIONS ON RHETORIC

1. What does Toffler mean in paragraph 1 when he says that language is "convulsing"? What image does "convulsing" bring to mind? How appropriate do you find the image?

2. Toffler uses the repetition of key words as a transitional device. What other transitional devices does he use? Provide several examples of each.

3. What types of evidence does Toffler use to substantiate his argument concerning the future of language?

VOCABULARY

conjectures	proposition	contempt
criteria	diffusion	defiance

CLASSROOM ACTIVITIES

1. A recent attempt to create a new language is found in Anthony

Burgess's *A Clockwork Orange,* a futuristic novel set in England. Here is how the novel begins:

"What's it going to be then, eh?" There was me, that is Alex, and my three droogs, that is Pete, Georgie, and Dim, Dim being really dim, and we sat in the Korova Milkbar making up our rassoodocks what to do with the evening, a flip dark chill winter bastard though dry. The Korova Milkbar was a milk-plus mesto, and you may, O my brothers, have forgotten what these mestos were like, things changing so skorry these days and everybody very quick to forget, newspapers not being read much neither. Well, what they sold there was milk plus something else. They had no license for selling liquor, but there was no law yet against prodding some of the new veshches which they used to put into the old moloko, so you could peet it with vellocet or synthemesc or drencrom or one or two other veshches which would give you a nice quiet horror-show fifteen minutes admiring Bog And All His Holy Angels And Saints in your left shoe with lights bursting all over your mozg. Or you could peet milk with knives in it, as we used to say, and this would sharpen you up and make you ready for a bit of dirty twenty-to-one, and that was what we were peeting this evening I'm starting off the story with.

How would you describe the language in this passage? What impressions does it create? Is it unintelligible?

NOTE: Writing assignments for "Our Changing Language" appear on p. 291.

2
Hot Language
and Cool Lives

ARTHUR BERGER

Have you ever wondered just how big "Giant King Size" actually is or what "terrific" really means? These are examples of what Arthur Berger, an expert on pop culture who teaches at San Francisco State University, calls "hot" language, a mode of speech that he feels is increasingly being used to hide, even from ourselves, the "cool" or less-than-exciting lives most of us lead.

There is a fish that always delights me whenever I take my children to the aquarium. It is a slender rather trivial thing that has the ability to puff itself up into a big ball and scare off (hopefully) other fish that might wish to attack it. It is literally a big windbag, yet this defense mechanism works—well enough, at least, for other windbags to be born and survive.

The whole business is quite absurd except that it does work, and what is more fantastic, with people as well as with fishes. A lot of people are leading rather luke-warm lives, if not cool (and not in the sense of "good" as some use the term) or tepid lives, yet they describe themselves and their actions in terms of what might be called "hot" language.

I can recall once overhearing two bored youths at a tennis court. Said one of them, "Let's split," a phrase much in usage these days, in fitting with the schizophrenic nature of the times. Somehow "splitting" from a place is much more exciting than "going someplace else" or "leaving."

Is it not possible that there is a direct correlation between a growing sense of powerlessness and futility in our lives and the jazzed-up language we use? The more you feel yourself diminished the more you "build yourself up" by using hot language, showing

281

that you are in some kind of an "in" group, and know what's going on. It is only natural to try to represent oneself in the best possible light, but if we study the way people do this, we find that this hot or inflated language is somewhat self-defeating.

As everything becomes inflated and *tremendous*, the word loses   5
its currency. What is normal becomes tremendous. What then do we say about something that really is tremendous? It seems that the more we use hot language to add color to our otherwise colorless lives, the less utility the hot language has; it becomes devalued, and we have to work harder for less, so to speak. What used to be large is now "giant king size," and we have reached the point of no return.

Perhaps there is some kind of a searching for the infinite at work.   6
In a recent advertisement from a humane society, various kinds of memberships were announced: Annual $5, Patron $10, Life $100, Perpetual $250. A lifetime is no longer enough. We must have a rate for those who would be immortal. On the opposite side of the fence death must be made more final, somehow. Thus we find ads for insecticides claiming that they "kill bugs *dead!*"

It may be that we can now think of killing without death—for as   7
everything grows out of control and the fantastic becomes the commonplace (men on the moon on prime-time television), the old words like the old lifestyle become, somehow, inadequate. We need more and more emphasis and must be told that when something is killed it will be dead.

Television commercials have bred within the average American   8
a skepticism that must somehow be overcome. We find all about us claims that are obviously absurd: on menus, travel brochures, book jackets, etc. The law of diminishing returns is at work. Since people now believe less and less, you have to promise more and more to come out even. In this sense advertising is self-defeating for it (more than anything else) has created this skepticism, which it keeps attacking and forcing at the same time.

The use of this hot language is symptomatic of a certain malaise   9
affecting people, which leads them to believe that life must at all times be exciting, vital, dazzling, full of "fabulous" experiences. This is nonsense, obviously. Everyone—even "world historical figures" such as leaders of great nations or movie celebrities—spends a great deal of his time doing routine, ordinary things. Thus, the use of hot language makes us *devalue* our lives, since we take a rather absurd conception of what is normal, measure our lives against this false norm, and find ourselves wanting. We all want to lead Giant

King Size lives in an age when there are few giants or kings. Since we cannot, we then define ourselves as leading lives of quiet desperation, describe life as absurd and meaningless, and try to escape from all this by consumerism, drugs, or some other kind of narcoticism.

A distinguished sociologist, Leo Lowenthal, has discussed a   10
form of hot language, the use of "superlatives," in the following manner:

> This wholesale distribution of highest ratings defeats its own purpose. Everything is presented as something unique, unheard of, outstanding. Thus nothing is unique, unheard of, outstanding. Totality of the superlative means totality of the mediocre. It levels the presentation of human life to the presentation of merchandise.

He wrote this in reference to the tendency of contemporary writers to use superlatives in biographies done for popular magazines. Lowenthal noticed that there was a change from early biographies that didn't use superlatives and dealt with heroes of production to recent biographies (around 1940) that used superlatives and were about heroes of consumption. On first sight the superlatives didn't seem very significant, until their real function was discovered. This was, Lowenthal suggested, to create "a reign of psychic terror, where the masses have to realize the pettiness and insignificance of their everyday life. The already weakened consciousness of being an individual is struck another heavy blow by the pseudo-individualizing forces of the superlative."

This was written in the forties, when we had "stars." How does   11
the ordinary man feel in the seventies, in an era when being a "star" is no longer significant, since we now have "*superstars*"? When the star is relegated to mediocrity, what do we say about the average citizen? The fact is significant that we now use terms such as the "little guy"; his stature and significance are diminishing greatly, and he is on the verge of becoming a "forgotten" American.

QUESTIONS ON CONTENT

1. What is "hot language"?

2. Do you agree with Berger's suggestion that the verb *split* is appropriate for the "schizophrenic nature of the times"? In general, does slang reflect the culture of which it is a product? Explain.

3. How might Paul Stevens (pp. 75–85) react to Berger's statement that "since people now believe less and less, you have to promise

more and more to come out even"? Is advertising really "self-defeating"? Explain.

4. Berger points to the power of language in shaping reality. Can "hot" language make a dull existence exciting? Explain.

QUESTIONS ON RHETORIC

1. What is the purpose of paragraph 1, and how does it function within the context of the entire essay?

2. What is Berger's thesis, and where is it found?

3. Berger uses a number of rhetorical strategies in this essay: definition, narration, cause and effect, comparison and contrast. Locate an example of each and explain the way it functions in the essay.

VOCABULARY

schizophrenic	skepticism	pettiness
inflated	symptomatic	mediocrity
infinite	consumption	

CLASSROOM ACTIVITIES

1. Discuss the implications of Lowenthal's statement (paragraph 10) about "superlatives" for students' grades, job evaluations, reviews of movies and books, and personal compliments.

NOTE: Writing assignments for "Our Changing Language" appear on p. 291.

3

The Limitations of Language

MELVIN MADDOCKS

In the following essay from Time, *Melvin Maddocks reports on the epidemic proportions in the United States of an old disease. "Semantic aphasia," or "that numbness of ear, mind and heart—that tone deafness to the very meaning of language," is something more than the pollution of language that Orwell warned us about in the 1940s. Semantic aphasia results from the overloading and consequent jamming of our individual communication networks. Although he offers some hope for the prevention of semantic aphasia, Maddocks is not very optimistic about its elimination.*

In J. M. G. Le Clézio's novel *The Flood*, the anti-hero is a young man suffering from a unique malady. Words—the deluge of daily words—have overloaded his circuits. Even when he is strolling down the street, minding his own business, his poor brain jerks under the impact of instructions (WALK—DON'T WALK), threats (TRESPASSERS WILL BE PROSECUTED), and newsstand alarms (PLANE CRASH AT TEL AVIV). Finally, Le Clézio's Everyman goes numb—nature's last defense. Spoken words become mere sounds, a meaningless buzz in the ears. The most urgent printed words—a poem by Baudelaire, a proclamation of war—have no more profound effect than the advice he reads (without really reading) on a book of matches: PLEASE CLOSE COVER BEFORE STRIKING.

If one must give a name to Le Clézio's disease, perhaps semantic aphasia will do. Semantic aphasia is that numbness of ear, mind and heart—that tone deafness to the very meaning of language—which results from the habitual and prolonged abuse of words. As an isolated phenomenon, it can be amusing if not downright irritating. But when it becomes epidemic, it signals a disastrous decline in the skills of communication, to that mumbling low point where language does almost the opposite of what it was created for. With frightening perversity—the evidence mounts daily—words now seem to cut off and isolate, to cause more misunderstanding than they prevent.

Semantic aphasia is the monstrous insensitivity that allows gen-   3
erals to call war "pacification," union leaders to describe strikes or slowdowns as "job actions," and politicians to applaud even moderately progressive programs as "revolutions." Semantic aphasia is also the near-pathological blitheness that permits three different advertisers in the same women's magazine to call a wig and two dress lines "liberated."

So far, so familiar. Whenever the ravishing of the English lan-   4
guage comes up for perfunctory headshaking, politicians, journalists, and ad writers almost invariably get cast as Three Horsemen of the Apocalypse. The perennially identified culprits are guilty as charged, God knows. At their worst—and how often they are!—they seem to address the world through a bad PA system. Does it matter what they actually say? They capture your attention, right? They are word manipulators—the carnival barkers of life who misuse language to pitch and con and make the quick kill.

So let's hear all the old boos, all the dirty sneers. Paste a sticker   5
proclaiming Stamp Out Agnewspeak on every bumper. Take the ribbons out of the typewriters of all reporters and rewritemen. Force six packs a day on the guy who wrote "Winston tastes good like . . ." Would that the cure for semantic aphasia were that simple.

What about, for example, the aphasics of the counterculture?   6
The ad writer may dingdong catch phrases like Pavlov's bells in order to produce saliva. The Movement propagandist rings his chimes ("Fascist!" "Pig!" "Honky!" "Male chauvinist!") to produce spit. More stammer than grammar, as Dwight Macdonald put it, the counterculture makes inarticulateness an ideal, debasing words into clenched fists ("Right on!") and exclamation points ("Oh, wow!"). Semantic aphasia on the right, semantic aphasia on the left. Between the excesses of square and hip rhetoric the language is in the way of being torn apart.

The semantic aphasia examined so far might be diagnosed as a   7
hysterical compulsion to simplify. Whether pushing fluoride toothpaste or Women's Lib, the rhetoric tends to begin, rather than end, at an extreme. But there is a second, quite different variety of the disease: overcomplication. It damages the language less spectacularly but no less fatally than oversimplification. Its practitioners are commonly known as specialists. Instead of unjustified clarity they offer unjustified obscurity. Whether his discipline is biophysics or

medieval Latin, the specialist jealously guards trade secrets by writing and speaking a private jargon that bears only marginal resemblances to English. Cult words encrust his sentences like barnacles, slowing progress, affecting the steering. And the awful truth is that everybody is a specialist at something.

If the oversimplifier fakes being a poet, the overcomplicator   8
fakes being a scientist. Perhaps it is unfair to pick on economists rather than anybody else—except that they are, after all, talking about money. And as often as not it turns out to be our money. Here is a master clarifier-by-smokescreen discussing the recruiting possibilities of a volunteer army if wages, military (W_m) are nudged seductively in the direction of wages, civilian (W_c): "However, when one considers that a military aversion factor must be added to Wc or subtracted from Wm, assuming average aversion is positive, and that only a portion of military wages are perceived, the wage ratio is certainly less than unity and our observations could easily lie on the increasing elasticity segment of the supply curve." All clear, everyone?

The ultimate criticism of the overcomplicator is not that he   9
fuzzes but that he fudges. If the cardinal sin of the oversimplifier is to inflate the trivial, the cardinal sin of the overcomplicator is to flatten the magnificent—or just pretend that it is not there. In the vocabulary of the '70s, there is an adequate language for fanaticism, but none for ordinary quiet conviction. And there are almost no words left to express the concerns of honor, duty or piety.

For the noble idea leveled with a thud, see your nearest modern   10
Bible. "Vanity of vanities, saith the Preacher . . ." In one new version his words become, "A vapor of vapors! Thinnest of vapors! All is vapor!"—turning the most passionate cry in the literature of nihilism into a spiritual weather report. The new rendition may be a more literal expression of the Hebrew original, but at what a cost in grace and power.

Who will protect the language from all those oversimplifiers and   11
overcomplicators who kill meaning with shouts or smother it with cautious mumbles? In theory, certain professions should serve as a sort of palace guard sworn to defend the mother tongue with their lives. Alas, the enemy is within the gates. Educators talk gobbledygook about "non-abrasive systems intervention" and "low structure-low consideration teaching style." Another profession guilty of nondefense is lexicography. With proud humility today's dictionary editor abdicates even as arbiter, refusing to recognize any standards but usage. If enough people misuse *disinterested* as a synonym for

uninterested, Webster's will honor it as a synonym. If enough people say *infer* when they mean *imply,* then that becomes its meaning in the eyes of a dictionary editor.

Con Edison can be fined for contaminating the Hudson. Legisla- 12
tion can force Detroit to clean up automobile exhausts. What can one do to punish the semantic aphasics for polluting their native language? None of man's specialties of self-destruction—despoliation of the environment, overpopulation, even war—appears more ingrained than his gift for fouling his mother tongue. Yet nobody dies of semantic aphasia, and by and large it gets complained about with a low-priority tut-tut.

The reason we rate semantic aphasia so low—somewhere be- 13
tween athlete's foot and the common cold on the scale of national perils—is that we don't understand the deeper implications of the disease. In his classic essay, "Politics and the English Language," George Orwell pointed out what should be obvious—that sloppy language makes for sloppy thought. Emerson went so far as to suggest that bad rhetoric meant bad men. Semantic aphasia, both men recognized, kills after all. "And the Lord said: 'Go to, let us go down, and there confound their language, that they may not understand one another's speech.' " Is there a more ominous curse in the Bible? It breathes hard upon us at this time of frantic change, when old purposes slip out from under the words that used to cover them, leaving the words like tombstones over empty graves.

How, then, does one rescue language? How are words repaired, 14
put back in shape, restored to accuracy and eloquence, made faithful again to the commands of the mind and the heart? There is, sadly enough, no easy answer. Sincerity is of little help to clichés, even in a suicide note, as Aldous Huxley once remarked. Read, if you can, the Latinized techno-pieties of most ecologists. Good intentions are not likely to produce another Shakespeare or a Bible translation equivalent to that produced by King James' bench of learned men. They wrote when English was young, vital and untutored. English in [the 1970s] is an old, overworked language, freshened sporadically only by foreign borrowings or the flickering, vulgar piquancy of slang. All of us—from the admen with their jingles to the tin-eared scholars with their jargon—are victims as well as victimizers of the language we have inherited.

Concerning aphasia, the sole source of optimism is the logic of 15
necessity. No matter how carelessly or how viciously man abuses the language he has inherited, he simply cannot live without it. Even Woodstock Nation cannot survive on an oral diet of grunts and expletives. Mankind craves definition as he craves lost innocence.

He simply does not know what his life means until he says it. Until the day he dies he will grapple with mystery by trying to find the word for it. "The limits of my language," Ludwig Wittgenstein observed, "are the limits of my world." Man's purifying motive is that he cannot let go of the Adam urge to name things—and finally, out of his unbearable solitude, to pronounce to others his own identity.

QUESTIONS ON CONTENT

1. What, according to Maddocks, is "semantic aphasia"?

2. Politicians, journalists, and ad writers are among those who spread semantic aphasia. Who suffers from this disease? Give some examples of semantic aphasia.

3. What two varieties of semantic aphasia does Maddocks identify? Give an example of each. Explain his statement, "If the oversimplifier fakes being a poet, the overcomplicator fakes being a scientist."

4. Why are people so indifferent to semantic aphasia? Are its effects harmless?

5. What hope does Maddocks offer for the rescue of language?

QUESTIONS ON RHETORIC

1. In developing his argument, Maddocks makes use of illustration, classification, definition, analysis, and cause and effect. Identify and discuss his use of each rhetorical technique.

2. What is the effect of the short question "All clear, everyone?" at the end of paragraph 8?

3. What is Maddocks's attitude toward his subject? Where is this attitude most clearly revealed?

4. Comment on the freshness, effectiveness, and complexity of the following figure of speech from paragraph 7: "Cult words encrust his sentences like barnacles, slowing progress, affecting the steering."

VOCABULARY

deluge	manipulators	fanaticism

proclamation	compulsion	sporadically
insensitivity	culprits	expletives
hysterical		

CLASSROOM ACTIVITIES

1. Maddocks asks, "What can one do to punish the semantic aphasics for polluting their native language?" How does he answer his own question? What answers do you and the other members of your class have? For example, is it farfetched to think of enacting verbal pollution laws? Are "truth-in-advertising" statutes examples of such laws?

WRITING ASSIGNMENTS FOR "OUR CHANGING LANGUAGE"

1. Each of the articles in this section presents a different view of the state of English. Write a paper in which you review and evaluate the three assessments of the language. Support your evaluations with evidence drawn from your own experience.

2. Ludwig Wittgenstein's statement "The limits of my language are the limits of my world" is often quoted. Write an essay in which you illustrate Wittgenstein's hypothesis. Support your generalizations with carefully selected details.

3. It has often been said that language reveals the character of the person using it. Write an essay in which you attempt to analyze the character of a particular writer (or writers).

NOTE: Suggested topics for research papers appear on p. 293.

NOTABLE QUOTATIONS

The following quotations are drawn from the articles in this section. They are presented as additional topics for classroom discussion or for writing assignments.

"Were Shakespeare suddenly to materialize in London or New York today, he would be able to understand, on the average, only five out of every nine words in our vocabulary. The Bard would be a semi-literate." *Toffler*

"Is it not possible that there is a direct correlation between a growing sense of powerlessness and futility in our lives and the jazzed-up language we use?" *Berger*

"Since people now believe less and less, you have to promise more and more to come out even." *Berger*

"Semantic aphasia is that numbness of ear, mind and heart—that tone deafness to the very meaning of language—which results from the habitual and prolonged abuse of words." *Maddocks*

"Words now seem to cut off and isolate, to cause more misunderstanding than they prevent." *Maddocks*

"Whenever the ravishing of the English language comes up for perfunctory headshaking, politicians, journalists, and ad writers almost invariably get cast as Three Horsemen of the Apocalypse. . . . They are word manipulators—the carnival barkers of life who misuse language to pitch and con and make the quick kill." *Maddocks*

"What can one do to punish the semantic aphasics for polluting their native language?" *Maddocks*

TOPICS FOR RESEARCH PAPERS

The following is a list of suggested research paper topics. Because each topic area is broad, you will need to limit and focus the subject you choose for your paper.

1. the language of college catalogs
2. how children learn language
3. the differences between the language of males and of females
4. synthetic languages (e.g., Esperanto, Volapük, and Interlingua)
5. stereotyping in the language of cartoons
6. the values conveyed by song lyrics
7. the language of political propaganda
8. names and naming: people, places, or products
9. advertising and children
10. the language of the funeral industry: death, dying, or burial
11. insults, taunts, and jeers
12. greeting-card verse
13. advertising jingles
14. obscenities
15. censorship
16. Bowdler and bowdlerization
17. the Sapir-Whorf hypothesis
18. college slang
19. sports jargon
20. language games (e.g., pig Latin, rhyming slang, and "op" languages)
21. the language of menus
22. language pollution
23. public doublespeak
24. nonverbal communication
25. medical jargon: the language of doctors, dentists, and nurses
26. the language of science fiction
27. the language of disc jockeys
28. the language of soap operas
29. black English
30. words in English borrowed from other languages

31. social or regional dialect variations
32. the language of legal documents (e.g., insurance policies, sales agreements, and leases)
33. language in women's magazines and men's magazines
34. body language and advertising
35. the jargon of a subculture
36. how a dictionary is made
37. figures of speech
38. English as a world language
39. the future of language
40. the language of public-service advertising

Acknowledgments (continued from page iv)

II POLITICS AND DOUBLESPEAK

"Politics and the English Language" by George Orwell. From *Shooting an Elephant and Other Essays* by George Orwell, copyright, 1945, 1946, 1949, 1950, by Sonia Brownell Orwell; copyright © 1973, 1974, by Sonia Orwell. Reprinted by permission of Harcourt Brace Jovanovich, Inc., Mrs. Sonia Brownell Orwell, and Martin Secker and Warburg.

"Gobbledygook" by Stuart Chase. From *The Power of Words*, copyright, 1953, 1954, by Stuart Chase. Reprinted by permission of Harcourt Brace Jovanovich, Inc.

"On Beholding and Becoming" by Terence P. Moran. Originally published as "Public Doublespeak: On Beholding and Becoming" in *College English* (October 1974). Copyright © 1974 by the National Council of Teachers of English. Reprinted by permission of the publisher and the author.

"Telling It Like It Isn't," *Time* (September 19, 1969). Reprinted from *Time*, The Weekly Newsmagazine; Copyright Time Inc.

III THE LANGUAGE OF ADVERTISING

"Bugs Bunny Says They're Yummy" by Dawn Ann Kurth, from *The New York Times* (July 2, 1972). © 1972 by The New York Times Company. Reprinted by permission.

"Weasel Words" by Paul Stevens. From *I Can Sell You Anything* by Carl P. Wrighter (pseud., Paul Stevens). Copyright © 1972 by Ballantine Books, Inc. Reprinted by permission of Ballantine Books, a Division of Random House, Inc.

"Intensify/Downplay" by Hugh Rank, from *Teaching About Doublespeak*, edited by Daniel Dieterich (NCTE, 1976). Copyright © 1976 by the National Council of Teachers of English. Reprinted by permission of the publisher and the author. "Intensify/Downplay" schema, copyright © 1976 by Hugh Rank. Reprinted by permission of the author.

Pennwalt ad reprinted by permission of the Pennwalt Corporation.

Volvo ad reprinted by permission of Volvo of America Corporation. Copyright 1977 Volvo of America Corporation.

E. F. Hutton ad reprinted by permission of E. F. Hutton & Company Inc.

"Ford Motor Company Correspondence" by Marianne Moore. (Nine letters by Marianne Moore to David Wallace of the Ford Motor Company.) From *A Marianne Moore Reader* by Marianne Moore. Copyright © 1957 by The New Yorker Magazine, Inc. Originally appeared in *The New Yorker* magazine. Reprinted by permission of the Viking Press. Letters of David Wallace, courtesy of Ford Motor Company.

IV THE LANGUAGE OF RADIO, TELEVISION, AND NEWSPAPERS

"The Death of Silence" by Robert Paul Dye, from *Journal of Broadcasting*, Vol. 12, no. 3 (Summer 1968). Reprinted by permission of the *Journal of Broadcasting*.

"Bunkerisms: Archie's Suppository Remarks in 'All in the Family' " by Alfred Rosa and Paul Eschholz, *Journal of Popular Culture*. Reprinted with permission of the editor of the *Journal of Popular Culture*.

"Fast as an Elephant, Strong as an Ant" by Bil Gilbert, from *Sports Illustrated* (April 25, 1966). Copyright © 1966 Time Inc. Reprinted by permission.

"Football Verbiage" by William Eben Schultz, reprinted from *American Speech*, XXVI (October 1951), by permission of Columbia University Press and Jane Schultz. Mr. Schultz died April 16, 1964 in Bloomington, Illinois, at the age of 77. At that time he was teaching English at Illinois Wesleyan University and was also college historian.

"A Vivacious Blonde Was Fatally Shot Today or How to Read a Tabloid" by Otto Friedrich, from *American Scholar*, 28 (Autumn 1959). Reprinted by permission of William Morris Agency, Inc. Copyright © 1959 by Otto Friedrich.

"Little League Series Bans Foreigners: No More Chinese HR's" from the New York *Daily News*, November 12, 1974. Copyright 1974 New York News Inc. Reprinted by permission.

"Little League Series Bars Foreigners," from *The New York Times*, November 11, 1974. © 1974 by The New York Times Company. Reprinted by permission.

"Must a Great Newspaper Be Dull?" by Walter Gibson. From *Tough, Sweet and Stuffy: An Essay on Modern Prose Style* by Walter Gibson (1966). Reprinted by permission of Indiana University Press.

V   JARGON, JARGON, JARGON

"CB Radio: The Electronic 'Toy' " by Thomas Fensch. Excerpts from *Smokeys, Truckers, CB Radios & You* by Thomas Fensch (New York: Fawcett Publications, 1976), reprinted with permission of the author.

"Is Your Team Hungry Enough, Coach?" by Edwin Newman. From *Strictly Speaking*, copyright © 1974 by Edwin H. Newman. Reprinted by permission of the publisher, The Bobbs-Merrill Company, Inc.

"The Language of the Law" by David Mellinkoff. From Chapter 15 of *The Language of the Law* by David Mellinkoff (Boston: Little, Brown copyright © 1963) by David Mellinkoff. Reprinted by permission of Little, Brown and Company.

"Occupational Euphemisms" by H. L. Mencken. From *The American Language*, fourth edition, by H. L. Mencken. Copyright 1919, 1921, 1936 by Alfred A. Knopf, Inc. and renewed 1964 by August Mencken and Mercantile-Safe Deposit & Trust Co. Reprinted by permission of the publisher.

VI   PREJUDICE AND LANGUAGE

"The Language of Prejudice" by Gordon Allport. From *The Nature of Prejudice* (Reading, Mass.: Addison-Wesley, 1954). Reprinted by permission of Addison-Wesley Publishing Company.

"Words with Built-In Judgments" by S. I. Hayakawa. From *Language In Thought and Action*, third edition, by S. I. Hayakawa, copyright 1972, by Harcourt Brace Jovanovich, Inc. Reprinted by permission of the publishers.

"How 'White' Is Your Dictionary?" by William Walter Duncan. Reprinted from *ETC*, Vol. XXVII, No. 1 by permission of the International Society for General Semantics.

"UN Group Urges Dropping of Words with Racist Tinge," from *The New York Times*, December 13, 1968. © 1968 by The New York Times Company. Reprinted by permission.

"Sexism in English: A Feminist View" by Alleen Pace Nilsen. From *Female Studies VI: Closer to the Ground*, edited by Nancy Hoffman, Cynthia Secor, and Adrian Tinsley. Copyright 1973, The Feminist Press, Box 334, Old Westbury, N.Y. 11568. Reprinted by permission of The Feminist Press.

VII CENSORSHIP AND TABOOS

"Verbal Taboo" by S. I. Hayakawa. From *Language in Thought and Action*, third edition, by S. I. Hayakawa, copyright, 1972, by Harcourt Brace Jovanovich, Inc. Reprinted by permission of the publishers.

"Four-Letter Words Can Hurt You" by Barbara Lawrence, from *The New York Times*, October 27, 1973. © by The New York Times Company. Reprinted by permission.

"The Corporate Censor" by Nicholas Johnson, from *TV Guide* (July 5, 1969). Mr. Johnson is also the author of *How to Talk Back to Your Television Set* (Boston: Atlantic-Little, Brown & Company, 1970; New York: Bantam, 1970) and *Test Pattern for Living* (New York: Bantam, 1972).

" 'Nigger' Can Be Erased in Maine," from *The Burlington Free Press* (June 4, 1977). Copyright 1977 by The Associated Press. Reprinted by permission of The Associated Press.

"Obscenity—Forget It" by Charles Rembar, from *The Atlantic Monthly*, Vol. 239 (May 1977). Copyright © 1977, by The Atlantic Monthly Company, Boston, Mass. Reprinted by permission of The Atlantic Monthly Company, the author, and the author's agents, Scott Meredith Literary Agency, Inc. 845 Third Avenue, New York, New York 10022.

"Bowdler in Oregon," from *Time* (December 11, 1972). Reprinted by permission from *Time*, The Weekly Newsmagazine; Copyright Time Inc. 1972.

VIII POEMS ON LANGUAGE

"Some Frenchmen" by John Updike. Copyright © 1963 by John Updike. Reprinted from *Midpoint and Other Poems*, by John Updike, by permission of Alfred A. Knopf, Inc. First appeared in *The New Yorker*.

"The Naked and the Nude" by Robert Graves, from *Five Pens In Hand* (New York: Doubleday, 1958). Reprinted by permission of Curtis Brown, Ltd. Copyright © 1958 by Robert Graves.

"Notpoem" by Adele Aldridge. From *Notpoems*, second edition, Magic Circle Press, out of print. Material available from third edition, Artists & Alchemists Publications, 215 Bridgeway, Sausalito, California 94965. Reprinted by permission of the author.

From *Knots*, by R. D. Laing. Copyright © 1970 by The R. D. Laing Trust. Reprinted by permission of Pantheon Books, a Division of Random House, Inc. By permission of Associated Book Publishers Ltd.

"O Cheese" by Donald Hall. Reprinted by permission of the author.

IX OUR CHANGING LANGUAGE

"The Acceleration of Language Change" by Alvin Toffler. From *Future Shock*, by Alvin Toffler. Copyright © 1970 by Alvin Toffler. Reprinted by permission of Random House, Inc.

From *A Clockwork Orange* by Anthony Burgess. Selection is reprinted with the permission of W. W. Norton & Company, Inc. Copyright © 1962 by Anthony Burgess. Copyright © 1963 by W. W. Norton & Company, Inc. by permission of the British publishers, William Heinemann Ltd, Publishers.

"Hot Language and Cool Lives" by Arthur Berger, from *ETC.*: Vol. XXVIII (1971). Reprinted by permission of The International Society for General Semantics.

"The Limitations of Language" by Melvin Maddocks, from *Time* (March 8, 1971). Reprinted by permission of *Time*, The Weekly Newsmagazine; Copyright Time Inc.